THE LOST WAR

Letters from British Officers
during the American Revolution

THE LOST WAR

*Letters from British Officers
during the American Revolution*

Edited and Annotated by
MARION BALDERSTON
and DAVID SYRETT

Introduction by
HENRY STEELE COMMAGER

Horizon Press   New York

To the kindest person I have ever known

Library of Congress Catalog Card Number: 75-18570
ISBN Number: 0-8180-0813-x

Printed in the United States of America

Contents

INTRODUCTION
Henry Steele Commager

Most of the letters from Army and Navy officers which poured in on Basil Feilding, Sixth Earl of Denbigh during the American War of Independence, had to do not with military or naval affairs, but with patronage or perhaps we should say with politics and patronage. They illustrate and bear out what Marion Balderston says in her brief preface to the collection which she has put together with such skill, that "gentlemen did not fight for King or country, they fought for promotion and more pay." And why not? It was not, after all, their war; England was not threatened nor, for that matter, the King. They were as truly mercenaries of the King as were the Hessians and Brunswickers hired to fight in the American wilderness, though both their conditions of service and their rewards were somewhat more advantageous than those of the Germans shanghaied to fight in a cause they knew not of.

These letters which Mrs. Balderston has rescued from oblivion illuminate the workings of the patronage system—a system which encompassed, needless to say, not just the military but the Church, politics, the bureaucracy and to some degree the scientific and learned community too, and influenced, if it did not control, votes in the Commons on most major issues, and which had a profound influence on colonial administration in America. With these matters David Syrett has dealt sufficiently in his lively and penetrating introduction to these letters, and I need not elaborate upon them.

Letters are always miscellaneous, and these are no exception. Inevitably they illuminate more than the patronage system. They deal with military and naval affairs; they record, in a somewhat astigmatic fashion the attitude of British officers towards the war and the American rebels, and they suggest some answers to the fascinating question why the greatest military power of its day should have found, in the American wilderness, only defeat.

The first—the attitude of Lord Denbigh's protegés towards the war —is interesting not only in itself, but because it reminds us that the psychology of the Americans in Vietnam has long antecedents. Mrs. Balderston assures us that the British did not "hate the rebels," and that the attitude even of Lord Denbigh himself was more that of "an irate father who demands instant obedience and cannot understand why he is not getting it," than of an enemy. The letters from America do not wholly bear out this somewhat benign view. There was, in fact, a good deal of bitterness towards the rebels, and especially towards Boston which, by precipitating the conflict and by providing the first defeat for the British, had earned the special enmity of its victims. Here is Lieutenant William Feilding writing his patron that when the British evacuated Boston "they should have burned it to the ground" and, a bit later, confessing that "I would be content to lose a leg and an arm to see them totally defeated and their whole country laid waist." A year later he was as embittered as ever. Every day, he wrote, "I curse Columbus and all the discoverers of this Diabolical Country, which no earthly compensation can put me in Charity with." Lord Sandwich, too, whose matchless mismanagement of the Navy was one of the major causes for British defeat, held a special grudge against the Bostonians and asserted that he was not prepared to grant peace to the colonials without first giving "due correction" to the wicked Bostonians. This was not a wholly new attitude inspired by humiliation; it had emerged even before the outbreak of hostilities, and expressed that almost instinctive contempt of the British upper classes for colonials. Even before Bunker Hill Lord Sandwich had assured his compatriots that the Americans were "raw, undisciplined, and cowardly" while one General Clark, otherwise unknown to fame, announced in the presence of Benjamin Franklin that with but a thousand Grenadiers he could march from Maine to Georgia and "geld all the males, some by force and the rest by a little coaxing."

The analogy to American experience in Vietnam can be read not only in the contempt which so many British displayed towards the Americans—a worthless lot, a rabble, without discipline and without courage, running away from battle, deserting to the British ranks, leaving Mr. Washington with no army at all. With the Rebels so wretched and so incompetent, so scattered and dispersed, it was clear that, whatever the vicissitudes of war, they could not last long. Victory for the British (as for the Americans in Vietnam) was always just around the corner, and always inevitable. As early as June 1776 Lieutenant Feilding wrote confidently that "this summer probably will put an end to their rebellion," and Captain Bowater was sure that the British would be home by Christmas. Nothing daunted, before the disaster at Saratoga the Captain reaffirmed his confidence in immediate victory. "As we have three considerable armies in motion" he wrote Lord Denbigh, "my next, I hope, will inform your Lordship of provinces Subdued. We shall certainly come home this winter." Back in England there was the same infatuation with British invincibility. Lord Denbigh, writing, this time, after the defeat at Saratoga reported that "we are not in the least dejected. Parliament will make it all good." It was all logical enough, just as American self-deception in Vietnam seemed logical enough. It was all logical enough. Britain, in 1776, like the United States, in 1964, was the greatest military power in the world. How could a raw, undisciplined and impoverished enemy win? How indeed: the question will not down. How did it happen that thirteen colonies on the fringe of civilization, as it were, with perhaps half a million males of fighting age, without military resources, without leaders, without even a national government, a national army, a national treasury, brought the mightiest of European powers to its knees, and wrung from it concessions beyond the avarice of conquerors?

None of our letter writers address themselves to this question: after all they did not anticipate defeat and scarcely acknowledged it. But the letters themselves, if they do not provide an answer to this importunate question, do provide interesting annotations to such an answer.

This question, how the Americans won their war of independence, has bemused moralists and historians from the beginning. The first answer was at once the most agreeable and the most irrefutable: victory was Providential, for God favored the American cause. Not surprisingly the British never embraced this explanation, but Americans have never wholly abandoned it: after all they still retain Annuit

Coeptis on their seal. Since Bancroft, however, the conjectures about American victory have become somewhat more sophisticated. There was what we may call the secular version of the Providential explanation: that Nature and Geography fought on the side of the Americans —as indeed they did. How ridiculous, said Tom Paine, to suppose that a continent should belong to an island! How, in fact, was Britain to deal with the logistics of a war three thousand miles from home! In the winter of '75 only eight out of thirty-five ships carrying provisions to the British Army in America actually reached their destination; in 1777 American cruisers captured or destroyed over three hundred British merchant ships; in 1780 the French and Spanish fleets captured no less than sixty-one ships and three thousand men in a single outbound convoy. But even if provisions were somehow available (and the British might have lived off the country) how could Britain conquer a territory ten times her size, or conquer armies which, when defeated, simply melted away, only to assemble again in the face of emergency? For what was perhaps most baffling—it is reflected here in many letters—is that the Americans could lose Boston, New York, Philadelphia, Charleston, without losing the war (imagine Britain losing London, Bristol, Manchester and Liverpool!) for in America cities did not really count. America made a mockery of the rules of war; again and again America—or Nature—wrested victory out of defeat.

A fourth explanation is, again, one that finds some support scattered throughout these pages of letters: that Britain lost the war because of incompetence and corruption. As Philip Guedalla reminded us, half a century ago, Lord Sandwich and Lord George Germaine have some claim to be honored as Fathers of the American Republic, for their contributions to American military victory were as valuable as those of any American military men except Washington himself. This is a consideration that Professor Syrett brings out with great persuasiveness.

A fifth, and as many historians now believe, decisive consideration is touched on here only tangentially, for more and more, after 1778, these letters are preoccupied with the problem of patronage. This was, of course, the fact that the war with the American colonies burgeoned, almost overnight, into a world war. After 1778 Britain was confronted not merely with a handful of ragged Continentals in the American wilderness, but with the formidable coalition of France, Spain and the Netherlands. She was forced to fight in the Atlantic, in the Caribbean, even in distant India; she was forced to fight for her life. Appropriately enough it was Yorktown that was decisive—Yorktown which was won by the French fleet and almost eight thousand French soldiers under Rochambeau—"O, God, it is all over," cried the luckless Lord North when he heard the news. It was indeed, as far as North, and his American war, were concerned. But—unlike most countries —Britain learned from her mistakes in the American war, and she was not to be defeated again in the next two centuries of her history.

—H.S.C.

PREFACE
Marion Balderston

For nearly two hundred years they had stayed there in the library of the Earl of Denbigh's home in Warwickshire, England—buried treasure, too heavy to lift easily and the writing inside difficult to read. But they are pure gold to students of the late eighteenth century, and to anyone interested in why England lost her most important colony.

The Denbighs had moved from the great Elizabethan house to a smaller, more manageable home at nearby Pailton House. The two enormous tomes went to the Warwickshire County Record Office, to be filmed and kept safely. As it happened I got to Warwick before the volumes were returned, and the friend I was visiting, who was a member of the staff of the Record Office, remarked casually that she had recently read some letters from Englishmen fighting in the American Revolution. Naturally very excited, I asked if the Record Office would let me see the manuscript. They would.

The Record Office is staffed by very pleasant and helpful young people; my friend and hostess Monica Ory was one. They brought out two immense books, so heavy I could not lift even one; they put them on a table for me and found me a high chair so I could read more easily. They also adopted me into their official family, which meant coffee "elevenses" in the morning and tea in the afternoon, and we walked home through the park watching the progress of the new building into which they were waiting to move.

Meantime I explored this treasure. There was so much to read and my time was short! The books, the property of the eleventh Earl, contain the letters written way back in the eighteenth century to his ancestor the sixth Earl, a member of the household of King George III. They present a dramatic narrative of the revolutionary era and are unique in revealing the conflict as seen through the eyes of Englishmen fighting a long way from home in a war traditionally thought of from the American viewpoint.

The letters were fascinating. The natural tendency in thinking about war is to assume that the enemy hates you and is to be hated in turn. It was not true of the American Revolution. The rebelling colonies had thousands of friends in the British Isles, many of whom doubtless felt like a mother who grieves when her child leaves, but recognizes his right to leave and live his own life. This attitude was not true of the high Tories such as Lord Denbigh, who acted more like an irate father who demands instant obedience and cannot understand why he is not getting it.

It was not a popular war, few came forward to enlist, hence George III had to purchase many thousands of men who had little alternative but to fight without knowing why.

The young officers whose letters are included here were gentlemen without a gentleman's income. Their alternatives were the army, the navy or the church. They did not fight for King or country; they fought for promotion and more pay. They knew the country was not behind them; the religious groups, including the Quakers, did not want the war, nor did the merchants who were losing a profitable trade with the colonies. The participants shared the same language, the same basic beliefs, and viewed the high principle of individual freedom in much the same way. Why level a gun at another man's head?

All this I felt as I read the antique script. The letters contribute to the humanizing of the British fighting man, giving a personal interpretation of that tragic period, showing how like the American, fighting and dying away from home, he must have been.

In the midst of reading these exciting letters, I realized I could not stay to finish them. But with Lord Denbigh's permission, I was entrusted with the microfilm of them and I had the whole winter in California to read and transcribe the letters. Through them the war became more gripping as it neared its finish.

I should like to express my gratitude to Lord Denbigh, to Monica Ory whose casual remark brought out so much revealing history, to M.W. Farr, M.A., F.S.A., F.R. Hist.S, the County Archivist, and to the Warwick Record Office for their many courtesies, to Dr. Mason Louance who read the manuscript, and as always to the Huntington Library in San Marino, California.

—M.B.

THE HISTORICAL BACKGROUND
David Syrett

Basil Feilding, the 6th Earl of Denbigh, was a man of political importance in England during the age of the American Revolution. He was the titled head of a great landed family, a member of the King's household, and had extensive political interests in Warwickshire and the Borough of Leicester. He was also intensely concerned about events in America.

Throughout the American Revolution, Denbigh corresponded with several British junior officers who were under his political protection and saw to it that the letters he received from them were full of personal insights, opinions, and descriptions. Because he wanted reliable independent information, Denbigh set up what amounted to a private news gathering organization. He directed the officers to send him detailed accounts of the events they witnessed during the American War (Letters 44, 54), and even went so far as to arrange for some of their letters to be sent to England in the pouches reserved for official military dispatches (Nos. 9, 64). The result is a collection of correspondence, much of which is unique, for many of the letters contain vivid accounts of naval, military, and political events at the time of the American Revolution.

To encourage forthright accounts of what was happening in America, Denbigh directed two of the officers with whom he corresponded not to sign their letters to him (Nos. 44, 127). These letters, therefore, have a candidness and immediacy not found in the official dispatches written by senior officers. Writing openly to their benefactor, the officers fill their letters with everything from complaints about food and pay to anguish over friends lost in battle. While their primary concern is promotion and appointments, in their letters to Denbigh the officers reveal much of the world and time in which they lived. They tell, for example, of the humiliation and despair experienced by the British when they were first cooped up in Boston and then thrown out of the town by what they considered to be a mob of country bumpkins. They portray the euphoria felt by the British during the invasion of New

York in 1776. There are descriptions of battles and informed, and not so informed, discussions of major figures and events. There is gossip and speculation. Pieced together, the letters form a moving account of what it was to be a British officer at the time of the American Revolution.

In this collection, intermixed with discussions about promotions are firsthand accounts of some of the great events of the age. On occasion, the information contained in these letters made Denbigh one of the best informed men in England. He learned, for example, of the departure of d'Estaing's squadron from the Mediterranean in 1778 almost as soon as the Admiralty in London (No. 137). Periodically Denbigh thought the news contained in these letters of such importance that he would inform government officials, such as the First Lord of the Admiralty, of the contents of a letter (No. 18).

In an era which produced such masters of the art of jobbery as the Duke of Newcastle and Henry Dundas, the patronage endeavors of Lord Denbigh were not particularly extensive or unique. The following collection of his patronage correspondence, however, has an additional dimension of historical importance. It shows with exceptional clarity exactly how patronage worked in the British military and naval establishments during the eighteenth century.

Lord Denbigh supported the King's government in the House of Lords with his vote and backed the government's candidates with money, influence, and votes on election day, and in return he became the chief dispenser of the government's patronage in Leicestershire. The extent of Denbigh's influence is illustrated by the following letter written to a new First Lord of the Treasury, Lord North, on April 15, 1771:

> I have just received a Letter from Leicestershire acquainting me with the death of Mr Alleyne, Window-peeper of Loughborough, & as your Lordship's predecissors in the Treasury (especially since the D.[uke] of Rutland's family have been in opposition) have generally favoured me by taking my recommendations for the little offices under Gov.t that have become vacant in that Country, I flatter myself your Lords[hi]p will permit me on this occasion to recommend Mr. Ross Jennings to be Mr. Alleyne's successor which will greatly oblige [me].

> P.S.   I beg leave to hint to your Lords[hi]p that myself & friends spent above £20,000 at the Last Leicester Election, & tho we were then beat by Mr. Booth Grey, my friends of the Corporation have

taken such precaution, as must render our future success unavoidable. Be so good as to favour me with an answer directed to South Street.[1]

Those who held power in London always listened to and often complied with Denbigh's requests that his friends, supporters, and relatives be appointed to various government positions.

The basis of Denbigh's political power was his family, land, and an alliance with the Corporation of Leicester. He used all of these to assist his relatives and his dependents by supporting the government in power. On September 12, 1775, upon learning of the death of John Conyers, M.P. for Essex, Denbigh wrote to Lord Rochford, a secretary of state, saying that as soon as the government announced a candidate for the vacant seat he would mobilize his family, who had "pretty considerable property" in Essex, to support the ministry's nominee during the election.[2] Denbigh's estate was Newnham Paddox, Warwickshire,[3] and being a landed noble he was a power to be reckoned with in the county. During the Seven Years War, for example, Denbigh was the colonel of the Warwickshire militia.[4] Denbigh's greatest political asset, however, was his alliance with the Corporation of Leicester.

Until the Municipal Corporations Reform Act of 1835, the Borough of Leicester was governed by a self-elected oligarchy known as the Corporation. This body consisted of a mayor, twenty-three other aldermen, and forty-eight common councilmen. The mayor was elected annually from among the aldermen by a vote of the whole Corporation meeting in Common Hall. The aldermen, who served for life, were chosen by the mayor and aldermen from among the Common Council; and the common councilmen were selected in the same way from among the borough's freemen. There were several ways in which a man could become a freeman of the Borough of Leicester. The freedom could be bought by payment of a fee of about £20, depending upon the Corporation's financial needs. In most cases, all sons of freemen were automatically freemen. All young men apprenticed under an indenture entered into before the mayor and subsequently enrolled became freemen upon coming of age.[5] This created an electorate which numbered about 2,500 at the time of the American Revolution and included those who had the franchise because they were householders and paid scot and lot.[6] The Corporation, however, could increase the number of voters who were friendly to it by creating honorary freemen. Denbigh himself and a number of his dependents were honorary freemen of Leicester.[7] Denbigh, however, did not think that the power to make honorary freemen should be "wontonly exercised," but it was used during close elections.[8]

Sidney and Beatrice Webb in their monumental study of English local government thought that the Corporation of Leicester, because it did not appear to be the least interested in such things as public improvements, was among the worst of its type of governing bodies in the Kingdom.[9] However, this is beside the point, for the real function of the Corporation of Leicester in the late eighteenth century was not the running of a local government in the modern sense, but rather the maintenance of a political system for the benefit of a particular group of people within the Borough of Leicester. In this period Leicester was divided into two warring political factions which were called by each other the Whigs and the Tories. In the context of Leicester politics, the labels Whig and Tory denote religious as well as political differences.[10] The Tories were Anglicans and, because the Test and Corporation Acts excluded from government positions men who were not members of the Church of England, this faction completely controlled the Corporation of Leicester. The Tory faction in Leicester tended towards conservatism in political and economic matters, specifically, they opposed any measure which would weaken their political and economic hold on the borough. An example of this can be seen in their stand against mechanization of the Leicestershire hosiery industry. The Corporation's ignorance and conservatism concerning this issue was heightened by the fact that a number of its members were knitters and feared the loss of economic power. Control of the Corporation was used by the Tories as a weapon in their incessant political battles against the Leicester Whigs, who can best be defined as those people in the Borough of Leicester who for various reasons opposed the actions of the Corporation. The Leicester Whigs were mostly Dissenters, who because of their religion could not be members of the Corporation; and as the hosiery industry at Leicester grew in size and became increasingly mechanized, its leaders tended to be Dissenters and Whigs. The Leicester Whigs also drew political support from the Whig gentry and aristocracy of Leicestershire, most notably from the Earls of Stamford and the Dukes of Rutland. The political opposition to the Tories who controlled the Corporation of Leicester was a powerful combination of Dissenters, industrial interests, and landed Whig aristocratic families.[11]

The strong political alliance between the Whig landed aristocrats of Leicestershire and the Whigs of the Borough of Leicester does much to explain the alliance between the Corporation of Leicester and the 6th Earl of Denbigh. The aristocrats and gentry who came into Leicester at election time in an attempt to place their own nominees in the borough's two seats in Parliament were against the policies of the government in power and not sympathetic to George III and his court. The Corporation of Leicester, however, approved of the policies of the government and showed this by not petitioning for repeal of the Stamp Act[12] and by passing a resolve supporting the government's policy of suppressing the rebellion in America by force of arms.[13] Denbigh, while apparently having no interest in Leicester other than the Corporation itself, was a natural ally, for he was a high Tory.[14] Politically, Denbigh supported everything that the Rutlands, Stamfords, and other Leicestershire Whig aristocrats despised. The practical advantages of an alliance between Denbigh and the Corporation of Leicester are obvious. Denbigh had wide ranging connections among the ruling elite in London and acted as a link between the Corporation of Leicester and the government. Furthermore, Denbigh's control of the bulk of the government's patronage in Leicestershire resulted in the political enemies of the Corporation being systematically denied appointments to minor government positions. Denbigh also derived much from the alliance, for his connection with the Corporation of Leicester gave him considerable political influence in a large provincial city, which in turn undoubtedly increased his political stature in London.

Denbigh employed political and personal influence to obtain commissions, promotions, appointments, and other favors for his relatives, his friend's relations, persons nominated by his political allies, and the sons of genteel families in Leicestershire and Warwickshire. Throughout the American War, Denbigh received a constant stream of letters asking for his assistance in obtaining appointments and promotions in the military and naval services. For the most part, the requests with political overtones came from either the Mayor and the Corporation of Leicester or the members of Parliament for Leicestershire (E.g., nos. 19, 28). There were as well distant relations, such as Captain William Feilding of the marines, who depended on Denbigh's influence (E.g., nos. 1, 3). Even a future relative, Thomas Farnham, was assisted by Denbigh in gaining a promotion (Nos. 170, 196). A number of down and out officers also tried to enlist Denbigh's support in various schemes which would obtain their own advancement (E.g., no. 167). The three Bowater brothers represent perhaps the best example of Denbigh lending his assistance to forward the careers of the sons of a genteel family. John, William, and Edward Bowater were the second, fifth, and seventh sons respectively of Richard and Mary Bowater of Stivichall, Warwickshire. Mary Bowater was the daughter of an M.P., while Richard Bowater's younger brother served as sheriff of Warwickshire and his older sister was the first wife of Arthur Gregory, a Gentleman Usher of the Privy Chamber.[15] Although they did not have much in the way of money, the three Bowaters were clearly the sons of a member of the gentry. Denbigh's oldest son, Lord Feilding, was in a class by himself among the recipients of his father's influence. In the space of seven years, he rose from behind a school desk to the head of a regiment of dragoons (Nos. 94, 207). In the course of the American War, Denbigh wrote scores of letters to generals, admirals, and the heads of various military and naval establishments in an attempt to further the careers of these men.

The army, the navy, the marines, and the ordnance each had different qualifications, standards, and procedures for commissioning and promoting officers. These differences resulted in the officer corps of each branch of the British military being recruited from different economic and social groupings within the British ruling classes. In many respects the branch of the service a young man entered was a matter of economics. In 1776, for example, the price of a cornet's commission in the dragoons was officially listed at £1,102.[16] It would have been unwise and unfair to procure a commission in a fashionable regiment such as the dragoons for a son of a respectable but impoverished member of the gentry; for even if the money for the purchase of the first commission could be raised, the young man would not be able to live on his pay and would be barred from further promotion by the cost of each successive commission. Conversely, placing the son of a great aristocrat in a corps such as the marines where promotion was notoriously slow and where there existed "a strong hereditary element among both officers and men,"[17] would be equally disastrous since the young man would never be able to obtain quickly enough the rank to which he and his family would think he was entitled.

Intermixed with these social and economic considerations was the whole question of interest. In the infantry, cavalry, and navy in order

to obtain steady and regular promotion up through the lower grades
—midshipman to post captain and ensign or cornet to lieutenant
colonel—an officer needed what in the eighteenth century was called
interest. That is, a young officer, if he was to have a successful career,
needed somebody of importance and power who would use his influence with the great and mighty to gain the necessary appointments
and promotions. Ability and luck alone were not sufficient.[18] Indeed,
interest was so important that there was not much point in obtaining
a commission in the infantry, cavalry, or navy for a person without
interest because it was almost certain that he would never be promoted. In the eighteenth century, both the army and navy were full of
aged lieutenants who lacked interest and had thus failed to gain promotion. The great importance of interest can be seen in the careers of
Lord Nelson and the Duke of Wellington. Neither man would have
ever received a commission let alone gained fame and fortune without
the assistance of interest. In the case of Nelson, the interest was his
uncle, Captain Maurice Suckling, the Comptroller of the Navy;[19] and
Wellington's commission was obtained through the influence of his
older brother, Richard Wellesley, 2nd Earl of Mornington.[20] Denbigh
was well aware of the importance of interest, and in the case of Edward Bowater, Denbigh himself was Bowater's interest and his Lordship constantly sought appointments and promotion for him (E.g., no.
118). There were, however, other cases where young men did not
have a powerful backer and Denbigh did not want to supply the interest himself; these men would be directed to the Royal Military
Academy at Woolwich, where artillery and engineer officers were
trained, or to the marines. Promotion in the artillery and engineers
was by seniority,[21] as was also the case in the marines.[22] Because of his
close friendship with Lord Sandwich, the First Lord of the Admiralty
during the American War, it was to the marines that Denbigh turned
when he wanted a commission for a person without interest or money.
Lord Feilding was first commissioned in the 7th Regiment of Foot
(No. 94), while the sons of aldermen of Leicester and people such as
William Feilding's penniless nephew were made second lieutenants in
the marines (E.g., nos. 89, 205).

The particular method and strategy used by Denbigh to obtain a
promotion, a commission, or an appointment varied among the different branches of the military and naval services and according to circumstances. It would have been useless for Denbigh to attempt to ob-

tain a commission in the marines by writing to the Secretary at War, for that official had nothing to do with marines. It would have been equally futile for Denbigh to try and get a favor from an official or officer with whom he had neither personal nor political influence (E.g., nos. 76, 80). Also, it would have been unwise for Denbigh to try and obtain an appointment or promotion for a person who clearly did not have the qualifications, such as enough time in grade, to be eligible for the position or rank (E.g., no. 80). The trick was to cast around the hierarchy of the naval and military establishments in order to find a person who had the authority to do the required favor and was as well a personal or political friend.

On February 26, 1776, Edward Bowater was commissioned a lieutenant in the Royal Navy.[23] Before receiving his commission, Bowater had served twelve years as a midshipman (No. 83), six years more than required by regulations to be eligible for commissioning. The legal requirements for receiving a lieutenant's commission were:

> [to have] passed their Examination; which if not already done at the *Navy-Office*, the Commander in Chief may authorize any three of his principal Commanders to examine them; and if they have served six Years at Sea, two of the said six rated as Midshipmen or Mates, produce regular Journals, good Certificates, and are not under twenty Years of Age, they may be preferred.[24]

Why it took Bowater six additional years to become a lieutenant is unclear. Maybe it was a lack of interest or an inability to get the required time at sea in the peace-time navy. Bowater was twenty-four[25] when he was commissioned a lieutenant, apparently having entered the service when he was twelve years old which was not uncommon. Nelson first went to sea at age twelve and Collingwood and Cornwallis at eleven.[26]

There is no mystery about how and why Bowater was commissioned a lieutenant—Denbigh arranged the promotion. At the request of Denbigh, Rear Admiral Robert Duff, commander-in-chief at Newfoundland, made Bowater an acting lieutenant (Nos. 27, 29). Upon being informed of his success in this matter, Denbigh then got his friend and political ally, the Earl of Sandwich, who was the First Lord of the Admiralty, to have the Admiralty direct that Bowater be sent a lieutenant's commission (No. 29). Nowhere is there any mention of Bowater presenting his journals and certificates to the Navy Office or being examined either in London or at Newfoundland. Nevertheless, because of Denbigh's interest, Edward Bowater had entered the ranks of commissioned officers of the Royal Navy and had begun the long climb upward in rank which would culminate in his promotion to the rank of admiral in 1819.[27]

It required both luck and interest for a lieutenant to be promoted to the rank of master and commander[28] in the Royal Navy. A master and commander commanded small ships—fireships, bomb ketches, and sloops—which were smaller than 6th rates. The power to appoint a master and commander to a ship stationed in England lay with the Admiralty, but the commander-in-chief of a squadron serving overseas could make a master and commander simply by appointing a lieutenant to command a ship of a size which required that her captain be a master and commander;[29] once appointed to the command, the lieutenant would automatically become a master and commander. The rate at which lieutenants were promoted to master and commander obviously depended upon the number of such commands available at any given time and the rapidity with which they were vacated. If no master and commander in a squadron was promoted, died, or left the service, then the commander-in-chief could not appoint any.

Lieutenants would pull strings and employ influence to get assigned to a particular ship or squadron where their chances for promotion to master and commander would be best (E.g., nos. 118, 133). One of the surest roads to promotion to the rank of master and commander was for a lieutenant to serve in the flag ship of an admiral who had an interest in advancing the junior officer's career. For example, Edward Bowater, in a flight of political fancy, suggested that Denbigh use his influence to get him assigned to the flag ship of Admiral Augustus Keppel, the commander-in-chief of the Channel Fleet, not realizing that Keppel and Denbigh were in opposing political camps (Nos. 76, 80). If an appointment to a flag ship could not be managed, the next best thing was an assignment in a squadron commanded by one of Denbigh's friends and political allies (E.g., no. 118).

Edward Bowater's career as a lieutenant is an excellent example of how the system worked. Commissioned a lieutenant in February 1776, Bowater spent that summer serving in the squadron at Newfoundland. Upon his return to England in the autumn of 1776 (No.

76), Bowater was appointed at Denbigh's request to H.M.S. *Terrible*, a ship-of-the line commanded by Captain Sir Richard Bickerton (No. 79). H.M.S. *Terrible* was part of the Channel Fleet, and for the next four years Bowater served in her, building up seniority as a lieutenant. At times during this period various schemes were brought forth to gain promotion for Bowater, but nothing ever came of them (Nos. 118, 133, 145). Then at the end of 1779, H.M.S. *Terrible* was placed, along with other units of the Channel Fleet, under the command of Vice-Admiral Sir George Rodney to take part in the first relief of Gibraltar. Rodney was a friend of Denbigh's, and on October 11, 1779, his Lordship wrote the admiral a letter requesting that Bowater be promoted (No. 176). Rodney answered on October 13, promising Denbigh that Bowater would be made a master and commander as soon as possible (No. 177). Thus, when H.M.S. *Terrible* arrived at Gibraltar, Bowater thought his chance had come at last. Adding to his optimism was the fact that a battle had been fought, a great victory gained, and there was to be a general round of promotions in the squadron. Much to Bowater's disappointment, however, Rodney did not promote him.

Still a lieutenant and bitterly disappointed, Bowater transferred out of H.M.S. *Terrible* and returned to England (Nos. 178-180). If Bowater was to gain promotion to master and commander, he would have to go overseas and serve under a flag officer who would have the opportunity and inclination to promote him. So Bowater was soon on his way to the Lesser Antilles as a lieutenant in H.M.S. *Alcide* (No. 181). Denbigh again wrote to Rodney, then commanding the squadron in the Leeward Islands, making it clear that he expected the admiral to promote Bowater to the rank of master and commander (No. 182). This time Denbigh's interest worked and on February 13, 1781, Bowater was appointed to the command of H.M.S. *Salamander*, a fireship (No. 195).[30]

There was nothing out of the ordinary in the way that Edward Bowater became a master and commander. In fact, Bowater's promotion was very ordinary. It was the middle of a great war, he had a good record, five years seniority as a lieutenant, and had a powerful interest behind him. Bowater was not the only navy officer to receive Denbigh's backing in gaining a promotion from lieutenant to master and commander during the war, for his Lordship wrote to a number of admirals in support of his friends and relations of friends (E.g., no.

4). What is interesting is that Denbigh appears rarely to have solicited promotions in the Royal Navy from his friend Lord Sandwich (E.g., no. 71), but rather from admirals commanding squadrons overseas. Perhaps the reason for this was that there were so many people begging the First Lord of the Admiralty to promote lieutenants that the chances for success were very slight.

To reach the rank of post captain was the dream of every navy officer. A post captain commanded ships in size from 6th rates up to the largest of the ships-of-the-line; and unlike the two lower commissioned ranks in the Royal Navy—lieutenant and master and commander—a post captain was at the same time both a rank and a position. A lieutenant could not become a master and commander by seniority alone, nor could seniority transform a master and commander into a post captain. But once a man was made a post captain he was placed in a position or post, and by means of longevity alone he could rise up through the post captains' list, then through the ranks of rear admirals and various grades of vice-admirals, and then up to the top of the admirals' list, to become at an extremely ripe old age admiral of the fleet—the highest rank of all.[31] Edward Bowater, for example, last went to sea in 1801 as captain of H.M.S. *Magnificent* and, though unemployed during the Napoleonic Wars, rose by seniority from post captain to full admiral in 1819.[32]

The process by which a master and commander was promoted to the safe haven of post captain was exactly the same as that used to promote lieutenants to the rank of master and commander. In England the Admiralty promoted a man to post captain, while overseas when a captaincy became vacant in a ship of the size of a post captain's command, the commander-in-chief of the squadron promoted a master and commander into the position.[33] As in the case of promotions to master and commander, influence or interest and the availability of ships requiring captains all played a part in the promotion process. Thomas Farnham, the brother of the second Countess of Denbigh, wrote to Denbigh three times requesting assistance in becoming a post captain (Nos. 196-198). Apparently Denbigh was successful, for Farnham was made a post captain on March 27, 1782; and though there is no available correspondence on this, Denbigh most likely had a hand in gaining promotion to post captain for Edward Bowater, who was promoted to that rank on January 16, 1783.[34]

Interest was decisive in reaching the rank of post captain in the

Royal Navy. One needed interest to gain a lieutenant's commission, to gain promotion to master and commander, and then to post captain. The great role of interest in navy promotions led to such absurd situations as when in 1780 Rodney promoted his fifteen-and-a-half-year-old son, who had been at sea less than two years, from lieutenant to post captain in ten days.[35] On occasion, however, there were merit promotions such as John Bourmaster, who had been seventeen years a lieutenant, being made a master and commander in 1776 at the request of General Howe as a reward for his work as agent for transports at Boston.[36] But it takes more than one lucky stroke to make it up from midshipman to post captain. Even Nelson, a man of known ability and luck, required interest to reach the rank of post captain. Thomas Farnham rightly proclaimed in a letter concerning his promotion to post captain, "nothing but interest will do." (No. 197)

The marines were the single greatest source of commissions for Denbigh's dependents. Perhaps the main reason for this was the extreme ease with which Denbigh could procure marine commissions. The marines were a small self-contained army administered by the Admiralty and as such Lord Sandwich, the First Lord, had complete control over the granting of second lieutenant's commissions. Furthermore, the strength of the marines was increased from 10,129 men in 1776 to 25,291 men in 1782,[37] with the result that a large number of second lieutenants were commissioned in the course of the war. Indeed, all Denbigh had to do in order to obtain a second lieutenant's commission in the marines for a person was to write a note to his friend Lord Sandwich (Nos. 40, 108).

Certain idiosyncrasies peculiar to the marines made it advantageous for Denbigh to procure commissions in that corps for certain of his dependents. In 1763 Lieutenant John MacIntire naively advised that the young marine officer should study his profession so that he would "be capable of doing Honour to any Promotion, that Fortune or Interest may favour him with."[38] In fact, interest was almost worthless in the marines and as for promotion, there was practically none. Denbigh's interest could only get Lieutenant William Feilding made an adjutant of one of the marine divisions so that he could get a little extra pay. Promotion was almost totally by seniority and terribly slow. In eight years of wartime service William Feilding was promoted once, from lieutenant to captain, and captain he stayed until January 11, 1789, the day he died of a "paralytic stroke" at Portsmouth.[39] Only through longevity could one gain promotion in the marines. From Denbigh's standpoint this was ideal, for once he got a person a marine commission, unlike the case of Edward Bowater, he did not have to use his interest again to gain promotions.

The career of a marine during the American War was a study in frustration, as the letters of Captain William Feilding and Major John Bowater so richly proclaim. The root cause of this frustration was a lack of promotion brought about by the structure of the officer corps of the marines. In 1776 there were seventy marine companies and a total of only seventy-one second lieutenants, fifteen captain lieutenants, and fifty-five captains. In the table of organization there were only seventeen positions for marine officers above the rank of captain of marines.[40] By 1782 the strength of the marines had increased to one hundred and fifty-one companies with a total of two hundred and ninety-two second lieutenants, twenty-five captain lieutenants, and one hundred and twenty-three captains, yet the positions above the rank of captain open to marine officers had only increased to twenty.[41] This table of organization, which called for scores of lieutenants and captains and a mere handful of field grade officers, when combined with no system of retirement resulted in aged marine officers serving in ships "with boys to command them, who were not born when they were made captains." Such marine officers were "obliged to serve old and infirm until they fell into the grave." [42] The entire system was made even more complex and redundant in that all the marine officers, from the twelve most senior captains up through the colonel commandant were given brevet ranks in the army. John Bowater, for example, was commissioned a brevet major in the army on August 24, 1777, yet he was still a captain in the marines and did not become a major in the marines until two years later on August 27, 1779. Moreover, all marine colonels were generals in the army.[43] The officer corps of the marines was so constituted that while a few men at the top gained high rank, the vast majority of officers commissioned during the American Revolution were doomed to serve out their careers as captains and lieutenants.

The whole sad situation in the marines can be seen in the importance date of commission made to the careers of John Bowater and William Feilding. Bowater was commissioned a captain in the marines in 1760, and Feilding made captain in 1776. Because of the difference between these two dates, at the end of the war William

Feilding was one captain among one hundred and twenty-three while Bowater was one major among ten.[44] Feilding died a captain, while Bowater lived to age seventy-one and became a lieutenant general in the army and a colonel in the Royal Marines.[45] Luck, seniority, and longevity made the difference between Bowater's and Feilding's careers, and they also explain the great importance that marine officers placed on such things as William Pitcairn being jumped ahead in rank (Nos. 9, 26), as well as their concern over how the officers who were killed at Bunker Hill were to be replaced (No. 26), and under what conditions officers on half-pay were to be permitted to return to active duty (No. 30). All these things were terribly important to a marine officer because of the way in which the marines were organized.

Denbigh very rarely attempted to obtain for his friends and distant relations army commissions or other favors from the War Office, and for the most part the few attempts that Denbigh did make at soliciting army commissions and promotions for friends failed. Denbigh's two successes were obtaining a cadetship at the Royal Military Academy for John Harding (No. 8) and an ensign's commission in the 29th Regiment for William Buckley, on condition that he procure twenty-nine recruits for the army and that his father grant him an allowance of £40 per year (Nos. 35, 46). Denbigh, however, must have regretted obtaining the latter commission, for Buckley's father later wrote begging his Lordship to use his influence to get young Buckley sent immediately to America so that he would not be put in jail (No. 95).

The reasons for Denbigh's lack of success at and interest in obtaining army commissions for friends and dependents are not hard to fathom, for they would have had to have money as well as interest to enter the army and to gain promotion. In 1781 the official price of an ensign's commission in an unfashionable infantry regiment was listed at £400, while becoming a cornet in a regiment of horse would cost £1,600.[46] There were, however, greater obstacles than money and interest. The King, the location of the war, and Irish politics all conspired to limit the amount of jobbery a man such as Denbigh could exercise with the army during the American War. With the vast bulk of the British army deployed overseas, the various commanders-in-chief controlled most of the promotions among the lower ranks of army officers (E.g., no. 70). Also, the military establishment in the British Isles was divided on paper into the British and Irish establishments.[47] In the Irish establishment promotions and commissioning were controlled by the Lord Lieutenant of Ireland. On several occasions Denbigh wrote to the Lord Lieutenant and the commander-in-chief of the army in Ireland requesting promotions or commissions for various people (Nos. 2 1, 2 2, 24, 68, 1 2 2), but each time he was rebuffed with the excuse that Irish politics required that Irish patronage be used in Ireland (Nos. 70, 1 24). In Britain itself, much to the dismay of the politicians, the granting of commissions and promotions was in the hands of the King. George III considered the army to be part of his personal prerogative and for the most part insisted on standards and qualifications for commissioning and promotion in the army.[48]

To every rule there are exceptions and while George III was fairly successful in fending off politicians who wanted to use army patronage to influence elections, he usually succumbed when it came to titled aristocrats demanding rapid promotion for their sons. A case in point is William Robert, Viscount Feilding, Denbigh's oldest son, who entered the army at age seventeen, was elected to Parliament at age twenty, and was placed in command of the 2 2nd Light Dragoons at age twenty-two. Such a career was one of the advantages of money, influence, and noble birth in eighteenth-centuryEngland.[49]

Lord Feilding was commissioned a lieutenant in the 7th Regiment on March 4, 1 7 7 7.[50] Although in 1 776 Denbigh had written to Lord Barrington, the Secretary at War, about obtaining a cornet's commission in the dragoons for Feilding (Nos. 8 2, 84), apparently he was made a lieutenant without ever serving at the rank of ensign or cornet. Denbigh arranged for his son to circumvent the rank of ensign or cornet by having Lord Feilding commissioned a lieutenant by selection directly by the King (No. 9 3). Commissioning by selection occurred when an officer died, for a commission could not be inherited, and upon the death of its holder the commission reverted back to the crown to be given to another person. There were also a few cases where an officer relinquished a commission which he had not purchased, and since a man could not sell a commission he had not purchased it reverted to the crown.[51] Apparently, a lieutenant in the 7th Regiment which was stationed in Canada had died and Denbigh got the King to give the commission to Feilding. Denbigh then obtained a leave of absence for his son so that he did not have to join his regiment in Canada and could remain in school (No. 9 3).

A few months after Lord Feilding was commissioned a lieutenant, Denbigh began intriguing to obtain for his son either a promotion to captain or a transfer to a more fashionable unit such as the cavalry (Nos. 122, 123, 125). Circumstances plus a good dose of his father's money and influence combined to gain Lord Feilding a promotion to captain less than a year after he had been commissioned a lieutenant. At the end of 1777, in response to the loss of Burgoyne's army at Saratoga and the impending entry of France into the war, the British government decided to raise twelve additional regiments of infantry.[52] These new regiments were to be raised at the expense of municipal corporations and great aristocrats who, with the permission of the King, could appoint most of the officers in exchange for paying the expenses for recruiting the men.[53] At the beginning of 1778 Lord Feilding, aged eighteen, was given a commission in one of these new regiments, the 75th Foot, in exchange for paying for recruiting a company of infantry (No. 130). This practice is known as recruiting for promotion, and it was a fairly common way for officers to gain promotion during wartime. It was also a way of shifting the expense of recruiting a wartime army away from the Treasury and into the pocketbooks of various municipal corporations and aristocrats. Recruiting for promotion has been bitterly attacked by military historians, such as Sir John Fortescue, who claim that it was a way in which young men with money and no military background gained rapid promotion to the detriment of the army.[54] Lord Feilding undoubtedly fits into this category, but he is an exception because of his father's influence. During the American War George III generally insisted that the officers promoted for recruiting these new regiments had much more time in grade than did Lord Feilding.[55]

To Denbigh, Lord Feilding joining the 75th Regiment was nothing more than a device by which to obtain a captain's commission. One wonders if Feilding ever joined the regiment at all,[56] for if he did serve with the 75th it was for a brief period: on May 17, 1778, he was appointed one of Major General Lord Percy's aides-de-camp (No. 136). Denbigh's next objective was to get his son transferred as a captain lieutenant into the cavalry and thereby prevent his being sent overseas on active service, for not only were cavalry regiments more fashionable but also, with few exceptions, they were kept in Britain.[57]

The necessity for Feilding transferring out of the 75th Regiment into the cavalry became pressing when, at the beginning of November

1778, Denbigh heard rumors that the 75th was going to be ordered to India. Denbigh was appalled at the prospect of his oldest son being sent to India "to fight against climet only"; and on November 2nd he wrote to Barrington begging the Secretary at War to get Feilding exchanged out of the 75th Regiment into either the Guards or dragoons (No. 154). Barrington replied to Denbigh on November 4th with a soothing note saying that the 75th Regiment was not going to be sent to India and that when Denbigh next came to London he, Barrington, would "be happy to Consult with You what can be most Advantagious to such an Heir of such a family as Lord Feilding" (No. 155). Apparently the result of this exchange was an offer of a commission in the Guards, which Denbigh turned down on the grounds of its being too costly (No. 158).

Denbigh wanted a captain lieutenancy in the dragoons for his son, and he made it perfectly clear to Lord Amherst, the Commander-in-Chief, that he would settle for nothing less (No. 158). And so in midst of a great war, it became the task of the Commander-in-Chief of the Army to find Lord Feilding a captain lieutenancy in the dragoons (No. 160). On January 16, 1779, Amherst came up with a scheme to remove Feilding from the 75th Regiment into a captain lieutenancy in the 10th Dragoons. Two other officers would have to be transferred and Denbigh would have to pay £600, which was the official difference in the purchase price between a company of infantry and a troop of dragoons (No. 162). Denbigh readily accepted Amherst's plan and paid the £600 even though Lord Feilding would be reduced in rank from a full captain to a captain lieutenant (No. 163); for Denbigh knew that once his son was a captain lieutenant in the dragoons it would be easy to obtain a captain's commission. And indeed on May 4, 1779, Feilding was made a captain by purchase in the 3rd Dragoon Guards (No. 169).

The practice of promotion by purchase, like that of promotion for recruiting, has been attacked by both contemporaries and historians as a system by which rich aristocrats pushed themselves forward in the army at the expense of more talented but poorer officers.[58] Ridiculous as the system of purchasing army commissions appears to twentieth-century man, it nevertheless fulfilled social functions in eighteenth-century England. For example, the purchase of army commissions was a way of insuring that the English ruling classes controlled the officer corps of the army. This was a matter of no little importance in a so-

ciety obsessed with vested property rights. Also, since any commission
that had been purchased could be sold, the system permitted old and
deserving officers, in an army without pensions, to retire with a lump
sum of money from the sale of their commissions.[59] Further, as one
historian has observed, it is difficult to "generalize" about the effects of
the purchase system, for while it discriminated against men without
money and placed rich young incompetents in positions of responsi-
bility, it also produced some of the best combat soldiers of the century.[60]

It was not Denbigh's ambition for his son to make a career of the
army. To be a mere soldier by profession was, to Denbigh's way of
thinking, beneath Lord Feilding's position in society. All the buying
and selling and exchanging of commissions and the transferring from
regiment to regiment in order to gain rank was designed not to make
Lord Feilding a soldier, but to give him status. Denbigh wanted his
oldest son to be called first "Colonel Lord Feilding," then "General
Lord Feilding," and finally, "General the 7th Earl of Denbigh." In
fact, Denbigh's ambition for his oldest son ran far beyond the army
right on to the center stage of British politics. For the next twenty
months, while his father was preparing the coup which would insure
his promotion to lieutenant colonel and propel him into the very
center of political affairs in Britain, Lord Feilding remained a captain
in the 3rd Dragoon Guards. During this period, Denbigh rejected a
plan to make Feilding a major by raising a regiment (Nos. 171, 173),
and conducted a correspondence with the Earl of Pembroke about
how best to get both their sons promoted from captains to majors
(Nos. 185-187). Then on December 2, 1780, Feilding, although un-
derage, was returned unopposed in a by-election as a member of the
House of Commons for Bere Alston. Lord Feilding's election to Parliament was the direct result of a deal made between his father and
the Duke of Northumberland, who controlled the Borough of Bere
Alston, which had an electorate of under thirty voters (Nos. 188-
190).[61]

Lord Feilding, though a member of the House of Commons for sixteen years, never became an important figure in Parliament. Being in
the House, however, had its rewards. Feilding doggedly supported
North's government to the end, and one of the last acts of that ministry before its fall was to appoint Feilding a major in the 19th Light
Dragoons (Nos. 199-200). Feilding then supported the new govern-

ment, and on January 30, 1783, ten days before he voted, without apparently noticing any ideological inconsistencies, for Shelburne's peace preliminaries, he was made a lieutenant colonel and commandant of the 22nd Light Dragoons (No. 207). For the next five years he generally supported the government, although he did vote with the opposition during the Regency Crisis in 1788-1789. At the beginning of the French Revolutionary War, Feilding raised and became the colonel of a regiment of light dragoons; and before his death in 1799, he rose by seniority and without seeing any active service to the rank of major general in the army.[62] To Denbigh, who outlived his oldest son by a year, Lord Feilding's career must have been somewhat of a disappointment, for the viscount never became great, powerful, or even important. In fact Feilding's life was almost a caricature of the young aristocrat who is pushed forward too quickly only to flop when he reaches the point in life where judgement and action count for more than interest and money.

Richard Pares has shown that present day readers tend to "sneer" at eighteenth-century patronage practices while overlooking the fact that they fulfilled legitimate social and political functions.[63] The endless wire pulling and the feeling that nothing is sacred in a world where every position from a church living to a commission in the marines is subject to jobbery boggles the modern mind, which would like to believe that now such positions are obtained only through merit. The twentieth century, however, is far distant in time and thought from the eighteenth century when inheritance of landed estates was governed by a modified form of primogeniture and when men of good family—younger sons, cousins, and the like—needed to follow a career in order to support themselves as gentlemen. Yet whole categories of professions exist today which were unknown two centuries ago. To be a surgeon in the eighteenth century was one step removed from being a barber. Employment by the government, either in the military, the church, or what is now called the civil service, was one of the few careers in which a person without independent means could maintain the status and rank of a gentleman. The government was looked upon by the heads of the great landed families of England as the employer of last resort for their relatives and other dependents, and it was for the most part through the operations of the patronage system that these families maintained themselves.

Patronage was also the glue which held politics together in the

England of George III. In an age before the rise of the modern political party, politics in Britain were to a great extent personal and non-ideological. It is true that at various times there were events, such as the war in America, which inflamed men's passions, but for the most part politics was reduced to a question of "the ins and the outs." A majority of the members of Parliament looked upon themselves as a group of "independent country gentlemen" who gathered at Westminster to support the King's government and who decided each question on its merits and not as a member of a party or faction.[64] This, of course, was a myth for in reality there were men in Parliament who were placemen, professional politicians, soldiers, lawyers, and men who openly belonged to various political factions, yet it was how the average member of Parliament saw himself and his colleagues. One of the few ways in which a politician could maintain a majority in the House of Commons, when its members looked upon themselves as free agents, was through a judicious use of patronage to cement together the incredibly diverse and even hostile personalities and political groups which made up 18th-century British governments. Patronage ran like a golden thread through all the complex twists and turns of British politics during the reign of George III.[65]

—D.S.

1. Warwick County Record Office, Denbigh Letter Books, vol. I, p. 286.

2. *Ibid.*, vol. I, p. 459.

3. *The Victoria History of the Counties of England: Warwick* (London, 1951), pp. 174-5, 284.

4. J.R. Western, *The English Militia in the Eighteenth Century* (London, 1965), p. 168.

5. R.W. Greaves, *The Corporation of Leicester, 1689-1836* (Leicester, 1970), pp. 8-9, 20-60.

6. Sir Lewis Namier and John Brooke, *The History of Parliament: The House of Commons, 1754-1790* (London, 1964), vol. I, p. 322.

7. John Bowater, Lord Feilding, Edward Miller Mundy, William Feilding, Ralph Milbank, George Buckley, Sir Charles Halford, Lord Wentworth, Edward Roe Yeo, and Charles Jackman were all honorary freemen of the Borough of Leicester. Henry Hartopp, ed., *Register of the Freemen of Leicester, 1169-1770* (Leicester, 1927), pp. 362-5; Henry Hartopp, ed., *Register of the Freemen of Leicester, 1770-1930* (Leicester, 1933), pp. 3, 10, 16.

8. Warwick County Record Office, Denbigh Letter Books, vol. I, p. 322.

9. Sidney and Beatrice Webb, *English Local Government: Manor and Borough* (London, 1908), vol. II, pp. 475-6.

10. Sir Lewis Namier and his disciples have tended to minimize, if not deny, the existence of a meaningful doctrine of policy differences between political parties in England at the time of the American Revolution. Moreover, where religion is concerned, they have stressed the extent to which Whigs and Tories were committed to the Anglican settlement of 1689. See for example, Sir Lewis Namier, *England in the Age of the American Revolution* (London, 1930), pp. 206-47. Namier and John Brooke have pointed out that in certain constituencies, Leicester among them, Dissenters played an important role in Parliamentary elections. They tend to dismiss, however, the larger political role of Dissenters, seeing them only in terms of their opposition to the Test and Corporation Acts and to the American War and classifying them as a political force "without parliamentary ambitions" made up of "artisans, small freeholders, or merchants." *History of Parliament*, vol. I, pp. 113-18, 322-4. The Borough of Leicester, however, appears to have been politically divided among religious, economic, and political lines into two factions which were called Tories and Whigs. This suggests that in the particular case of Leicester the traditional or "Whig" interpretation of eighteenth-century politics might be closer to the truth than the Namierite one.

11. The best accounts of Leicester politics during the late 18th century are Greaves, *op. cit., passim*; A. Temple Patterson, *Radical Leicester: A History of Leicester 1780-1850* (Leicester, 1954), pp. 21-8; *The Victoria History of the Counties of England: Leicester* (London, 1954), pp. 124-5.

12. Greaves, *op. cit.*, p. 103.

13. Warwick County Record Office, Denbigh Letter Books, vol. II, pp. 463, 464, 467.

14. See for example, W.S. Lewis, Grover Cronin, Jr., and Charles Bennett, eds., *Horace Walpole's Correspondence with William Mason* (New Haven, 1955), vol. I, p. 81n.

15. Joseph Jackson Howard, ed., *Miscellanea Genealogica et Heraldica* (London, 1877), vol. II, pp. 177-82.

16. E.E. Curtis, *The Organization of the British Army in the American Revolution* (New Haven, 1926), p. 60.

17. Michael Lewis, *A Social History of the Navy, 1794-1815* (London, 1960), p. 239.

18. Lewis, *ibid.*, pp. 202-27; Curtis, *op. cit.*, pp. 24-8.

19. Geoffrey Bennett, *Nelson the Commander* (New York, 1972), p. 12.

20. Elizabeth Longford, *Wellington: The Years of the Sword* (London, 1969), pp. 21-2.

21. Richard Glover, *Peninsular Preparation: The Reform of the British Army, 1795-1809* (Cambridge, 1963), p. 143.

22. Paul Harris Nicolas, *Historical Record of the Royal Marine Forces* (London, 1895), vol. I, p. xi.

23. [National Maritime Museum], *The Commissioned Sea Officers of the Royal Navy, 1660-1815* (London, 1954), vol. I, p. 88.

24. William Mountaine, *The Seaman's Vade-Mecum, and Defensive War by Sea* (London, 1756), pp. 39-40.

25. Howard, *op. cit.*, vol. II, pp. 180-1.

26. Lewis, *op. cit.*, pp. 155-74.

27. John Marshall, *Royal Naval Biography* (London, 1823), vol. I, p. 272.

28. In 1794 the modern name of the rank was introduced when the Admiralty dropped the word "master" from the title. Lewis, *op. cit.*, p. 194.

29. Lewis, *ibid.*, pp. 193-4.

30. Public Record Office, ADM/6/22, p. 405.

31. Lewis, *op. cit.*, pp. 186-9.

32. Marshall, *op. cit.*, vol. I, p. 272.

33. Lewis, *op. cit.*, pp. 203-4.

34. *Commissioned Sea Officers*, vol. I, pp. 88, 307.

35. David Spinney, *Rodney* (London, 1969), pp. 353-4.

36. Robert Wilden Neeser, ed., *The Dispatches of Molyneux Shuldham* (New York, 1913), p. 259.

37. Nicolas, *op. cit.*, vol. I, p. xiii.

38. John MacIntire, *A Military Treatise on the Discipline of the Marine Forces, when at sea: together with short Instructions for Detachments sent to attack on Shore* (London, 1763), p. 276.

39. *Gentleman's Magazine*, vol. 59, p. 89.

40. *A List of the General and Field-Officers, As they Rank in the Army. . .* (London, 1776), pp. 193-4, 196.

41. *A List of the Officers of the Army . . .* (London, 1782), pp. 191-3, 197-200.

42. National Maritime Museum, SAN/T/7, John Graham and Charles Jackman to Sandwich, April 3, 1779; The Memorial of the Field Officers, Captains, and Subaltern Officers of His Majesty's Marine Forces, [July 1779].

43. *A List of the Officers of the Army. . .* (London, 1782), p. 191.

44. *A List of the General and Field-Officers, As they Rank in the Army. . .* (London, 1776), pp. 193-4; *A List of the Officers of the Army. . .* (London, 1782), pp. 191-3.

45. *A List of all the Officers of the Army and Royal Marines* (London, 1810), pp. 4, 472.

46. Thomas Simes, *The Military Guide for Young Officers* (London, 1781), pp. 292-3.

47. Curtis, *op. cit.*, p. 2.

48. The papers of Charles Jenkinson during the period when he was Secretary at War [British Museum, Add. MSS., 38210-38217], reveal the enormous amount of time and effort George III put into supervising army promotions. See also, *The History of Parliament*, vol. I, p. 139.

49. Feilding's career was not atypical for a person of his social status. Lord Herbert, for example, the oldest son of the Earl of Pembroke and one year older than Feilding, entered Parliament at the age of twenty-one and was placed in command of the 2nd Dragoon Guards at age twenty-four. Both

Feilding and Herbert, when ages eighteen and nineteen respectively, were captains together in the 75th Regiment. *History of Parliament*, vol. II, p. 610.

50. *A List of the General and Field Officers, As they Rank in the Army. . .* (London, 1778), p. 61.

51. Glover, *op. cit.*, p. 144.

52. The 72nd-84th Regiments. Eric Robson, "The Raising of a Regiment in the War of American Independence with Especial Reference to 80th and 94th Regiments," *The Journal of the Society for Army Historical Research* (Autumn, 1949), vol. XXVII, p., 107.

53. Curtis, *op. cit.*, p. 68.

54. J.W. Fortescue, *A History of the British Army* (London, 1915), vol. IV, pp. 212-16.

55. For example, the captains of the 80th Regiment, which was raised at the same time as the 75th Regiment, had an average of 4.2 years service as lieutenants before being promoted to captain. Robson, *op. cit.*, p. 111.

56. Captain Lord Feilding was a member of the 75th Regiment such a short time that his name does not appear in the Army Lists as a member of the regiment. *A List of the General and Field Officers, as they Rank in the Army. . .* (London, 1778); *A List of all the Officers of the Army. . .* (London, 1779), pp. 36, 144.

57. Only the 16th, 17th, and 23rd Light Dragoons served overseas during the American War; while out of one hundred and three infantry regiments only eighteen remained in the British Isles throughout the war.

58. E.g., Hugh Thomas, *The Story of Sandhurst* (London, 1961), p. 20.

59. Glover, *op. cit.*, pp. 144-6.

60. Correlli Barnett, *Britain and Her Army, 1509-1970* (London, 1970), p. 238.

61. *History of Parliament*, vol. I, p. 251; vol. II, pp. 416-17.

62. *History of Parliament*, vol. II, pp. 416-17.

63. Richard Pares, *King George III and the Politicians* (Oxford, 1953), p. 5.

64. For an account of the cult of the country gentlemen, see Sir Lewis Namier, *Crossroads of Power: Essays on Eighteenth-Century England* (New York, 1962), pp. 30-45.

65. For discussion of patronage, see Pares, *op. cit.*, pp. 6-7, 10-11, 16-30, 79-80.

NOTE

Throughout the text Denbigh's surname appears as Feilding, although his Lordship occasionally spelled it Fielding. Denbigh's contemporaries, scholarly opinion, and the family itself seem equally divided on the spelling of the name. The army list of 1776 records the name Lieutenant William Fielding,[1] yet in Denbigh's letter books the lieutenant appears as Feilding. One of the most famous members of the family, the author of *Tom Jones*, spelled his name Fielding. In his study of the peerage, Arthur Collins favored the spelling Fielding for the whole family;[2] while *The Commissioned Sea Officers*, seems to divide the family at random into Fieldings and Feildings.[3] Most modern authorities, however, among them Sir Lewis Namier and John Brooke,[4] opt for Feilding as the correct spelling of the surname of the 6th Lord of Denbigh; and the present Earl of Denbigh spells his surname Feilding.[5]

Because it is not uncommon in the documents which follow to find several different spellings of the same word, to avoid confusion, when individuals first appear in the text they are identified whenever possible by full name, rank, title, and position held at the time, and the correct spelling of the surname kept throughout the volume. All warships and place names have also been given their correct spelling throughout the text. There are a few instances in which the punctuation and spelling have been altered for the sake of clarity. The form in which the letters are presented to the reader has been standardized, and the complimentary close, generally a phrase such as, "I am your Lordship's most humble & obedient servant," has been removed in order to avoid constant repetition. In all other cases the original spelling and punctuation of the documents have been retained.

1. *A List of the General and Field-Officers, As they Rank in the Army. . .* (London, 1776), p. 193.
2. Arthur Collins, *The Peerage of England* (London, 1812), vol. III, pp. 244-80.
3. *Commissioned Sea Officers*, vol. I, pp. 311, 316.
4. *History of Parliament*, vol. II, p. 416.
5. *Who's Who, 1971-1972* (New York, 1971), p. 823.

THE LETTERS

I

March 1775-March 1776

For the British, the first twelve months of the American War was a time of humiliation and defeat. One by one all their illusions about America and Americans were cruelly shattered. The first blow came on April 19, 1775, with Lexington and Concord. Until this time, the British had believed that the revolutionary movement in America could be quelled by a display of force at Boston, but the beginning of fighting in Massachusetts signalled the end of royal authority in America and left the British army trapped in Boston by the New England militia. There were, however, those among the British, men such as Major John Pitcairn of the marines, who still thought that "a smart action, and the burning two or three of their towns, will set everything to rights." Yet it was soon evident that this was another illusion, for the fighting of a battle and the burning of towns would not break the American will to resist royal authority. On June 17, 1775, an inconclusive and bloody battle in which 226 British soldiers were killed was fought at Bunker Hill, and in the following months the Royal Navy burned to the ground the towns of Falmouth, Maine and Norfolk, Virginia. Nothing was gained for the British from either the battle or the burning of towns, and on into and through the winter of 1775-6, the British in America remained for the most part passive spectators as they were overtaken by events.

During the winter of 1775-1776, nothing seemed beyond the reach of the American rebels. Their forces invaded Canada, overran the province, and laid siege to Quebec City while the British army remained penned up in Boston. Even the Royal Navy, which had a tradition of victory, seemed helpless during the first year of the war. It could not prevent the Americans from raiding Nassau in the Bahamas, from capturing British supply ships almost within sight of Boston, or from blowing up the lighthouse at the entrance to Boston Harbor. It was a grim time indeed for the British. Defeat and impotence gave rise to feelings of rage and despair among the British soldiers trapped in Boston as they watched the King's empire in America being destroyed by a force they considered to be no more than an armed rabble.

On March 17, 1776, the British army suffered the ultimate humiliation when it was forced to evacuate Boston. The army withdrew to Halifax to prepare to invade New York later that spring; they left behind them no vestige of British authority. An empire which had once stretched from the Atlantic to the Mississippi and from Hudson's Bay to the Gulf of Mexico had crumbled and dissolved.

1. From Lieutenant William Feilding[1]

Plymouth Mar. 23. 1775

My Lord

I took the liberty of acquainting your L[or]ds[hi]p from Portsmouth of my Mother's distressful situation[2] which gives me many very uneasy hours. Your Lordsps unparalelled marks of friendship & benevolence I ever shall have a most grateful sense of. I have not the least doubt but that your Ldsp. will do every thing towards making a permanent provision for my unhappy family. I have this day sent my Mother the last four guineas I could spare.

The Transports with the Portsmouth Marines arrived here last tuesday & on saturday the Plymouth Marines embark & sail the next day for America.

1. Lieutenant William Feilding, Adjutant of the Portsmouth Division of Marines. Great, great grandson of George Feilding, 1st Earl of Desmond, second son of the 1st Earl of Denbigh; and remotely related to the 6th Earl of Denbigh.
2. Lieutenant Feilding's father, Rear Admiral William Feilding, died on September 23, 1773, leaving his widow, Mary; his daughters, Elizabeth, Sarah, and Frances, and three grandchildren without support. Denbigh attempted to obtain a rear admiral's pension for the widow, but Feilding had been a post captain, superannuated with the pension and title of a rear admiral but not the rank. Thus, his widow was not eligible for a rear admiral's pension on the ordinary establishment of the navy and could only petition the Admiralty for a very small pension as a sea officer's widow.

2.   From Lieutenant William Feilding

Boston June 1775

My Lord

I take the opportunity to acquaint your Lordsp. by the *Cerberus* (who lately arrived with the general Officers[1]) that we arrived here the 22d. of May after a very disaggreeable passage of 7 weeks with very hard hard gales of wind. We were much surprized to find a different face of affairs to what we expected, the inhabitants having left the Town & retired to their estates in the Country, many of whom (I am told) were under a necessity of so doing to preserve their property, as the Yankeys had threatned destruction to all Estates belonging to persons who wished well to the British Government, but far the greatest part of them are inveterate Enemies to the Mother Country. I suppose yr. Ldsp has heard ere this of the attack on the Troops on the 19th of Apr. last[2] & make no doubt that American Writers will do all in their power to make the public believe that the Troops went out on purpose to attack them & that we were the first that fired; they have endeavoured to do so in this country by a number of Affidavits which they have published from people who were not at the attack: but your Lordsp. may be assured that these reports are entirely false, as our Troops acted on the defensive. The Grenad[iers] & light Infantry under the command of Col. Smith & Maj. Pitcairn[3] were ordered to Concord to destroy a Magazine: which they did; & on their return were attacked the whole way by numbers who fired out of houses, thro bushes & over stone Walls, but did not destroy so many of ours as might be expected from their situation, as they fired entirely under cover & wou'd never attack openly. The Rebels are now close to our lines & will not suffer any fresh provisions to be brought into the Town so that the Comunication with the Country is shut up. The whole winter the Town abounded with all kinds of fresh provisions & extremely cheap but now it is quite the contrary: not even a bit of vegetables is to be seen tho they are in the greatest quantity in the Country. The Rebels centries & Ours are so close that they sometimes talk to each other. They burn & destroy every thing on the Islands in the Harbour to destress us. Our Troops I believe would be very glad to give them a good drubbing as they are upon all occasions firing at us (particularly at the *Glasgow* who lies between shores[4]) but without effect as they want to provoke her to fire. In all the American papers they exult much at the victory which they say they have gained over the Parliament Troops, as they call us & themselves the King's loyal & faithful subjects. Our Numbers killed & wounded they multiply to thousands, but if thousands were on any side it was theirs: tho it is supposed they lost considerably less than 1000. Our Troops are pretty healthy & are encamped on the common round the Town & have lost very few men by desertion. My time as Adjutant is far from being idle. I do assure your Lordsp. I seldom sit down to dinner: however I am happy in a good state of health & have not as yet found the least inconvenience from being fatigued or wet in my tent as we have had some very heavy showers. I have sent your Lordsp. a printed account of the attack on our Troops & likewise the resolutions of the Congress. I shall write by all opportunities.

1. Major Generals William Howe, John Burgoyne, and Henry Clinton.
2. Lexington and Concord.
3. Lieutenant Colonel Francis Smith of the 10th Regiment and Major John Pitcairn of the Marines.
4. Between Boston and Charlestown.

3.   **Donald Mackinnon[1] to Lieutenant William Feilding**

Newnham[2] June 6th. 1775

Dear Sir

I have the pleasure to acquaint you by my good Lord Denbigh's directions that his Ldsp. has at last procured some small provision to be made for a part of your Family. The Queen has granted to Mrs. Farrell[3] a pension of £75 pr. an. neat money, out of her own privy purse, to be paid in quarterly payments & the first of them to be made this Midsummer.

I am also to acquaint you that L[a]dy Denbigh[4] at his Ldsp's request has taken your youngest Sister[5] into this Family with a view to qualify her for some useful & active station in life. She is not (I am certain) upon the footing upon which you would wish your Sister to be; for She does not mess in the Parlour, but I can assure you that Lady Denbigh treats her with particular tenderness & affection, &

from the attention paid to her by all here I have reason to believe that she will spend the time agreeably & profitably. His Ldsp. & all here heartily wish your safety & to hear from you as oft as possible.

1. Denbigh's private chaplain and secretary.
2. Newnham Paddox, Warwickshire.
3. Sarah Feilding Farrell. Lieutenant William Feilding's married sister.
4. Mary Cotton Feilding, Countess of Denbigh.
5. Frances Feilding.

4. To Lord Sandwich[1]

Newnham June 17th. 1775

My dear Lord

I have been so much out of Order since I have been here that I fear it will not be in my power to attend the Birth-day[2] when I intended in person to have most earnestly applied to you to give a Sloop to Captn. [Thomas] Underwood who is now perfectly restored to health & languishing to go to sea. As I think it very likely that more Sloops will be put into Commission I flatter myself you will be able to give him One before the expiration of the Summer. What makes me hope that your Lordsp will not think me unreasonable in this request is, that you know that Mr. Underwood's misfortune not his fault prevented his benefiting of your former good intentions to promote him.

I take it for granted American business will bring you from your tour visiting the Sea ports & Dockyards sooner than you intended. The Rubicon is now passed & matters are become very serious indeed. I should be very glad of a line from you for my own satisfaction as well as that of all this Country which is in great anxiety.

1. John Montagu, 4th Earl of Sandwich. First Lord of the Admiralty, 1771-1782.
2. The King's official birthday, the celebration of which was put off from the 4th until the 22nd of June in 1775.

5. From Lieutenant William Feilding

Charles Town hill June 20th. 1775

My Lord

I have just time to acquaint your Lordsp that on saturday the 17th inst. part of our Troops under the command of Genl. Howe[1] landed at Charles Town to take a redoubt which the rebels had that morning thrown up; & have the satisfaction to acquaint your Lordsp that the bravery of our Officers & Soldiers is not to be equalled on the attack & storming the redoubt & in following the Rebels off that peninsula.[2]

We have lost several men & Officers. The Account I have not been able to get. Our Corps have suffered very much—have lost Major Pitcairn two Captains & three Lieuts. killed, & three Captains & five Lieuts. wounded very much. Your Lordsp will have a better account of it from the letters sent by the General. I hope your Lordsp will excuse this scrall as my time is not my own.

1. Major General the Hon. William Howe, commander-in-chief of the British army in America, 1775-1778.
2. The Battle of Bunker Hill.

6. **From Lord Sandwich**

Portsmouth June 23d. 1775

My dear Lord,

I am always happy when the requests of my friends are such as it is in my power to comply with. I cannot indeed promise any particular Sloop, but I hope before the Summer is ended to be able to find employment for Capt. Underwood.

7. **From Lieutenant William Feilding**

Heights of Charles Town near Boston America
July 18 1775

My Lord

In my last [No. 5] I was not able to give you any account of the Attack of the Rebel redoubt & strong holds on the heights of Charles

Town June 17 for I assure your Lordsp the duty of an Adjutant at that time & place was not a little fatiguing & afforded very little rest even at night as we are often alarmed at the Rebels firing at the lines; this I hope will sufficiently apologise for me. The particulars of that action your Lordsp has heard from better hands already. I can only say from the oldest soldiers here say that it was the hottest fire they ever saw not even the battle of Minden which was reckoned one of the greatest actions ever gained by British Troops was equal to it. And for the honour of the British Troops, many of whom had never seen a Ball fired, they behaved with the greatest courage; & tho, considerably inferior in numbers as well as advantage, boldly ascended the hill jump'd into the ditch, mounted the redoubt, carried it, drove the Rebels from their strong breast works & gained a complete victory. In ascending the hill our Major commandant[1] was killed, 5 Officers of the two Marine Grenadier Companys were killed & wounded & as many of the two light companies, besides several in the Battallion, in the whole 1 Major. 2 Capts. & 3 Sub[altern]s Killed. 4 Capts. & 4 Sub[altern]s very badly wounded none of whom are yet recovered. The night of that day, the Troops were employed in throwing up entrenchments near Charles Town neck to secure themselves from the Rebels who kept firing at them the whole night, to very little effect as they only killed one Officer & slightly wounded some of the men, which Officer unfortunately had a wife & children in Boston. The loss of our Major Commandant was not only a loss to his Family as one of the best of Husbands & Fathers; but a great loss to the Marines & the Army in general as a brave soldier & an excellent Officer. For this loss the Corps of Marines went into mourning for six weeks, as well as for the rest of the Officers killed.

The Rebels have thrown up many large redoubts strongly fortified upon the heights from Dorchester neck round to Charles Town neck besides breast works from one hill to another well finished & extremely well planned by Engineers supposed to be French & Swedes. Their numbers are about 17000, commanded by Generals appointed by the continental Congress. Washington Generalissimo, Ward, Lee & Putnam Major Generals,[2] besides several Brigadiers. Their army is said to be above half Irish & Scotch, but far more of the former than the latter, chiefly Emigrants who have settled in this Province since the last war, & have been compelled to take up Arms Against their Sovereign & Country under false pretences of having their property & liberty secured to them.[3]

State of our Loss. Killed in the Action & dead since, 4 field Officers 9 Capts. & 12 Sub[altern]s. Wounded in the Action. 3 Field Officers, 26 Capts. & 39 Sub[altern]s. The non-commissioned & Rank & File killed & wounded are above 900.[4] Many of the wounded are since dead & they continue dying daily but some have recovered.

The Rebels must have lost a much greater number as near 200[5] were found on the field of Battle & they were discovered carrying their dead in carts before they retreated. Their wounded also must be considerable. Among their killed at the redoubt was the famous Dr. [Joseph] Warren a Major Genl. & President of the [Massachusetts Provincial] Congress; a man who inflamed the minds of the people from the Pulpit several times in this Town.

It is reported to day, that the Genl. of the Rebel Army had sent to the several Towns in this Province for their Minute Men to join them immediately as they meant to attack the Town of Boston; & that their Answer was that they never meant to attack but to defend their own Towns & that they would do *this* to the utmost, but refused the Summons.

I thank God I never enjoyed a better state of health. I hope your Lordsp. Lady Denbigh & the young Gentlemen are all well.

1. Major John Pitcairn.
2. Major Generals Artemas Ward, Charles Lee, and Israel Putnam.
3. Throughout the war it was widely believed among the British that the American army was largely comprised of renegade Irishmen.
4. 226 killed and 826 wounded.
5. 100 killed, 271 wounded, 30 captured.

8. From Lord Townshend[1]

Rainham Augt. 7th. 1775

My dear Lord

It is now in my power to place Mr. John Harding at the royal academy[2] as your Lordsp. wished, therefore I beg you will send him immediately if qualified according to the printed rules I had the honour to transmit to your Ldsp. some time ago; but if that should not be the case he had better stay a little longer for another vacancy to obtain the degree of instruction therein mentioned. I must tell your

Lordsp. that the youngest Cadet is without pay from a disagreeable insolvency of an Officer which has fallen upon the Corps, but this inconveniency to Mr. Harding will be but of short duration as this confounded War in America will occasion but too many vacancies on our establishment.

1. George Townshend, 4th Viscount Townshend, Master General of the Ordnance.
2. Royal Military Academy, Woolwich, where artillery and engineer officers were trained.

9. To Lieutenant William Feilding

Newnham Augst. 8. 1775

Dear Grenadier

I received yours of the 20th. of June [No. 5] some time ago & it gave us all great pleasure to hear of your escape & welfare. I have since seen Lord Sandwich & did not fail to try if any thing could be done with him to forward your promotion. I had the satisfaction to find his Lordship, from the accounts he receives of you from other quarters as well as from me, very well disposed towards you. He tells me that all promotions in the Marines will be given according to seniority to the Officers on the Actual service where vacancies happen, & assures me that you may depend upon the strictest justice according to this rule;[1] & that Major Pitcairn's Son (whose case is very particular) being put over all your heads is not to be looked upon as a precedent.[2] To this I will add that nothing shall be wanting on my part at all times to make good your claims & to render every service to yourself & Family.

As you are always to send your letters to me in Lord Dartmouth's packet[3] there is no danger of their being opened, I therefore must desire you not only to be very particular in your facts but also to give your opinion freely as well of past transactions as of what is likely to happen in futurity. We are all very much surprized here to find that you are still blocked up within the Walls & peninsula of Boston, where if you continue without fresh provisions, I fear you will lose many of your Men by sickness & desertion, & as the Rebels are I fear in possession of Dorchester hill you are liable every day to have the

Town knocked about your ears. What is all this owing to? Surely you have troops enough to force a communication into the Country & oblige the Rebels to raise ye seige. And it would be more to the credit of a British Army to die in the field than to be starved within an entrenchment. Another thing surprizes me still more, how General Gage[4] could neglect taking possession of the heights of Charles Town before the Rebels had entrenched themselves on them. But of this & many other things he will have to give an account himself very soon in this Country. Ten more British Regiments are just ordered to be sent to you, five of them from Ireland & the other five from Minorca & Gibraltar. The latter are to be replaced by Troops from Hanover.

Our papers are full of complaints against Admiral Graves,[5] but I flatter myself there is no room for them as he has always bore the best of Characters.

1. The promotion of a marine officer below the rank of colonel was, with few exceptions, by seniority. In 1775 there were three categories of marine officers: those serving ashore with two marine battalions at Boston; those assigned to warships; and those on the half-pay list. Sandwich, however, apparently told Denbigh that marine promotions at Boston would be by seniority among the officers of the two battalions alone. But this policy was not followed, and the marine officers who had served ashore at Boston believed they had been treated badly when the vacancies created by their casualties at Bunker Hill were filled by seniority from among the whole marine officer corps.

2. First Lieutenant William Pitcairn was commissioned on March 2, 1773, and William Feilding was commissioned on January 22, 1763. At the time of the death of his father, William Pitcairn was 109th in seniority among the first lieutenants of the marines; Feilding was 58th. After Bunker Hill, Pitcairn was promoted over the heads of 108 first lieutenants to the rank of captain lieutenant with a commission dated July 27, 1775.

3. William Legge, 2nd Earl of Dartmouth and Secretary of State for the Colonies, August 1772-November 1775. On June 6, 1775, Denbigh made arrangements for Feilding's letters to be sent to England in official military dispatch pouches.

4. Lieutenant General Thomas Gage, commander-in-chief of the British army in America until October 10, 1775, when he left Boston to return to England.

5. Vice-Admiral Samuel Graves, commander-in-chief of the Royal Navy in America until he was relieved on December 30, 1775.

10.   **From Lord Sandwich**

Admiralty Augst. 10th. 1775

My dear Lord

I have the pleasure to inform you that Capt. Underwood is appointed to the command of the *Atalanta* Sloop; her destination is not yet settled.

My best respects attend Lady Denbigh, I hope the Pike arrived safe & proved a good one.

[P.S.] Mr. [William] Bowater[1] Junr. of the Marines is promoted to a first Lieutenancy.

1. Fifth son of Richard Bowater of Stivichall, Coventry, Warwickshire.

11.   **To Lord Townshend**

Newnham Augst. 12th. 1775

My dear Lord

I have just received the favour of Yours of the 7 Inst. [No. 8] & am very much obliged to you for the appointment of Mr. John Harding into the Royal Academy. I accept of the present vacancy as he is now exactly of the proper age as your Lordsp will find by the Certificate of his Age which was sent to the Ordnance in 1773. I have accordingly desired his Father to fit him out & carry him to the Academy for Examination. He will call upon Mr Courtney[1] at the Ordnance Office to receive his commands as he goes thro Londn.

1. John Courtney, Secretary to the Master General of the Ordnance.

12.   **To Judd Harding**

Newnham Augst. 12th. 1775

I have the pleasure to acquaint you that by a letter [No. 8] I have this received from the Master of the Ordnance your Son John Harding is appointed into the Royal Academy at Woolwich. It is therefore necessary that he should be presented for examination immediately & fitted out according to the enclosed printed directions.

I sent your Name to the Lord Lieut. of this Country to be inserted in the new Commission of the Peace that is about to be made out.[1]

1. Denbigh requested that Judd Harding be made a justice of the peace.

13. To Lord Sandwich

Newnham Aug. 12th. 1775

My dear Lord

I return you my sincere thanks for the very handsome & expeditious manner in which you have been so good as to give my friend Captn. Underwood a Sloop, & I flatter myself he will make it his Study to deserve the many favours [he has] received from your Lordsp. He shall come up to Town next week & wait on Mr [Philip] Stephens[1] to take out his Commission & receive your Lordsps further Orders. The Pike was an exceeding good one for which Lady Denbigh sends you her thanks & desires me to tell you how happy you have made her by the promotion of her Protogée the young [William] Bowater to a first Lieutenancy of Marines.

1. First Secretary to the Lords of the Admiralty.

14. From Lieutenant William Feilding

Boston Augst. 13. 1775

My Lord

Since my last [No. 7] nothing extraordinary has happened, except the Rebels burning the Light Houses on cape Ann & the light house at the entrance of Boston. The latter was afterwards repaired & an Officer of Marines with 30 men from the Admiral's Ship sent to guard it. On the 31st. of July before day about 400 rebels landed on the Light House Island, killed the Lieut. & ten Marines & took the rest prisoners with several Carpenters. The Men of War's boats manned & armed followed the Rebels to the opposite shore but were not able to take any of them;[1] some of the Carpenters made their escape, the rest of the prisoners were obliged to drag a piece of cannon up their hill. They still continue to fortify every height & their camps are seen all over the Country. Our Troops have been attacked with severe fluxes & many have died for want of fresh provisions which have been so very scarce that when any have been procured for the Hospitals, they allowed only 4 ounces pr. Man Officers included. I have eat fresh meat but 3 times these six weeks. Fish & Salt pork are our constant Food. A supply of about 30 head of cattle & 50 sheep was brought here in a vessel taken by the cruiser, the whole of which was purchased for the use of the sick which I was not sorry for. I keep my health at present very well tho not quite so stout as when at Newnham.

N.B. Two Captns. of Marines died yesterday.

1. American accounts of the burning of the lighthouse at the entrance to Boston Harbor list British casualties as seven killed and twenty-three captured.

15.　**From Thomas Dicey**

Claybrook Augst. 14. 1775

My Lord

My Father being still in such a situation as to prevent my leaving him even for an hour I beg leave to take this method of applying to your Lordsp in behalf of a very near connection who has been very hardly treated to serve Government.

The case of my friend & the favour I solicit for him & which I shall consider as conferred on myself are briefly thus. Some time in the course of last year a Company in the 33d. Regt. became vacant by Death. In consequence of which Lord Cornwallis[1] the Coll. recommended the Captn. Lieut. to succeed to the Company & my friend Lieut. [John] Kerr the Senr. Lieut. to the Captn. Lieutcy. urging Mr Kerr's services as the chief ground of both recommendations. The Lord Lieutenant of Ireland where the Regt. is answered Lord Cornwallis that the Company should go in the Regt. but that the Capt. Lieutcy. must be given to a Lieut [the Hon. Robert] Peckenham (a younger Officer than Lieut. Kerr & of a younger Regt.) who was Member for an Irish County, a friend of Government & Bro. to Lord

Longford.² Lieut. Kerr therefore was disappointed to serve Mr. Peck-enham & Govt. & the favour I request of your Lordsp is to procure a company of Foot for Lieut. Kerr, whose merits as an Officer shall be fully & satisfactorily certified to your Lordsp or Lord North³ (to whom I wish your Lordsp to apply rather than to Lord Barrington⁴) by Lord Cornwallis. Mr. Kerr has been in the service ever since Aug. 1760 has never been 2 years absent from the Regt. during that time & was the Chasseur Officer of the 33d. Regt. from the first establish-ment of that detachment to the conclusion of the war.

I particularly apply to your Lordsp at this juncture because by the many vacancies that have lately happened & the augmentation of the Army that is daily talked of I conceive a promotion of this sort to be more practicable than in a time of profound peace and tranquility.

1. Charles Cornwallis, 2nd Earl Cornwallis, Major General and Colonel of the 33rd Regiment.
2. Edward Michael Pakenham, 6th Baron Longford, Captain in the Royal Navy, M.P. in the Irish Parliament, and member of the Irish Privy Council.
3. Frederick North, Lord North, First Lord of the Treasury, 1770-1782.
4. William Wildman Barrington, 2nd Viscount Barrington, Secretary at War, 1757-1778.

16. **To Thomas Dicey**

Newnham Augst. 14 1775

Lord Denbigh's Comp[liment]s to Mr. Dicey, shall always be happy to have it in his power to obey any commands of his, but upon the present occasion can assure him that all promotions in the Army on the Irish establishment are entirely in the Lord Lieutenant of Ireland & that neither Lord North nor the Secry. at War have the least share in them. But as the present Lord Lieut is a very intimate friend of Lord D's he will write to him to recommend Mr. Kerr in the strongest manner for a Company when any new Regts shall be raised in Ireland.

17. **From Lord Sandwich**

Admiralty Augst. 26 1775

My dear Lord

Captain Underwood is ordered to the coast of Guinea from whence he ought to bring Lady Denbigh a collection of curious birds. I shall be obliged to you if you will write to him immediatly to tell him I shall take it as a favour if he will give the Writer of the inclosed[1] a Midshipmans birth on board the *Atalanta*: he will be no incumbrance upon him being a stout seaman & just returned from India with Sir Robt. Harland.

1. Not entered in the letter book.

18. **To Lord Sandwich**

Newnham Augst. 28 1775

My dear Lord

I have received yours [No. 17] & have by this post wrote to Captn. Underwood[1] who I am confident will take great pleasure in obeying all your commands, particularly those respecting your Midshipman whose letter I have enclosed to him. As Underwood's state of health has been bad so lately I could have wished it had been convenient for you to have sent him to a healthier climate; tho I dare say he will very cheerfully go to the coast of Guinea or the Coast of H ll if his service requires him so to do.

I have this day had a letter [No. 7] from Adjutant Feilding dated July 18th. He says nothing new has happened since the Action of the 17th. June, but that the Rebels have thrown up many large Redoubts strongly fortified upon the heights from Dorchester neck round to Charles Town neck, besides breast works from one hill to another well finished & extremely well planned by Engineers supposed to be French & Swedes; that the Rebels are in numbers about 17000, said to be above half Irish & Scotch Emigrants settled there since the War. If this last circumstance is true Is it not high time to stop emigration?

P.S. Lord Craven[2] tells me that in case Southwell[3] gets his Peerage Geo. Berkley[4] will be a Candidate for Gloucestershire, & I most sincerely hope he will be beat as the D. of Beaufort⁵ nominates a very worthy friend⁶ to Governt. in opposition to him.

1. Not entered in the letter book.
2. William Craven, 6th Baron Craven.
3. Edward Southwell, M.P. for Bridgewater, 1761-1763; Gloucestershire, 1763-1776. He vacated his seat when raised to the peerage as 21st Baron de Clifford.
4. Lieutenant the Hon. George Cranfield Berkeley, R.N., M.P. for Gloucestershire, 1783-1810. In 1774 Berkeley was a candidate at Cricklade but withdrew before the election; and in 1776 he stood and narrowly lost in Gloucestershire against W.B. Chester in a very expensive campaign.
5. Henry Somerset, 5th Duke of Beaufort.
6. William Bromley Chester, M.P. for Gloucestershire, 1776-1780.

19.   From John Peach Hungerford¹

Dingley Septr. 4th. 1775

My Lord

I have the honour of your Lordsp's letter enclosing that from Mr. Bowlby for which I return your Lordsp. thanks. The Names of the young Gentlemen who wish to obtain your Lordsp's patronage to get into the Army are Thomas Moor Hall of Shakestone Leicestershire & Richard Roberts of Thurnby in Northamptonshire. By the papers it appears that some new Regiments are going to be raised in Ireland, if that should prove true they will be very happy to be a Commission in one of them.

1. M.P. for Leicestershire, 1775-1790.

20.   From Thomas Dicey

Claybrook Septr. 8 1775

My Lord

As the answer [No. 16] I had the honour of receiving from your Lordsp. to my last letter [No. 15] gave me room to believe that your Ldsp. wished to serve me in the request I made I again take the liberty to renew my application & to inform your Lordsp. of some circumstances which were then unknown to me.

My Friend Lieut. Kerr at the very time I wrote had got the Captn. Lieutenancy & consequently the rank of Captn. by the death of Capt. Pakenham. At least the recommendations were gone over from the Ld. Lieut. for his Majesty's approbation, so that I would hope the difficulty of getting a company for him *now* would not be so great as when he was only Lieutenant. All the Regiments serving in America or that are ordered thither are to be immediatly augmented with two Companies so that no less than sixty two will be disposed of, & very few half pay Officers whatever have yet offered in consequence of the Advertisements in the Gazette. The 33d. (Captn. Kerr's) does not go & therefore a Company in any other Regt upon any service or Station is what I solicit, & what I shall always think myself particularly obliged to your Lordsp. to obtain. It is material to observe another circumstance, viz. that all the Regts. to be augmented come upon the British Establishment, because it does not [take] place till they quit Ireland: most of them indeed are already upon the British establishment, namely those now in America; the Lord Lieut therefore has nothing to do with those Companies, such is the unanimous opinion of all the Military people in Ireland, & that no applications but to Lord North will avail. I leave that however to your Lordsp's better Judgment & information. With regard to my friend's character as an Officer I will engage that it shall be authenticated in the most honorable manner by his Coll. Lord Cornwallis to any quarter your Lordsp may be pleased to point out.

21. **To Lord Harcourt**[1]

Newnham Septr. 9th. 1775

My dear Lord

As I find some corps are to be raised in Ireland I shall take it a great favour if your Lordsp will give a pair of colours[2] in one of them to a very worthy young fellow & friend of mine Thomas Moor Hall Esq. I have for this long time studiously avoided importuning your Lordsp & therefore hope you will the sooner gratify me in this small matter which I have very much at heart.

1. Simon Harcourt, 1st Earl Harcourt, Lord Lieutenant of Ireland, October 9, 1772-January 25, 1777.
2. The two flags, one royal and one regimental, belonging to a regiment, hence the appointment to an ensigncy.

22. To Lord Cornwallis

Newnham Septr. 9th. 1775

My dear Lord

I am very desirous of assisting Lieut. Kerr of your Regt. who I am told is lately become Captn. Lieut. in getting a Company. I therefore wish you would point out to me the most effectual method of doing this; whether by an application to the Secretary at War at home or to the Lord Lieut. of Ireland. And as Mr. Kerr is in your Lordsp's own corps, your putting in a word for him will be great service to him.

23. From Lord Harcourt

Dublin Castle Septr. 15. 1775

My dear Lord

There are no new corps raising in Ireland, nor do I understand that it is his Majesty's intentions to raise any new Regiments but to augment those that are on the British & Irish Establishments: but if contrary to my expectations any new Regiments should be raised I shall be very happy to have it in my power to oblige your Lordsp's friend Mr. Moor Hall.

24. To Lord Harcourt

Newnham Septr. 25. 1775

My dear Lord

I am perfectly well apprised that no new Regiments are to be raised in Ireland but that the present ones are, to be augmented by additional Companies, every one of which must have an Ensign. I therefore cannot help thinking the Earl of Harcourt could have no great difficulty in giving a pair of Colours to the recommendation of his very old acquaintance & sincere friend.

25.   From Lord Cornwallis

Dublin Septr. 28. 1775

My dear Lord

The Additional Companies are only raised for the Regiments serving in America, consequently they are given away by the Secretary at War. I understand that it is regulated by the King's Order that One of these Companies should go in each Regiment, & the Other from half-pay. If that should be the case, your Lordsp's endeavours to serve Captain Kerr must in the present instance prove ineffectual. If any Companies should be added to my Regiment he will certainly succeed.

26.   From Lieutenant William Feilding

Boston Oct. 8th. 1775

My Lord

I was favoured with Mr. Mackinnon's letters [No. 3] by the *Cerberus* which has been the first Ship with any Accounts from England even concerning the former Action of the 19th Apr. Since my last [No. 14] we had no Attack with the Rebels, but they very often insult us by firing at our guards & working parties to very little effect. An Officer of the 59th. & a private Soldier of the 4th. Regt. lost their legs & 5 or 6 other Soldiers slightly wounded. Our shells & shot I believe have done much execution. Their Works are extended for Miles extremely well planned & executed, with several pieces of Cannon in them mostly 3 & 4 pounders, some few 24 & 18 pounders but not sufficient to fill all their Ambresures. We hear the Cannon which they have taken from the batteries at N.[ew] York are upon the Road for this Place. We are fortifying the Town within the Houses on the neck which will secure the Town from their Approaching this Winter. Several of their shot have gone thro the houses on the Neck but done no other damage.

Some Transports under the direction of the *Canceaux* Capt. Mowatt[1] with a detachment of a Capt. 2 Sub[altern]s & 50 Marines, from the Army 2 officers & some Artillery with plenty of all kinds of Ammunition, are to sail in a few days, the destination of which is a secret, but supposed to be to burn some Towns on some of the Rivers to the Eastward, where ships have landed warlike stores.[2] I hope they will meet with success & distress those rebellious Rascals before the winter sets in, of every thing that can be of use to them in cold weather & flatter myself they are badly provided already with warm clothing for a large Army which I believe will cause great discontent.

It is reported that the clothing of the 22d. & 40th. Regts with the Cloaks of the latter which unfortunately fell into their hands at Philadelphia, they have died brown, as they do not chuse to appear like the *Parliament's Army.* The Deserters which have lately come in are badly clothed. The Heights of Charles Town are very strong with lines & redoubts, & a Citadel is going to be built to hold the Troops for the Winter. It has often been reported that the Rebels intended to attack the lines at Boston neck and Charles Town. Attacking without cover is not their method of fighting as they would undoubtedly loose considerably by it. The Troops have suffered much for want of fresh provisions, especially the sick, but since the port has been open, some vessels have come in with stock which has been some relief to those who could afford to buy it. Some Transports with 100 men from the Army were went to some of the Islands to buy stock & were tolerably successful in getting 2000 sheep & about 100 head of Cattle the most part of which were kept for the sick to the satisfaction of every body. Three fleets of Transports are now out (under convoy of Men of War) after Provision, Forage & Wood for the Army; some of which are daily expected particularly those with Wood as Fuel is very scarce & the Weather beginning to grow cold.

Coll. [Arthur Tooker] Collins arrived in the *Cerberus* to command the Marines, & brought Commissions for Officers here to fill the Vacancies by the late Action, which have been filled up chiefly by Seniority of first Commission different from Lord Sandwich's usual plan [No. 9]. Had it been otherwise I should have been one of the first for promotion. I hope however thro your Lordsp's influence, Lord Sandwich may be prevailed upon to break thro *this new plan*, as his Ldsp. has not entirely stuck to it by promoting Mr. Pitcairn a very young 1st Lieut. to a Captn. Lieutenancy, which your Ldsp. may conclude did not a little mortify me; he having been very little more than 7 years in the Corps & I 17 not much under his Age! But I flatter myself as there are 4 more vacancies sent home that your Ldsp. will be able to procure me one of them.

I beg leave to return your Ldsp. my most grateful acknowledgements for the very friendly & humane Act of procuring a Pension for my Sister Farrell & Family, the unsettled situation of whom had given me much uneasiness. I am likewise extremely obliged to your Ldsp. & Lady Denbigh for the affection & tenderness which you shew to my youngest Sister, & who I flatter myself will merit your esteem.

I have just received Mr. Mackinnon's of June 6th. [No. 3] by the *Raven* who had long been expected here. I have the pleasure to acquaint your Ldsp. that tho the Army has been in general sickly, Officers as well as Men, I have had my health extremely well.

P.S. Lord Percy who has just received his appointment as Major General in America[3] is very well, & from whom I have received great Civilities desired his Comps to your Ldsp. The 4 vacancies that have happened since the Action are

Major [Stawet] Chudleigh	dead of his wounds
Captn. [Arthur] Walker	
Captn. [William] Sabine	
Captn. [Charles] Chandless in a violent fever cut his own throat	

1. Lieutenant Henry Mowat, R.N.
2. This force attacked and burned Falmouth (now Portland), Maine on October 19, 1775.
3. Hugh Percy, Lord Warkworth. On July 11, 1775, Percy was appointed a major general in America, and on September 29, 1775, he was permanently promoted to that rank.

27.   From Rear Admiral Robert Duff[1]

Portsmouth Novr. 14. 1775

My Lord

As Lieut [Bayntun] Prideaux who commanded the *Quebec* Cutter has on account of bad health been under the necessity of applying to me for leave to come to England I was glad to embrace so early an opportunity of shewing my inclination to serve Mr. [Edward] Bowater[2] whom your Ldsp. recommended to me & have given him an

Order to act as Lieut. & to command the *Quebec* Cutter at Newfoundland. As that climate does not agree with Mr. Prideaux's health he will not incline to return to his command, it will therefore contribute greatly to secure Mr. Bowater's appointment if your Ldsp. will as soon as convenient apply to Lord Sandwich to give me directions to send a Commission to Mr. Bowater in lieu of the Order he now acts by. Mr. Bowater is a young Gentleman of great merit whom your Lordsp. will always have a satisfaction in patronizing. I shall take an early opportunity of paying my respects to your Ldsp. after my arrival in London.

1. Governor of Newfoundland and commander-in-chief of the squadron there.
2. Seventh son of Richard Bowater.

28. From The Corporation of Leicester

Leicester Novr. 15. 1775

May it please your Lordship

We the Mayor & Aldermen of the Borough of Leicester beg leave to recommend to your Ldsp's notice William Buckley a Member of this Corporation, & beg your Lordsp will provide for him in such a department as will be most convenient & agreeable to your Lordsp. The favour will be acknowledged by My Lord your Ldsp's most obedt. humble Servants.

29. To Rear Admiral Robert Duff

Londn. Novr. 18. 1775

Dear Sir

I have received your letter [No. 27] & cannot sufficiently thank you for the attention you have paid to my recommendation of Mr. Bowater. I have applied to Lord Sandwich & have the pleasure to inform you that the Admiralty have given directions for sending Mr. Bowater a Commission.[1] I am very happy the young Gentleman meets with your approbation. When you come to Town I shall be exceeding glad to see you in South [Street]. . . .[2]

1. Edward Bowater was commissioned a lieutenant on February 26, 1776.
2. Illegible. Denbigh always gave the address of his London residence as "South Street," although his house was located on South Audley Street.

30. From Lieutenant William Feilding

Boston Novr. 20. 1775

My Lord

I was Honor'd with your Lordship's of the 8th. of Augt. [No. 9] the 8th. Inst: by the *Phoenix*. We have Remain'd quiet for some time, as the Rebels find whenever they insult us, they lose considerably by it: the 16th of Octr. they fired at the Guard going to Releive the Advanced Lines and kiled a Soldier of the 63 Regiment that kind of firing they had practised for some time, to very little Effect, tho several of their shot went thro' the Guard Room—one of which took off Capn. Poulets[1] leg of the 59 Regt. We always Returned their fire, with a treble discharge of Cannon from the Lines, and finding it impossable to dismount any of their Guns (as they allways draw them in as soon as fired and every person out of sight till loaded) fired at last on the Town of Roxbury, and have learnt by deserters, that the morning the Soldier of the 63rd was kiled we killd about thirty and wounded several, which put a stop to their insulting us in that quarter. The 16th of Octr. three Gundelos came down Cambridge River, between 8 & 9 oClock at Night, and fired very briskly for an hour at the Marines 40th and 22nd Regts. encampments, but fortunately no person was hurt, tho several shot went thro Tents where men were asleep, at last one of the Guns burst, which kill'd most of the Men in that Gundelos particular the Officer that Commanded, and wounded the Rest. They not being good Artilery men it was imagined they over charged their Guns, as the distance their shot Came was very great and must have had great Elevation as several shot went over the Camp and thro' Houses in our Rear.

They published in their papers, that all their fireings had Kill'd several of the Minesterial Army, particularly the last from the Gundelos, and had they made a general attack that Night should have carried the Town as they were inform'd, (by a person who had leave to go into the Country) the Officers were at a Ball and more intent on pleasing the Ladies, then defending their Camp; all which is without foundation, there being no Amusement of that, or any sort whatever, and if there was, it would be highly improper for Officers on Service to be at them or out of Camp after dark, and [I] can with great pleasure say the British Officers never were more Elert, and Attentive to their duty, then in this Army of which the Repeated thanks, they have Received from their Generalls in Publick Orders, is Sufficient to prove what I say, every person in this Camp is a Sleep between 8 and 9 oClock at Night, I can't say in Bed because those nights, where it is high Water, between the Hours of 9 and day light, we lay in our Cloaths, as it has been reported from their Deserters, they mean to make an Attack by water at Night: which is be leaved as we know they have some Hundreds of Whale Boats. I am of Opinion they would suffer considerably by such an Attack, as their Boats would be in great Confusion when fired upon, and wou'd not be able to make good a landing, but by a very considerable Loss. It has likewise been Reported, that Genl: [Charles] Lee had proposed to the Congress to attack the Town of Boston, and that he wou'd insure them Success, but that they must lay their loss in ten Thousand men which (tho a great number) wou'd be nothing to this Army, as he was sure the English would dispute every Inch of Ground but the Congress disapproved of it, however it is believed they will make a push before the time their men inlisted for is out, which is said to be the end of Novembr: and December, were we in their Situation we shou'd not (with their Numbers) lay so long inactive: I believe our troops in generall wish they wou'd Attack, tho sum are of a diffrent Opinion. Some times I wish for the first and some times from Reports & Conversations, I am led to give in to the latter, As an Army of twenty or thirty Thousand men Attacking a large Town on a Peninsula, with an Army under ten Thousand real Effectives, sick included (and the sick of this garrison is no small number,) would have but little Quarter were they *Obliged* to Retreat (a word the British Troops are not used to) from the Common to the Town, and that Town set on fire by the disaffected (who still Remains in the Town) to stop our Retreat. On the Other Hand a precaution has been Taken by our Generall who is in great Repute, and most esteam'd both for his Military genius, and care of his Army to prevent if Possable such accidents happening, that when the General Alarm is made some of the light Dragoons with the Town troops [are] to patrole the streets and put every person to death who shall be seen with fire arms, or firing out of Houses.

I must observe to your Lordship, that before the *Cerberus* return'd from England, it was Imagin'd we should have Evacuated this place and have gone Else where, perhaps to New York where we should have had an Open Country, and many Loyalists to have join'd the Army which in this province are very few: the Reason why this is beleived, Very little defencive works had been made to secure us for the Winter, till after that ship Arrived and G:[eneral] G:[age] ordered to England, it was then thought proper, (tho late in the year) to put the Town in the best state of defence before the Troops, returned in to Winter Quarters and have now finish'd four Redoubt on the Common which are very strong and Able, with about two Hundred men Each to defend them selves and prevent Thousands from passing between them, the Troops are to be Quarter'd in the Exterior parts of the Town Contiguous to post alotted each Corps. The Troops from Ireland with the four Companies of Artillery are coming in Dayly.[2]

The English papers I hear are full of Envectives against our Commander in Chief by sea [Graves], and not without Reason, that ever[y] person here thinks him the most improper person to Act in Conjunction with land forces in this important Ocasion, and beleive no Gencral in his Majesty's Navy is *less Respected*, tho no body Doubts his courage, but in Judgement. Your Lordship will be much surprised to hear that several Vessels have been Taken by the Rebels bound from England and Ireland to this Port with provisions &c. (The letters which have been taken in those ships have been opened and after keeping them some time have sent them in) and with in a few leagues of this Harbour, and particularly the other day when the first Transport with part of the 17th Regt. of foot arrived was Chaced & fired at by a Rebel Arm'd Schooner, Commanded by a deserter by the Name of O'Brian,[3] Carrying a flag at his Mast head and Wearing Colours of the Massachusetts Province a White field with a green tree; which schooner came close to the Harbour's mouth. At the same time many of His Maj.'s Frigates Sloop[s] Arm'd Schooners &c. were lying at Boston. I should not be surpris'd to hear some of our Transports with Military stores &c. on Board were taken. From this kind of Conduct which is publick talk here, I leave your Lordship to judge weather he deserves those invectives or not. Men of War should be constantly Cruizing between Cape Cod and Cape Ann, and some towards St. Georges Bank, to pick up our Transports, and other Vessels, and Convoy them in. The Expedition I mentioned in my last

[No. 26] of a party of One Capn: and fifty Marines, being orderd to Embark on board the *Canceaux*, was Augmented with another Captain and fifty men from the line, under command of Capn. [William] Forster of Marines, and saild about the time G:[eneral] G:[age] left this [place] And burnt the Town of Falmouth in Casco Bay, with several small vessels, and was to have destroy'd several Towns along the Coast of this place, including Salem and Marble Head, but the Vessels the Mortars Howitzers &c. were on board were so much shook by the fircings were Obliged to Return. The 9th. Inst. a party of light Infantry (about 300) under the Command of Lt. Col: [George] Clark landed on a neck of land call'd Phipps Farm, (which Neck at high Water is an Island) just under Mount Piscoe, where some Cattle were grazing and Brought off the whole about 13 in No. The Rebels from the Mount fired a few Shot at them, and as soon as the Troops Re'embark'd, and got a little distance from the shore, a very large body of Rebels Cross'd the Ford & fired at our men but fortunately no man was hurt. Several of the Enemy was kill'd by the Cannon for the *Scarborough*, (who lays between Phipps Farm & Bartons Points) the lines from Charles Town Heights and the Gondolos who Cover'd the Retreat, this farm lay on Cambridge Marsh. Tho' the Rebels have got Possession of Dorchester Hills we are under no apprehentions of their Raising Works to Anoy the Town, as our Advanced lines, the Battery on the Neck, (called the Block house.) and the Neck Battery wou'd flank them on one side, the Men of War on the other side and Hatches Warfe Battery in Front, behind the great hill they have a large Redoubt strongly Fortified, & Reinforced every Evening with a Considerable Number of Men. Since the leaves have fallen, we are able to see their Works, which are Very Extensive & strong: almost every Height Fortyfied, and every Pass in the Bottoms are Redoubts with lines of Communication, all the great Hills, as well with in the Walls of Cambridge are Covered with Barracks to hold some Thousands of Men.

The Town troops I mention'd, are His Maj: Loyal American Subjects Residing in the Town of Boston with their Adherents, who have offerd themselves to the General to serve their King & Country in defending the Town, and are form'd into three Companies under the Command of Brigadier Riggles,[4] and call'd the Loyal American Associators,[5] distinguish'd by a White sash Round their left Arm. Besides these are two Companies, Composed of Merchants and their ad-

herents, one call'd the Royal No. British Voluntiers,[6] distinguish'd by
a Blew Bonnet with a St. Andrews Cross, and the other Call'd the
Royal Irish Vols. Distinguish'd by a Cap with the Harps,[7] these five
Companies will be near five hundred men. Charles Town Height's
are made pretty strong with Lines and Redoubts, and Barrack for
about one Thousand Men. Fresh provisions are stil scarce, and dear
tho several Vessels have come in with stock which has been sold at
Publick Vendue, that the Inhabitants as well as the Millitary might
have an Equal share. About once a Week I eat a fresh dinner and
that not always a good one. Fish which was a standing dish is not to
be had, as the Boats are in danger of being Taken. Beef when it is to
be had is a Shilling a pound, it has been as low as Eight pence & nine
pence. Some Horse flesh has been sold at 6*d* per pound. I eat last
Week at Ld. Percy's some Cold, not much inferior to Veal. Geese has
been sold at twenty Shillings apiece, [starved] Fowls at 5 Shillings
apiece & every other Articles of eatables in proportion. We are still in
Camp & Ice 2 inches [thick] on the pond. Very Cold but fine Whole-
som Weather, and tho we have no fires in our Marquees, we are
Warmer at night than being in Houses at present. The Regiments are
this day gone into Winter Quarters. The Marines, Granidiers, 4th
and 44th Regiments Accepted (as they lay on good ground & [at a]
Particular post.) stay out a little longer till the Guard Rooms &c. are
finish'd in the Redoubts. Those Regiments who have Decamp't have
Supplied us with Tents to double our mens, which were estreamly
Cold without. Adml. Graves has just sent to Coll: Collins, he has
Receivd Directions from the Admiralty to Compleat the Marines on
Shore to one Thousand private[s]. I am Estreamly Oblig'd to your
Lordship for Useing your Utmost Endevours to serve me, but hope
your Lordship will Excuse my saying that I am Very Unfortunate,
that when I came near promotion some other plan is adopted, all
promotions in this Army has gone by Seniority in the present Corps,
the Method which L:[ord] S:[andwich] persued in England, and was
thought when the General Recommended the promotions to go in the
Marines serving in America, it would have gone in the same Channel,
but to my misfortune his Lordship fill'd the Vacancys by Seniority.of
former Commissions by which I, who stood second, became the Thir-
teenth, and when the last four Vacancys are fil'd up shall then be
fourth, and fear if any more Marines are sent out in the spring, I shall
still be further off promotion, as there are several (who have come

from half pay) Senior to me. Many who have been and are to be promoted, never Expected it before me, but I am now to wait the Isue of the Ensuing Campaigne. I wish for nobodys Death, it may be my Own lot, as every body in the Field has an Equal Chance.

I have given your Lordship an Account, freely of Affairs in generall and have only to add my sincere wishes for your Lordship Lady D:[enbigh] & the Young Gentlemens healths to whom I beg my best Respects with Complements to Miss M.:[8] &c. &c.

The Arrival of the store ship with Mortars shells &c. &c. has given much uneasyness for was she to fall into Hands of those Rascals they wou'd make our Lines to hot for us. Every Body is astonish'd that a Vessell of such Consequence shou'd not be sent out either under Convoy or the Direction of some Officer with Force to defend him self, which is Reported is quite the Contrary as she has not a Gun mounted, and might be Easyly taken. We likewise hear she is Commanded by a Yankee, if that should be the Case, I should not Wonder if he was to Carry the Vessell into an Other Port. A Vessel of that Consequence shou'd not be trusted to the Care of a Master of a Merchant Ship as those fellows in general have very little Honesty, & might be bribed to betray his trust; only part of the 17th Regt. of Foot is Arrived & the last of the four Companies landed the 26th inst: several has been seen of, but the badness of the Weather I fear has drove them of[f] the Co[a]st: nothing worse I hope. Lieut. Bowmaster Agent to the Transports & in a Transport with some Guns, Retook a brig, the 25th Inst. that was Taken by the Rebels Close to Boston light house, at which place Bowmaster was lying at Anchor to defend it till it was Repaired & put in a state of defence.[9] Lieut. [Michael] Seix of the 64th Regt. is a Volenteer with 40 men from the Line, to stay at the light house the Whole Winter.

1. Captain William Pawlett.
2. 17th Regiment.
3. Captain Jeremiah O'Brian of Machias, Maine.
4. Brigadier Timothy Ruggles. An American Loyalist from Harwick, Massachusetts.
5. Formed by order of General Howe on November 17, 1775.
6. This company was formed on October 29, 1775. It was made up of "some North British Merchants residing in town with their Adherents." This was the first Loyalist military unit formed by the British in America during the Revolution.

7. Officially formed by General Howe on December 7, 1775. The members of this unit were Irish merchants resident in Boston.

8. Hester Mundy, sister of Edward Mundy of Shipley Hall, Derbyshire, M.P. for Derbyshire, 1784-1822.

9. For recapturing this ship, Lieutenant John Bourmaster was promoted to the rank of master and commander and made Principal Agent of Transports.

31.   To Joseph Johnson[1]

South Street Novr 23d 1775

Sir

I have received a letter [No. 28] signed by you & several more of my friends of the Corporation of Leicester recommending Mr. William Buckley to my protection. Nothing can give me greater pleasure than to obey the commands of so many respectable Gentlemen: but the Candidates for preferment are so numerous & my friends have been so often gratified in the military department which I understand is Mr Buckley's line that I cannot take upon me to say when I shall be able to succeed for him, however nothing shall be wanting on my part of which I beg you will assure the rest of your body Corporate.

1. Mayor of Leicester.

32.   From Lieutenant William Feilding

Boston Camp Decem. 3rd. 1775

My Lord

I beg leave to send your Lordship some of our News papers with Articles of Inteligence from the Other Colony's: particularly the last of the 30th of Novembr, where your Lordship will see the Articles of [Capitulation] of St. Johns and Fort Chamblee [Chambly], which was not believ'd here till the Arrival of *Genl: Gage* Arm'd Schooner this morning from Quebec; who brings Accounts that St. Johns & fort Chamblee had been Taken before she sail'd, and that Montreal was Surrounded and the Rebels in sight of Quebec, and no Military Force in Town but *Lizard*'s Marines, but that the Merchant[s] and Canadians, had put the Town in a state of Defence, that it would be impossable to take it but by starving them out, as provisions was scarce and not sufficient for the Winter. We are in great trouble about the Ordnance Brigg, as the Rebels have offer'd great Rewards to any person who, shall either take or destroy her. Several Men of War are Cruizing for her, she has been seen by them, but parted Company in hard Gales of Wind. We flatter ourselves, shou'd she not be able to get in, she will go to the West Indies. This with my last of 30th of November[1] goes in the *Boyne*, under the care of Lieut. [Alexander] Brisbane Marines who goes home for the Recovery of his Wounds.

[P.S.] Genl. Burgoyne[2] who has been very Ill goes in the *Boyne*.

1. Not entered in the letter book.
2. Major General John Burgoyne served with the army at Boston from May 25 to December 5, 1775, when he returned to England. Burgoyne later served in Canada and commanded the army that surrendered at Saratoga on October 17, 1777.

33. From Lieutenant William Feilding

Boston Decem. 12th. 1775

My Lord

In my last [No. 32] I informed your Lordship the apprehension we were in for fear of the Ordnance Brigg[1] was taken and am sorry to Acquaint your Lordship that by Accounts from the Rebels, she was Taken a few days before the *Boyne* sail'd. The 7th Inst. the *Fowey* Return'd from a Cruize with [a] Rebel privateer Brigg[2] she had Taken two days before, Carrying 10 dutch five pounders, & 10 swivels, with a Captain two Leiutenants, a Master & two Mates, all Soldiers from the Rebel Army at Cambridge (except the Master & Mates) with Commissions signed by John Hancock, president of the Continental Congress & Instructions from Genl. Washington. The Captain says he saw the sea Morter (which was on Board the Ordnance Brigg) at Cambridge Common the Thursday before he was taken; and that from the Information of the Master, he was sent out to sea for a Powder Ship, which we have heard nothing of as yet. A deserter who came in a few days since, Says he saw all the Ordnance Stores safe Lodg'd at Cambridge last week. I am likewise sorry to Acquaint your Lordship of the following prizes the Rebels have taken within these 10 days. A Ship six weeks from London with all kind of provisions taken within a league and half of the light house, (with a fair wind,) and Carried into Salem. A Ship with Blanketts for the Army an Article much wanted this cold Weather, particularly to the Enemy, as they are in great want of warm Cloathing. A Brigg from Jamaica with Rum; A Ship with Coals and another from Scotland with warm Cloathing for the Soldiers; besides a ship we hear they have taken with Medicines & seven Surgeons Mates. Fuel & provisions I am told is Very Scarce, and that we shou'd soon be put to half Allowance of the former, and short Allowance of the latter, as we have very little hopes of having supply's, the Rebels with a few arm'd Vessels and Boats taking all our ships in sight of our port, where Men of War are lying: some of them have been at sea and have sufferd much from Hard Gales of Wind; which have been frequent with in these six weeks; but when it is Moderate they shou'd instantly go out, and endeavour if possable to stop those privateers, and Boats from Boarding our Vessells as they Come in with the land; besides some of the Ships of War, shou'd lie in Salem, Cape Anne and Cape Cod to prevent their Armed Vessels and boats going to sea, and to send all Vessels going into these Ports to Boston. When the two first Transports Arrived from England last May with Marines, the *Lively* was lying at Salem, who as soon as she discovered Vessels in the offing sent her Tenders with an Officer to pilot them into Boston, all which was exceedingly proper, but am sorry to say no Ships of War have been lying there for some months; I am told the Rebels have erected a Battery there to prevent them, but I have heard of Men of War going against a Battery in former Wars and destroying it; I need not say what are the Opinions of this Garrison, and the invectives thrown out against such proceedings.

The Remainder of the Troops went into Winter Quarters yesterday as Well as those from the Heights of Charles Town, they being Releived by six Hundred men under the Command of Lieut: Col. [James] Agnew, and Major [Richard] Bassett which Command is to be releived every fortnight. From the Severe duty and Troops have had this long Campaigne, as well from the badness of the Weather, and salt provisions, has Reduced them very much, and Nothing but a desire of Scourging the Insolent Rebels of our Country keeps up the Soldiers' Spirrit; what will be the Isue of the Winter God only knows.

[P.S.] This by the *Tartar*.

1. The ordnance storeship *Nancy*, which was captured on November 27, 1775, by the American armed schooner *Lee*. The *Nancy's* cargo consisted of, among other things, 2,000 muskets, 100,000 flints, 30,000 round shot, 30 tons of musket balls, and a large brass mortar.

2. The American armed schooner *Washington*, which was captured on November 5, 1775, off Cape Ann.

34. From Lieutenant William Feilding

Boston Jany. 19th. 1776

My Lord

Saturday 23d Decemr: the Rebels began a new work on the Peninsula calld Phipps's Farm, which they made in a state of defence that Night during which time we fired several shot & shells from Boston's Point Redoubts, some of which did Execution but not sufficient to deter them from finishing a Work of such Consequence to them, which seems to be a strong Redoubt with Ambrezures, and Lines of Breast work: As this work is not above 1200 yards they cou'd annoy us much, as some of their shot from a Heighth call'd Cobble hill, and near mount Pisgah, a much greater distance, went thro' a meeting House in new Boston near Barton Points where six Companies of Grenadiers are Quartered, but did no mischief. They have not as yet got any Cannon in this work: It is as been supposed they will fix the mortars which they took in the Ordnance Brigg, on this Height and endevour to Burn the Town, but every thing has Remained quiet for some time on both sides. Some Ladies and Officers for diversion, and for the Benefit of the sick and ma[i]med Soldiers in this Army, have Acted Plays; and Faneuil Hall (a famous place where the sons of sedition used to meet) is fitted up very Elegantly for a Theatre. And on Monday the Eight Instant was perform'd *The Busy Body*:[1] A new farce call'd *The Blockade of Boston* (written by Genl. Burgoyne)[2] was to have been introduc'd, but unfortunately as the Curtain drew up to begin the Entertainment, an Orderly Sergeant came on the Stage, and said the Alarm Guns were fired which Immediately put every body to the Rout, particularly the Officers, who made the best of their way to their Respective Corps and Alarm Posts, leaving the Ladies in the House in a most Terible Dilema. This Alarm was as follows, between 8 & 9 oClock at night, and Very dark about thirty Rebels

Cross'd the Mill bridge near Charles Town Neck and set fire to some Empty Houses and took a Sargeant and three men which lay in one of them not as a Guard but as a Convenience as they belong'd to the Deputy Quar[ter] Master General. Upon which the Troops in the Redoubts on the Heights fired very Briskly for a few minutes some small Arms & Cannon at the fire; but as [the] Enemy's number was so small and Retreated immediately as soon as they had set fire to the Houses, they escap'd without the loss of a man. This Alarm was so triffling that it displeased the General much, but on the other hand he was much pleased to see the Elertness of the men. The *Blockade* is soon to be Acted with the *Tragedy of Tamerlane*[3].

The 29th of Decemr. arrived Adml. Shuldham[4] who relieves Adml. G[raves] which gives much Satisfaction since his Arrival the *Fowey* has been sent to Marble Head; where she lays under a Battery of Eighteen Guns; the Rebels upon her Arrival laid up all their Privateers, and Genl: Washington sent Orders not to fire on the Man of War, and likewise sent her some fresh Provisions.[5] All the Men of War are gone to sea and none left but what is sufficient for the safety of the place. No Vessels of late have been Taken. A:[dmiral] G:[raves] sails soon for England, and believe no Commander ever left this [place] less regretted. Major [John] Maitland, with 2 Captains, 6 Sub[altern]s and 200 Marines including the two Light Companies, embark'd the 26 Decembr. and Sail'd soon After on an Expedition under the Command of Major [James] Grant 40th Regt. with the *Scarborough;* the Destination of which is not known, some Immagine to Rhode Island, others to Bermudas, where it is said the Rebels have a Magazine of Military stores &c.—supplied by the Dutch in the West Indies about seventy leagues distance, either of these places it is probable they are gone to.[6] Major Genl. Clinton[7] is Embark'd with the two light Companys of the 4th. and 44th. Regts: destined it is immagined to Virginia to Reinforce Lord Dunmore,[8] and take the Command of the Troops.[9] Captain Rawdon[10] a fine speritted Young Officer goes a Supernumerary Aid de Camp to the Genl. Several Vessels have Arrived with porter, potatoes and sour crout for the Army which is of infinite Service as many of the Soldiers are much Afflicted with the Scurvy. The sheep which these Vessels took on Board at London all died to very few as scarce a Ship brought in above 8 or 10 out of a Hundred and fifty each.[11] Fresh provisions are not to Scare as several Vessells of late have Arrived from Halifax, and Annapolis [Royal]

with quarters of Beef, Mutton &c.—which has been sold at the following most Exhorbitant prices. Beef 20*d*.—Mutton 2*s*.—Pork 2*s*.
per pound. Geese 12*s*. and Hares 3*s*. which with the Exchange of
Money is enough to Ruin the Subalterns of this Army. We are happy
to find the people of England have open'd a Subscription for sending
fresh Provisions to the Soldiers. Were the Soldiers Allow'd their Rations without paying for [them], it wou'd be of Infinite service in getting them Warm Clothing and other Nessissarys which at present the
Captains are Oblig'd to provide, to the Ruin of their pocketts and the
distress of the poor Soldiers, from the heavy Stoppages they unavoid-
ably are Obliged to be put under; during the last War the Soldiers
never paid for their Provisions, this method was only introduced since
the peace by Sr. Jeffery Amherst.[12] The price of a Ration to the Soldier is 2½[*d*.] which is but a tenth part of the Value as it cost Government, (I am inform'd) near half a crown. I shou'd imagine that 2½*d*.
can be of no great Consequence to Government, but of very great use
to the Soldier.[13] The Officers of His Majesty's Marine Forces serving
in No. America, were much shagrin'd upon the arrival of the
Chatham, to find that the Vacancy's which Happen here had been
Chiefly fill'd up by Officers at Home (by Lord S.[andwich's] former
plan) as they were informed that His Majesty had Order'd all Vacancys happening in America to be fill'd up in the Respective Corps,
which has hither to been the Case with the Regiments, and at first
with the Marines, but now find that the plan did not stand long with
us, which is distressing to Officers who have sufferd all the Hardships
and Fatigue of a long and Severe Campaigne, and have done their
duty with Spirit and Alacrity. The Corps have Represented it to Coll:
Collins, our Commandant. I am sorry to Acquaint your Lordship that
Lord S.[andwich] has not stuck either to Seniority of first Commission
in the Marines here, or Seniority of last Commissions in England as
by the last promotion, first Lieut. [Robert] Anderson (who was Kill'd
in a duel here) was promoted out of all line whatever; a man who
cou'd neither boast of being an Officer or a Gentleman, but by being
so styl'd in his Commission. Col: Collins some time since Acquainted
Ld. S:[andwich] that from the severe duty the troops had several Officers of the Army had sold out and that some Soldiers of the Regiments had deserted, but that his faithfull Marines Remained and that
he styl'd them faithfull, because both Officers and Men did their duty
with Cheerfullness, and that the Officers wou'd Rather perish than

think of Quiting the Men, when in defense of their King, Country, and Laws! and Requested his Lordship wou'd Continue to give them that Reward due to their merit, by promoting them to the Unfortunate Vacancys that happened here. The address of the Commons has been sent to the Rebells who says, its all a Lye, and made here on purpose to give to them. I am informed that Genl. [John] Thomas sent in word he had seen the divine speech from the Throne, That England may do the Worst, that they were prepar'd for the Spring: which I do not beleive, as they have discharg'd some of their Regiments with this Excuse that it was a great Expence to keep them at present: and numbers have deserted.[14] I have nothing more to add but my best respects to Lady Denbigh.

[P.S.] I have Received the following letters from your Lordship: June 6th [No. 3] the beginning of Sept by the packett from New York having been above three months from England. July 25th—the 28th Septr. by the *Cerberus*. Augt. the 8th [No. 9]—the 8th of Octr: by the *Phoenix*. Oct 12th—the 30th Decembr. by the *Chatham*.

1. A farce written in 1709 by Susanna Centlivre.
2. In 1774 Burgoyne wrote *Maid of the Oaks*, which was produced by David Garrick at Drury Lane in 1775. While in America, Burgoyne wrote a proclamation imposing martial law on Massachusetts which was issued under Gage's name on June 12, 1775. Towards the end of 1775 he turned to dramatic writing and wrote a prologue and epilogue for the tragedy *Zara*, which was performed at Faneuil Hall in December 1775. This was followed by the farce *Blockade of Boston*, performed in January 1776 after Burgoyne had left Boston.
3. Christopher Marlowe's *Tamburlaine The Great*, first produced c. 1587.
4. Vice-Admiral Molyneux Shuldham, later 1st Baron Shuldham, commander-in-chief of the Royal Navy in America from December 29, 1775, to July 12, 1776, and then commander-in-chief at Plymouth.
5. Rumors were rife among the British at Boston. Feilding probably heard a twisted account of Captain James Wallace successfully obtaining provisions at Newport, R.I. by threatening to destroy the town with naval gunfire.
6. This expedition went to Savannah, Georgia to obtain rice.
7. Major General Henry Clinton, second in command of the army in America. When General Howe returned to England in 1778, Clinton became commander-in-chief until after the Yorktown campaign.
8. John Murray, 4th Earl of Dunmore, the last royal governor of Virginia.
9. It was intended that Clinton meet an expedition from Ireland off North Carolina and that together they support the Loyalists in the American South.

10. Francis Rawdon Hasting, Captain Lord Rawdon.

11. In 1775 the Treasury let a contract to a London merchant, Anthony Merry, to ship livestock to the army at Boston. The undertaking was a failure, for at a total cost of £16,427.16s., only 105 animals out of the 290 dispatched arrived at Boston alive.

12. Jeffery Amherst, 1st Baron Amherst, commander-in-chief of the British army in America during the Seven Years War; subsequently a field marshal. From 1772 to 1778 he officiated as Commander-in-Chief of the British army, and from 1778 until the end of the war he held the position of Commander-in-Chief.

13. The pay of a British private soldier during the American Revolution was a racket in which everybody received money but the soldier himself. Each soldier was paid 8d. per day. This money was then divided into two parts called subsistence and gross off-reckoning. The subsistence amounted to 6d. per day and was supposed to be applied to the cost of a soldier's food. In reality, however, subsistence was used to pay for things which had nothing to do with provisions. For example, 6d. a week was used to pay for a soldier's shoes, stockings, and the repair of arms, while another 1d. per week was a fee split between the regimental surgeon and paymaster. The gross off-reckoning part of a soldier's pay amounted to 2d. a day, from which came a payment of 1s. in the pound on a full day's pay to the Paymaster General of the Forces; one full day's pay to Chelsea Hospital; and 2d. on the pound in the full pay to the regimental agent. What remained, if anything, was known as the net off-reckoning and was applied to the cost of the soldier's clothing. At the beginning of 1776, the government was paying 5¼d. per ration.

14. On October 26, 1775, Parliament opened at Westminster with the customary Address from the Throne by the King setting forth the policy of the British government. In his speech, George III stated that it was the intention of the British government to suppress the rebellion in America by force of arms; but when the Americans saw the error of their ways, the British were prepared to act with mercy. For this reason, the commanders-in-chief of the army and navy in America were made commissioners with the authority to grant pardons and to receive submission. After a debate, the Address was then overwhelmingly approved by the Commons 176 to 72 and by the Lords 76 to 33.

35. To Joseph Johnson

South Street Jan. 22. 1776

Sir

It is with great pleasure I can assure you that Government looks with particular approbation on the humanity & public spirit exerted by you and your Body Corporate & several more of your friends &

neighbours in contributing so liberally towards the relief of the distressed Widows & Orphans of those brave Men who have fallen or may fall in the service of their Country in America.

Mr. William Buckley whom your Corporation recommended [No. 28] so strongly to my protection some time ago having signified a particular inclination for the Army I applied to Lord Barrington in his behalf who has been so obliging as to promise me a Commission on the following condition, that Mr. Buckley raises 25 men from the age of 16 to 40 & in height 5 feet 5 or upwards. The Commission will be dated from the day the last raised man is attested & entered into any recruiting party. Now I should think that with the help & assistance of your Magistrates & our other friends at Leicester this might easily be done. Be so good therefore as to lay this before your body at your next meeting together with my best Comps.

36. From Lieutenant William Feilding

Boston Jany. 28th. 1776

My Lord

Since my last by the *Julius Caesar* nothing extraordinary has happened. Accounts has been Receiv'd here by Way of New York that the Rebells 5,000 men under the Command of Gen. [Richard] Montgomery in Canada, demanded the Surrender of Quebec, or they wou'd storm it which being Answer'd in the Negative; The[y] Attack'd and Carried the lower Town upon which Genl: Carleton[1] Assembled all his Forces, (which Chiefly Consisted of Inhabitants who had form'd themselves into five Companies, and about 200 Regulars at the utmost) Attack'd and drove them out of the Town and with his Artillery from the Heights of Abraham Flank'd them in their Retreat, Kill'd about 2 or 300 and took as many Prisoners.[2] Among the Slain was Genl: Montgomery (Formerly Captn. of Grenadiers in the 17th Regt:) and his Aid de Camp. Col. Arnot [Benedict Arnold], second in Command wounded and taken prisoner.[3] This stroke I beleive will hurt them much, as they were in great hopes to Carry Quebec, by which they wou'd be masters of Canada and make those proper Subjects to their Arbitrary Government, this news the Rebells here Acknowledge, a Circumstance they are not very fond of. Genl: Clinton is saild, supposed to the Southward. The day my last letter left this my

Friend [John] Bowater[4] Arrived in the *Centurion* who is in very good health, the Conformation of which he acquaints your Lordship in this letter. The *Blockade of Boston* has been perform'd twice, and Receivd (tho Short) with great Applause. The Characters of the Yankee General and Figure of his Soldiers is inimatable, the Genl: a man who can't Read but can Speachefie, and tell his soldiers they are to obey the Voice of the people in the streets, the Joy the Rebells are in, in reading the Resolves of the Mayor and City of London in favor of the Con-ti-nen-tal Congress[5] in Phi-li-del-phi-a pa-per is truly Characteristick. This letter goes by the *Canceaux*, Capt. Mowat who Adml. G.[raves] takes home, with him, and whose Return is much wished for, as being a man who has been Employ'd to assist Capt. Holland,[6] Surveyor Generall of America above twelve Years, and Whose Knowledge of the Coast Harbour, Rivers, Creeks Bays &c. &c. is much depended on Relative to the navigating any Expedition the General and Admiral Chuse to carry on by water.

1. Guy Carleton, Governor and Captain-General of Quebec, 1776-1778; and commander-in-chief of the army in America, 1782-1783.
2. In the abortive assault on Quebec City the Americans lost some sixty men killed and wounded, and about four hundred were captured.
3. Arnold was wounded but not captured.
4. Second son of Richard Bowater.
5. In the course of the dispute with America, various groups of merchants and several municipal bodies came out in support of the American position. For example, on July 8, 1775, the Court of the Common Council of the City of London presented an address to the King requesting suspension of hostilities against the Americans.
6. Samuel Holland, Surveyor of the Lands in the Northern District of America.

37. From Captain John Bowater

Boston Jany. 28 1776

My Lord

As my friend Mr. Feilding has mention'd [No. 36] my Arrival &c. &c. I have little to inform Your Lordship of except that of my Passage which was the longest and most disagreable I ever met with, and we was very near going to the West Indies & certainly shou'd if we had not had thirty Thousand pounds on Board of [ship for] the use of the Army.

I've Read the Coppys of many of the letters Mr Feilding has wrote to you & I can assure you I think he has given you the best Intelligence of every thing that goes on here. The frost has had such an Effect on my hands that I can hardly bend a finger but I was determind to make an Attempt, in Order to Assure your Lordship that I gratefully Remember my best friends in this Very dreadfull Situation.

P.S. We sailed from Portsmouth the first of October and Arrived here the 19th of Jany: & this is the first Oppertunity I've met with of sending a line. I never was in better health or spirits, but the Cold pinches me, having been so lately at Fayal, in excessive heat. I want for neither Meat Drink or Cloathing.

38.   From Judd Harding

Solihull Jan. 28. 1776

My Lord

I ordered my Son to wait upon your Ldsp on his return from the Academy at Woolwich, but being ignorant of the Town [London] & directed by a blockhead of a Porter who could not find your Ldsp's House I hope you will excuse his having omitted it. But I insist upon his waiting upon your Lordsp. now at all events to deliver this letter & to pay his dutiful respects.

I have the pleasure to acquaint your Lordsp. that he has obtained his warrant[1] that he has been upon full pay from the 13th. of Octr. last & that I have a favourable account of his behaviour from his Officers. I hope he will always behave in a manner not to make your Lordsp. repent of your Appointment & that he will ever gratefully remember & acknowlege the great favour you have conferred upon him. My Family join in offering best respects to your Lordsp, Lady Denbigh, Lord Feilding[2] & the Honble. Mr: Feilding[3] & that you may long enjoy health & happiness.

1. A cadet's warrant.
2. William Robert Feilding, Viscount Feilding. Lord Denbigh's eldest son.
3. Hon. Charles Feilding. Denbigh's youngest son.

39. **From Arthur Gregory**[1]

Warwick Jan. 29th. 1776

My Lord

The Papers mention that a Battalion is to be formed by a draught from the Guards under the command of Col. [Edward] Matthews to go to America I should therefore be much obliged if your Ldsp. would name a son of mine to our Royal Master for a Lieutenancy in that Battalion. He is anxious to retaliate his Brothers death, is nineteen, has been in our militia about 3 years & applied himself with diligence & assiduity the little time we were together & has quite a passion for the Military.

1. Gentleman Usher of the Privy Chamber to His Majesty. Gregory was a resident of Stivichall, Coventry, Warwickshire, and his first wife was Mary Bowater, the older sister of Richard Bowater.

40. **To Lord Sandwich**

South Street Jan. 30th. 1776

My dear Lord

As you are making a large addition of second Lieutenants of Marines your giving a Commission in that Corps to Mr. James Berkley who is nearly related to Lady Denbigh & much espoused by her & all her Family will very much oblige her.

41. **From Lord Sandwich**

Admiralty Jan. 31. 1776

My dear Lord

I cannot have a greater pleasure than in obeying Lady Denbighs commands, therefore as I have some way or other mislaid your letter of yesterday [No. 40], if you will remind me of the young mans name & age, I will carry a Commission this day to his Majesty to appoint him a Lieutenant of Marines. I dine at home & shall be glad of your Company.

42. From Captain Charles Jackman

Norwich Feb. 7. 1776

My Lord

My being still upon the recruiting service at this place your Ldsp's letter of the 3d. inst.[1] did not come to my hands till this day. I am extremely happy at the honour your Ldsp & Lady Denbigh intend me by putting under my care a Relation of her Ladysps & a youth of so promising a disposition. It will give me the greatest pleasure to receive Mr. Berkley under my own roof where there shall be the greatest care taken of his morals & every attention paid to his improvement & instruction that shall be in my power. I must beg to trouble your Ldsp. with these assurances & my humble respects to Lady Denbigh & if your Lordsp. will be pleased to add that I am proud of the honour her Ladysp. does me, & not withstanding I am at present from Chatham I beg you will assure her Ladysp that there will be the greatest care taken of him in my absence. I write by this post to Coll. Sheldon[2] to have every thing prepared for the young gentleman's reception at Rome House.

I am in hourly expectation & hopes of being relieved from this expensive & disagreable duty & flatter myself your Ldsp. will think with me that after recruiting 70 men in four months I have some title to be at home again at least for a short time. I shall certainly do myself the honour when I come to Town, of calling at South Street.

1. Not entered in the letter book.
2. Thomas Sheldon, Colonel-Commandant of Marine officers on half pay.

43. To Captain Charles Jackman

South Strt. Mar. 1. 1776

Dear Jackman

Our little friend Berkley setts out for Chatham to morrow morning & I flatter myself he will do credit to my recommendation & to the attention which you are so good as to pay to him. The Mother desires her son may go on with his Drawing & French Masters who will be regularly paid quarterly. I am very much obliged to you for your friendsp. in this matter & have nothing more to desire but that you will let me know what is to be paid for his board.

[P.S.] Lady [Denbigh] desires her thanks to you and joins me in Comps to you & Col. Sheldon.

44. To Lieutenant William Feilding

London March 2d: 1776

Dear Feilding

The last letter I Receiv'd from you was dated Jany. 19th: [No. 34] since which I find your Mother has receiv'd one dated Feby. 2d. but none came to me by that ship. Your Letters give great Satisfaction to all who see them, so continue to write to me boldly, & the truth but not sign your name. It is the fashion here to wish that Boston may be Attack'd as Genl. Burgoyne assures every Body, that if they do Attack, the Enemy must be Repulsed, however I do not like your Account of their last Redoubt & Battery being finish'd without your being able to prevent it. You will have in the Course of this Summer every Assistance this Country can give you; the House of Commons yesterday Voted 17000 Foreigners by a majority of 242 against 88. If our accounts from Quebec are true, I suppose an Exchange of prisoners will soon take place in some shape or other. Ld. Wentworth[1] has Receiv'd [John] Bowaters letter [No. 37] by which we are Glad to find he is Arrived safe.

Write by every ship, and enclose your letters to Lord George Germaine[2]—my wife & all friends here Join in Complements to yourself & Bowater. All yours are well at Brompton.

P.S. How do you approve of your new admiral pay my best Complements to Lord Percy, and tender him my Thanks for his kind attention towards you.

Just as I had finish my letter, I Receiv'd yours & Mr Bowaters Joint letter [Nos. 36, 37] of the 28th Jany. by the [blank][3] which makes us happy to hear you are both so well.

1. Thomas Noel, 2nd Viscount Wentworth, M.P. for Leicestershire, October 20-October 31, 1775, but raised to the peerage before he could take his seat.

2. Lord George Germain, Secretary of State for Colonies, November 1775 to January 1782.

3. *Canceaux.*

45. To Arthur Gregory

Mar. 2d. 1776

Dear Sir

The reason for my not answering your letter [No. 39] sooner was my wishing to see some day light by which to assist you with reguard to its contents. But upon enquiry I find that altho there have been many changes in the guards not above one Commission has been disposed of excepting by purchase, that was an Ensigncy. As to a Lieutcy. I could not get one for my own Son either by purchase or otherwise untill he had at first had a pr. of Colours for at least 2 years & they are not to be had in the Guards at a less price than 1000 guineas.

46. From George Buckley

Thornton Mar. 15. 1776

My Lord

I have this day had the pleasure to see your Lordsp's favour to my son William. Your Ldsp's proposal of the £40 pr. an. I am willing to comply with. I trust your Ldsp. will put him in such a Regt. as will be for his future advantage. What Orders come to the Officer[1] of the 29th he shall go by. It gives me great concern that your Ldsp. should have had so much trouble, but I hope he will merit your Ldsp's recommendation. I return your Ldsp. sincere thanks for this kind favour & shall be ready upon all occasions to serve your Ldsp. as much as lies in my power.

N.B. The letter to which the preceding was returned in Answer is not preserved. It notified to the son William Buckley Ld. D's having procured a Commission for him upon condition of his raising 25 recruits & provided his Father would settle £40 pr. an. upon him till he was further promoted.

1. The officer on recruiting duty in Leicester.

47.   From Lieutenant William Feilding

Boston Feby:[1] 1776

My Lord

I have just time to Acquaint your Lordsp. that the Rebels on the nights of the 3d and 4th: Instant from Roxbury, Phipps Farm, and Cobble hill, thro' several shells and a great number of Shot into the Town, and at the same Fortified Dorchesters hills, with two Very large Redoubts and lines and are working on all sides of Us with a prodigious body of Men. Six men[2] of the 22d Regt. lost their legs by one Shot as they were laying in their Barrack guard bed, some Horses of the light Dragoon's were wounded, and some few of the Inhabitants slightly hurt. The Genl. is going to leave the Town and take the Army to Halifax. The troops are Embarking their Stores and Baggage, and suppose in three or four days we shall leave it. Numbers of the Inhabitants are likewise going with the Army. The Hurry and Confusion the latter are in, is dreadfull. I don't Know weather the Town is to be distroyed or not.

P.S. as I have not time to write to my Mother, I beg your Lordship will let her know I am well.

1. This letter was written between March 5th and 16th, 1776.
2. The Deputy Adjutant General of the British army at Boston recorded that five men of the 22nd Regiment were wounded by the American bombardment.

48.   From Captain John Bowater

Centurion; King['s] Road, Boston March 25th. 1776

My Lord

I wrote to your Lordship by the *Preston*, Admiral Graves, which was the only Ship that has Saild from hence since my Arrival in

America. Neither has Any ship Arrived here since she saild nor have I
Received a line from any one since I left England. The Violence of the
Winds at this Season of the Year with the extream Coldness of the
Weather has prevented any ship Approaching the Coast. By a Sloop
that came in Yesterday from Antigua we have an account of three
men of War & Seventy sail of Transports Victualers & store Ships
being drove in there & was Refitting in order to join us as soon as
possable.[1] And we are now all looking with the utmost anxiety for
Vessels to Appear in sight as no one here is free from the dreadfull
Thought of famine as I am inform'd we have not a months provisions
Remaining for either Army or Navy. Tho we have been for this week
past put upon two thirds of Allowance, and I believe this was the
principal Reason for our Evacuating Boston, tho many others are Assign'd. The Rebels taking Possession of Dorchester Heights, & at last
made their Approaches within a Thousand Yards of the Town, it was
said to be no longer Tenable. Indeed at last the[y] Amused us with
both shot and shells in every part of the Town, but did no damage to
the Shiping. An other Reason Assign'd was, that by our being Embarked must puzzle the Enemy exceedingly as they wou'd not Know
where to guard most—And we might go to any place that wou'd
Joyn us heartily. The present orders says Halifax but that Cannot be
for any time as we have exausted that Country during the Winter.
Meat was rose to 10*d.* per pound all over the province two months
ago. We have three & twenty Battalions embarkt with us yet we have
not seven Thousand fighting men. But with Women & Children civil
Officers, followers of the Army, and many of the principal Inhabitants
of Boston, (who if they did not accompany us would be either hung or
sent to the mines) we are above twenty Thousand people to Receive
Victuals & drink.[2] The Transports are very much Crowded & a great
many Children was Sufficated the first night and [if] the Weather
turns Warm I am afraid the Troops will be sickly. It wou'd be a pitty
to loose any of them, as I never saw a more spirited sett of fellows—
and they have the greatest Confidence in their Generalls, if they
Lament any thing it is that they can die but once in the service of their
Country. The Cruelty Committed daily by the Rebels makes them
keen for Revenge.

   Mr. Feilding writes [No. 47] to your Lordship by this Oppertunity
and will give you an Exact Account of all the millitary motions
previous to the Retreat—as Every precaution was taken the same as if

the Enemy meant to anoy us. But they chose to save the Town as the principal seat of their Rebellion, and we wou'd not destroy it as the principal part of it belongs to the Friends of Government, also it might be Nessisary for us to retake it again for the next Winter Quarters. Tho I now think we shall go either to New York or Virginia, we have still a Regiment of light Horse with us which takes up as much Room as six Regiments of Foot and they never could be of the least service in any one of the Colonies, this with a Thousand other Absurdities which the wise heads at home have transmitted to us has laid us under the most dreadful misfortunes. Coals Porter & Potatoes have been brought out to us in great Plenty and in large Ships with twenty Guns & a hundred men. Brass Cannon, Mortars, Shells, Balls, flints, Powder &c. &c., have been sent out in small Briggs, with two & four Guns & ten or twelve men. And they have been taken by the Enemy who have beat us Very severely with our own Weapons. (The Board of Ordinance is in great disrepute with us at present.) If we are Expected to do any thing considerable we must have very great Reinforcements as the Rebels are so Numerous, they have above five & twenty Thousand Round us now & they take the utmost pains in Disciplining them, & they have got a great many Foreigners amongst them Runegadoes & partisans from all Countrys which are Very great Rascals but are generall[y] Very Clever fellows. We have not had any late Accounts of Genl. Carleton but we are in hopes he will be Able to hold out at Quebec untill we can send him a Reinforcement he has perform'd Wonders already.

My best Respects attends Lady Denbigh & family. The packett going in hast[e] obliges me to Conclude. Major Charles Stewart[3] is well we often Converse and he desires to be Remember'd to your Lordship.

You must not Expect to hear from me often as we are so often sent out of the way when any thing is going home & it is at least a Thousand to one you do not Receive this.

---

1. This is an overstatement, although out of thirty-five ships sent from England with army provisions during the winter of 1775, only eight actually reached Boston; the rest were either forced by weather to the West Indies or captured.

2. The British evacuated 8,908 troops and 924 Loyalists from Boston.

3. Major Hon. Charles Stuart, son of Lord Bute. Bute was a former First Lord of the Treasury and Denbigh's friend.

II

March 1776-December 1776

At the beginning of 1776, it was clear to anyone in Britain who read a newspaper that royal authority in America could only be restored by waging a war to conquer the continent. Accordingly, it became the intention of the British government to reconquer Canada and to end the rebellion with one mighty campaign aimed at New York. The general line of reasoning behind this scheme was that the Americans would be decisively defeated by a large number of European troops and then see the futility of further resistance; moreover, control of New York would provide the British with a base for future operations and open up the Hudson River, which runs along the western flank of New England, to British amphibious forces. It was thought in London that if New England, long considered the center of the rebellion in America, could be blockaded by the Royal Navy along the coast and cut off from the rest of the country at the Hudson River, it could be caught and held between the King's troops in New York and Canada.

Throughout the winter and spring of 1776, various government departments such as the Navy Board, Treasury, and War Office labored to assemble the thousands of troops and hundreds of ships required to carry the government's scheme into effect. During the spring and summer of 1776, the Royal Navy's strength in American waters was increased to about seventy warships; and some 27,000 troops were sent to America and Canada aboard four hundred transports.

The campaign to end the rebellion in North America opened on May 6, 1776, when H.M.S. *Isis* arrived at Quebec City with reinforcements from England and broke the American siege of that place. Then, as more and more British troops arrived in Canada, the American army, which had been greatly weakened by sickness, abandoned the province and began a retreat which ended on the southern end of Lake Champlain at Fort Ticonderoga. Meanwhile, the British were assembling another army at Staten Island in New York to crush

Washington's army. By August of 1776, this force had grown to some 25,000 British and German troops supported by scores of warships and transports carrying all the equipment required for the conduct of amphibious operations. As one observer noted, the British army at Staten Island was "one of the finest that was ever seen." Confronting the British at New York were about 17,000 ill-equipped, badly led, and untrained American troops stationed in indefensible positions. Clearly, the British at New York during the summer of 1776 had the best opportunity of the war to end the revolt in America by force of arms.

On August 22, the British bid for victory at New York began when the King's troops landed at Gravesend on Long Island. Victory followed victory as the British forced the Americans first out of Brooklyn, then New York City, and finally stormed the American stronghold at Fort Washington at the northern end of Manhattan, capturing its entire garrison. The campaign ended in December with the King's troops occupying a large region in New Jersey and setting up a string of posts along the Delaware River. The British victory at New York seemed complete, for prisoners were taken by the hundreds, a seemingly shattered American army had disappeared into Pennsylvania, and the King's troops occupied Long Island, Manhattan, and the Bronx; Newport, R.I. had been taken as well to be used as a naval base, and a large region from which to draw supplies had been overrun in New Jersey. At the end of the campaign of 1776, there were many among the British who thought that the rebellion in America would wither and die during the winter or at the most one more campaign would be required in 1777.

49.   From Captain John Bowater

On Board the *Centurion*, Halifax
April ye 12th. 1776

My Lord

I have taken Every Oppertunity that has offerd Since my Arrival in this Country to inform Your Lordship of our proceedings. But three ships have saild in each I have sent you a letter. I am now only to inform you that we had a very Short passage to Halifax & brought in all the Ships except three which I'm afraid are lost. This Place we found in a very distress'd Situation as to provisons & the fish that is their great support has not yet taken to the Harbours. The General has been Oblig'd from the very exorbitant price the Inhabitants set on their things to limit the price of provisions. Beef at one shilling per pound & every thing in proportion. The Country abounds in Game which will employ the Millitary. One third of the Troops are landed & Quartered on the Inhabitants & they are to stay a week & then relieve those on Board to keep the Troops in health as they was very much Crowded. We are in daily Expectation of a large fleet of Victualers, which have been drove to the West Indies And of some from England our situation at present is very far from Comfortable untill they Arrive. It is expected this Force will be divided part to go to Virginia & Joyn the Force's under Lord Cornwallis, the Rest to go up the River St. Lawrence and Endevour to Recover Canada. We are in great hopes Genl. Carleton wou'd be able to hold out at Quebec untill we send him a Reinforcement. Of all the Misserable places I ever saw Halifax is the Worst. Built with Boards & the streets not pav'd the worst House in [illegible] wou'd here let for three Guineas a week unfurnish'd.

My Friend Fielding has been much out of Order but is now recovered. I was yesterday with Major Stuart, he enjoys good health in this Country. And I was Yesterday very agreably surpriz'd with two letters from my Mother; have Receiv'd none before & these was of six months date. The Weather has been unaccountably severe upon us as well as the winds the ground is now Coverd with snow. I was made very happy on hearing my Brother Edward was made a Lieutenant & that your Lordship had got his Commission confirm'd. I shall not trouble you with a long line of Thanks but will say in a few words that I am infinately Oblig'd to your Lordship & will also promise it shall be the last trouble I shall give you on their Account, as I now hope the Rest of their preferments will be gain'd by their merits only.

I don't Know what the people of England will think of our Evacuating Boston, but it was Rediculous keeping a place that was [so] much Edg'd in that it wou'd Require a very large Army to force their lines and a much greater to Keep it after it was done, now we can Act where we please & they do not Know where to guard against us which will perplex them very much & put them to an Immense Expence to Remove their Cannon, Stores &c. &c. And as ours [is] an

Army on floate we can land when we have a mind & leave it at a short notice. The Ships Coming out have been very unlucky in losing Masts Yards &c. &c. but we shall have a powerfull squadron very soon & in good order. And they are in very good sperits since the Arrival of the proclamation for the division of the prizes.[1] Every day brings an Account of some of the Rebels Vessels falling into the Hands of our Cruizers & of late we have lost but few. I am better Situated then many of our Corps by not being disembarkt & of late have had Tollerable good health, if I stand the summer as well I shall be very happy. We sail to Morrow to the Southward & when we shall joyn the Squadron again I dont know Every thing is Kept a profound secret which is a great amendment in the American Affairs. The Generall and Admiral are on very good terms. I must now conclude this Epistle but not without Requesting your Lordship to present my Dutifull Respects to Lady Denbigh & my best Regards to her family and Friends.

1. The Capture Act, which declared the Americans to be in a state of open rebellion and that their ships and vessels were lawful prizes of war.

50. From Lieutenant William Feilding

Halifax 28th April 1776

My Lord

In my last [No. 47] I only inform'd your Lordsp: of the Generals intentions to Evacuate the Town of Boston, which took place the 17th of March: at 4 in the Morning we Paraded at ½ past 5 began to Embark the Army from the diffrent Wharfs in flat bottom boats and longboats to the transports which lay Contigious for that purpose, about 7 the Signal was made for the detachment at Charles Town under the Command of Lieut. Col. [Henry] Monkton to leave the Heights, about 8 the Rear Guards came off and the Transports with the Men of War Saild for King['s] Road. The Rebels were very numerous upon all the Heights from prospect hill near Charles Town, round to Dorchester hills, & never once Fire'd a Shot. It was Immagin'd they wou'd have Attack[ed] Lieut. Col. Monkton's detachment in their Retreat, but believe the[y] dreaded some Scheme was laid to draw them in, and very peaceably stood at a distance and never Attempted the Hills nor Boston lines till they saw the Harbour quite Clear of Ships and Boats. If they had the Town Certainly wou'd have been Burnt, as every thing was laid for that purpose, the Retreat was well plan'd and conducted with great Regularity & silence, as not a single word was heard from a Soldier during the Embarkation, which was very Astonishing, and had been Remark'd by old Officers that they Never saw an Army so Silent, Attentive and Obedient to their Officers as this, upon all Occasions. Tho the day was very fine (the situation of the Ships at Anchor and the Boats going off with the Army Afforded a most Beautifull picture) the scene was awfull and Malencholy; had the Town been Burnt the Conflagration wou'd have been dreadfull. I shou'd have been sorry to have seen the Town destroyd, tho I think its the only one on the Continent that ought not to be saved, as it was there the seeds of Sedition was first Sown, Nursed and Cherish'd. Mr. Washington when he enter'd the Town was much Surprised, that no Depredations or Plunder had been Committed by the Kings Troops but the Town has sufficiently paid for it since as the Goods in every shop was seiz'd and Many of the Inhabitants (that they thought was in the least favor of Government) confin'd some in Gaol, and others with sentries at the doors. The Army lay at King['s] Road and Nantasket about ten days, setting and Victualing the Troops, and proceeded for Halifax, where we Arrived the 2nd Inst. I believe the Scarcity of provision was the cause of the Army leaving Boston, as there was but one months provision left, when it was determin'd to quit the Garrison, and am sorry there is not a Sufficiency here to enable the Troops to proceed to the Southward.

A few days since our Detachment which saild the begining of Jany: under the Command of Majors Grant and Maitland, arrived from Savannah in Georgia where they had been for Provision &c. in their Return, the *Scarborough* with the Transports and other Vessells which they had taken, put into Rhode Island, where soon after she arrived was Attack'd by the Rebels, and Oblig'd to put to sea leaving two prizes loaded with Rice behind which the Rebels had Boarded and Seiz'd. Capn. [Tyringham] Howe of the *Glasgow* of 20 Guns Arrived here a few days since having been Attack'd near Rhode Island by five Rebel privateers (mounting between them near 100 Guns) and with much difficulty Escaped, having a Runing fight from 3 in the Morning till the Evening.[1] Captn. [James] Wallace in the

Rose has also been chaised by the same Vessels. When we quit this [place] is not known nor to which place. We hear Genl. Burgoyne is saild with ten Thousand Troops for Quebec, with four Companies of Artillery. That Major General Earl Cornwallis is gone with the like number to Carolina and that this Army (with an Augmentation) under Genl: Howe is destin'd for New York. An Army We hear is also to be left at Halifax. I hope none of the Marines will be left as I wish much to be where some thing will be done, and where I hope the Rebels will get heartily thrashed. I would be Content to loose a leg & an Arm to see them Totally defeated and their whole Country laid waist. Last week a packet Arrived from Falmouth with dispatches for Governor [Francis] Legge, who is Recalled to answer a Complaint made by the provence for Tyranny and Oppresion, &c.[2] A Transport from the West Indies with four Companies of the 55th Regt: is just Arrived and brought in a prize which she Chaced & took on the Banks. The Vessels was bound from Philadelphia with provisions to St. Eustatia and to Return with Warlike Stores and Amunition &c. A number of letters were taken on Board the Contents of which I have not been able to learn. I beg leave to Acquaint your Lordship that the Commanding Officers of the three divisions of Marines have always Allow'd the Benefit Arising from Recruits enlisted at Quarters to be Equally divided between the Adjutants and Quarter Master. On my leaving Portsmouth, the other Adjutant and Quarter Master told me I should share with them during my Absence as I still belong'd to the Division[3] and had the same right to it as when I was absent with leave. I am inform'd from those Gentlemen that supposeing I had a Share with the Staff in America (which is impossable) they had agree'd to my Sharing with them to the 30th of June last and no longer. I therefore shall Esteem it a favour [if] Your Lordship wou'd mention it to Lord S:[andwich]—and get an Order for my being Continued to share with them as Usial as I am under a Nessesity of Keeping a horse, and paying a most Exorbitant price for Forage &c. that little Benifit wou'd Assist me much my Brother Adjutant at Plymouth being served in the same manner, we have both wrote to Mr. Stephens to lay it before their Lordships. Your Lordsp doing me the Honor to back my Application wou'd (I am sure) be a means of my obtaining it. I am sorry to acquaint your Lordship that Lord S:[andwich] is determind to fill the Vacancys happening in America by the Lieuts. serving on board ships as well as on shore, by which plan I find there are more before me now for promotion, then when I left England.

I was made Very Happy the day we sailed from Boston by receiving a letter from Lord F:[eilding] in which he Acquainted me of your Lordship Lady Denbigh, and Family being in good health. I am likewise happy to find that what Accounts I can give your Lordship of the Military Operations here, meet with your Lordship's approbation. Bowater is well and at Sea Cruizing on the Banks for the Ships from Europe bound to Boston.

1. The *Glasgow* was attacked off Block Island on April 6, 1776, by a squadron of eight American warships under the command of Commodore Esek Hopkins of the Continental Navy.
2. Legge was sent as governor to Nova Scotia with instructions to investigate official corruption within the Province. He was so successful that a number of powerful officials and merchants at Halifax procured his recall by claiming that Legge was setting up a "tyranny."
3. The Marines were divided into three divisions based at Chatham, Plymouth, and Portsmouth.

51. From Lieutenant William Feilding

Halifax May ye 12th. 1776

My Lord

I have nothing particular to acquaint your Lordship of but that Lord G[eorge] G[ermain] in his letter to the Lieut. Govenor (Arbuthnot)[1] says he supposes he will apply for the two Battalions of Marines to stay in his Government; which I hear he is to have, tho I believe Contrary to the General's Inclinations, he having express'd a great desire of taking the Marines with him. Likewise all the Generals wish to have so fine a Body of Men with them, as the General has not declared what troops is to be left to Garrison this place the Corps is still in hopes of going with the Body of the Army. The two Battalions Consisting of above 800 Rank and file are to be Reviewd by the General next week, at which time I suppose we shall know our fate. The General is fortyfying the Town and Dock Yard with Redoubts on the Heights, and Bastions with Lines Round the Yard, which will be compleated in a Month, about which time the Camp Equipage[2] and Provisions is Expected to arrive, and the Army be in motion for the

Southward. A Vessel who Arrived a few days since from Jersey, says she saw twelve sail of Transports with Troops going into the River St. Lawrence. Every thing here is as dear as Boston, particularly Meat and that Rather Scarce.

PS This by the *Glasgow.*

1. Captain Marriot Arbuthnot, R.N. was also Commissioner of the Dock-yard at Halifax.
2. Personal equipment, other than arms and ammunition, needed by troops in the field.

52. From Lieutenant William Feilding

Halifax May 23d 1776

My Lord

I am Sorry to inform Your Lordship that the General [Howe] defer'd making a distrabution of the troops till he heard from home, which was last week where in the two Battalions of Marines were particularly Mention'd to be left at Halifax which has displeas'd the General much, as he wish'd to take the Marines who are almost Equal to three Regiments, extreamly well Appointed and Officer'd and a Body of Men that are not only fit for the field, but of infinite service in Case the Troops shou'd have much boat work, which is very probable. Why this Slight is put upon us from home we cannot find out. The Officers in General have Applied to go as Volenteers with the Army but that Could not be granted, however he [General Howe] has given Major Maitland the Command of the second Battalion of light Infantry and taken our Granadier Company's into the Granadier Battalions; and wou'd have taken the light Companies but Major Genl. Masse[1] beg'd he wou'd not. The General has likewise given some of our Young Subalterns Commisions in the [army] Regiments that go with him, and the General is Vastly Pleased with the sperit of the Corps; and says he never Met with a Corps whose Officers are so desireous of going into Actual Service and cou'd Reap so little Benifit from it. The Corps is so much hurt at being left behind that I believe that they will apply to be Recald and serve on board the Men of War. I do assure your Lordship that staying in Halifax Garrison has given me so much Uneasiness that I begin to think the

Marines the Worst Corps, for a Gentleman who has any sperit or feeling to stay in. A Merchant of Note who was at Montreal traveled from thence to New York, where he made his Escape on Board the *Hussar* Sloop of War. Arrived here last week; by him we learn that the Rebels under the Command of [Benedict] Arnold made a Most Extraordinary march in to Canada, the Middle of the Winter, and Attack'd Quebec about the 2d of April. Genl. Carleton after suffering them to take Possession of the lower Town, Attack'd and drove them out of it, with the loss of about thirty men; that the Enemy [lost] about 1600—Eight hundred of which was left dead in the feild 300 taken Prisoners and the Rest wounded. This second defeat in Canada is so Capital a stroke, that the Rebels are much Shagreen'd at it, and no man wou'd turn out Volunteers from their Army at Philadelphia and New York to Reinforce the Scatter'd remains of their defeated Army in Canada: by him we likewise learn that there are differences in the Congress, and the people about New York, much disatisfied. It is the Opinion of many that this Summer, and next winter will totally destroy their Army, and the Misled deluded people will at last be convinced that they have been drawn into Ruin, by a set of mock patriots, whom they find has now left them in the Lurch, to save them selves. A Confirmation of the Quebec news has been expected daily from Genl. Carleton, which delay is Imagin'd [owing] to the Ice not being broke in the River St. Lawrence. The Guards and Foreign Troops are Expected soon. The Troops Embark on Monday the 27th inst: their departure will (I believe) depend Chiefly on the Arrival of the Troops and Camp Equipage from England, as the Regiments that were at the last Campaigne at Boston are intirely without the latter. The Captain of the *Hussar* brought in a Vessel which he had cut out of the River near Rhode Island much to his Credit & the Honor of the Navy. I hope he will meet with preferment (he being an Old Master & Commander) for his sperited behavour. Nothing but the Idea (if I dare make use of the Expression) of the Rebels Coming here after the Army is gone Reconciles me to being left behind, which generally believ'd Mr. Arnold being an Enterprising Man, will attempt this Province as being his last Effort, as it will be impossable for him to bring Cannon thro' the woods or down the River. I think his Army must inevitally be cut to pieces of which I hope to have the Satisfaction of Acquainting you hereafter. And that the two Companies of the 14th Regiment and the two Battalions of Marines as Regulars, with the Royal Highland Emegrants,[2] and Fencible Americans[3] (who are training to be Soldiers) had totally defeated them. The Emegrants the most part are a good body of Men and may soon be brought into some kind of discipline, but the Fencibles not being all Cloth'd look so much like Yankee's that [shame] of doing with them gives me Horrors. A Ship Arrivd a few days since from London with the following articles as a Donation from the Society, for Relief, of Soldiers, Widows and Children of the Army at Boston. Shoes, Stockings, Bayes Waistcoats, Caps, flannel for socks, for the Soldiers; Shoes Stockings and other Articles for the Women and Children in Camp, which Donation from the people of England has a Very great Effect upon the Troops, and the General has mention'd it a very high manner in publick Orders. Every soldier will (I believe) receive one of the Above Articles which will be of infinate Use to them in the Ensuing Campaigne, besides these Articles a Quantity of money in Silver has been sent to be distributed to such Objects as the Commander in Chief thinks proper. Since my last [No. 51] I have Receiv'd the following letters from your Lordship, one dated 2d. March by the packet [No. 44], and a long letter dated 22d Novr.[4] which letter has been to the West Indies, in the last was a note to Earl Percy, who directed his best Respects to your Lordship. I am much oblig'd to your Lordship for the very friendly Attention you pay to my preferment, and am well Convinced of your Lordship['s] inclination to serve me, and I hope your Lordship will be Able to Accomplish it soon (as I hear L:[ord] S:[andwich] is going out of the Admiralty) into a higher office, two of our Captains, [Thomas] Groves, and [John] Hadden, are going home with the General's leave, being unfit for Service, the former being 76 years old and a soldier since he was sixteen, the latter from wounds he Receivd last war, is not able to march. I hope if these Gentlemen shou'd Retire from Service that L:[ord] S:[andwich] will pay Attention to the old Sub[altern]s in this Country. I am likewise Extreamly Oblig'd to your Lordship and Lady for the Very great Civility and Friendship and benevolence to my Mother & family and shall ever Retain a most greatfull Acknowledgement of the same.

P.S. Bowater has been at sea some time.

1. Brigadier General Eyre Massey, commander of the garrison of Halifax.
2. 84th Regiment of Foot, which was raised in Nova Scotia.
3. A Loyalist unit raised by Lieutenant Colonel Joseph Gorham.
4. Not entered in the letter book.

53. From Lieutenant William Feilding

Halifax June 7th 1776

My Lord

I have the pleasure to send your Lordship the Inclos'd[1] Account of the Seige of Quebec by the Rebels and of their flight at the sight of about 1200 Men, leaving their Camp standing, Cannon, &c. behind them. A Dinner was drest for Genl Thomas[2] and on the Table when they perceivd the British Troops, of which the latter feasted on. A French Gentleman met Thomas, who call'd to him, "Monsieur General, Vous etes bien pressés." This Account has given General Howe's Army great sperits, and are in great hopes that they shall do the same by the Rebels at New York, or where the Troops are destin'd for and that the two Army's may meet in some of the provinces; This Summer in all probibillity will put an End to their Rebellion. I am told, it is impossible to think of the Hardships they Under went in geting into Canada; many Died from fateague and Hunger, and were oblig'd to Kill Dogs and their Horses for provisions. General Howe with his Army Consisting of the following Corps sails tomorrow or next day. Viz. 17th. light Dragoons, Royal Artillery, 4th-5th-10th-17th-22d-23d-27th-35th-38th-40th-43rd-44th-45th-49th-52d-55th-63d   and 64th Regt: with the light Infantry and Granadiers of those Corps in two Batallions each including the two Marine Granadier Companies. The Whole is in good health and great Spirets and sorry I am that I cannot be with them. From the General Application of Officers and Soldiers (left in this Garrison) to serve as Volunteers with the Army that moves from hence, The General Mention'd in Publick Orders with thanks, highly Approved of their Spirrit, but as the Arrangement was made it was impossable to Alter it. Lord Howe[3] with British and foreign Troops, it is suppos'd will Join those from hence at Sea, as Several Men of War are seen Cruizing it is said for that purpose. Admiral Shuldham, and General Howe are upon Exceding Good terms, which gives great pleasure to the Army, and am sure no two Officers were ever in higher Estemation.

1. Not entered in the letter book.
2. Major General John Thomas, the commander of the American troops when the British broke the siege of Quebec City.
3. Vice-Admiral Lord Richard Howe. The brother of Major General William Howe. Admiral Howe was appointed commander-in-chief of the Royal

Navy in America on February 5, 1776, and relieved Shuldham on July 12, 1776.

54.   To Lieutenant William Feilding

Newnham June ye. 8th. 1776

Dear Will

I have Just Receivd yours of the 28th. of April last [No. 50] from Halifax. I will take the first Opportunity of laying your Greaveance before Lord Sandwich, and make no doubt of geting it Redress'd. I am Glad to find your self & Capn: Bowater Continue well I flatter my Self by this time that you are Reinforced by the Hessians and the Guards, and that you will make a prosperous Campaigne. We are all perfectly well here; I have no news to send you, but that this Country is determin'd to give Genl: Howe every Support in her power. Miss Hester Mundy, is just Married to Sr. Roger Newdigate,[1] it is a great Match for her don't fail to write by Every ship, and send a particular Account of what is become of Genl. Carleton and Quebec. The Report here from New York is that Genl: Carleton has Repulsed the Rebels a second time and has intirely defeated Genl. Woolster;[2] pray God this may be true.

P.S. my best Complement to Ld. Percy.

1. Sir Roger Newdigate, Bart., M.P. for Middlesex, 1742-1747, and for Oxford University, 1751-1780. Newdigate was a rich antiquary and a high Tory whom Horace Walpole once called "a half Converted Jacobite."
2. Brigadier General David Wooster, who succeeded to the command of the American army at Quebec after the death of Montgomery and the wounding of Arnold.

55.   From Captain John Bowater

On board the *Centurion* Halifax
June 8th: 1776

My Lord

I had the Honor of your Lordships letter dated the 20th of Novr.,[1] and I have wrot four [Nos. 48, 49],[2] the last was from Halifax in which I inform'd your Lord:p that we was then going [on] a Cruize off Boston in Order to prevent the Ships going to that place and to direct them here. We was very fortunate in meeting with about fifty sail which wou'd have fell into the Hands of the Rebels, we Remain'd on this duty five Weeks & then Went into Nantasket Road near Boston & staid a Week in Order to Observe the Enemys motions, they have fortyfied Fort hill & have Added more works to Bunkers hill & have Also mad[e] some Batterys on Castle William. By a deserter that we had who brought us some of their News papers, we find that as soon as we left it they divided their Forces, one half to New York & the other to Canada having only four Regiments in Boston under the Command of Genl. [Artemas] Ward. They have fitted out a number of small Vessels as Privateers, & have taken an other of our Powder Ships,[3] & I am afraid it was Occasion'd by the Treachery of the Master she was one of the largest & most Valueablest that was sent out, at Newby[4] they have a great many privateers & have taken many of our Small Vessels coming from the West Indies. At Portsmouth they have three stout Frigates, but they have not yet Ventured out & I am inform'd, they are in great want of Sails & Cordage. Their Paper Money is not well Establish'd, what is sold for two Shilling Specie you must give a Six Shilling note for. Our Men of War have taken Burnt, & destroy'd an Amazing number of their Vessels, some Hundreds, yet they stil persist in going to St. Eustatia & their good friends the Dutch supply them with both Arms & Ammunition. On our Arrival here the 6th of June we found all the Troops embarkt except the two Battalions of marines & some young Corps, which are to Garrison this Place in all about twelve Hundred. The Marines are Very much mortified at being left behind, & I think your Lordship will feel the loss, as your good Correspondent Feilding will be out of the way of sending you so early inteligence. The fleet & Army are Very healthy & in high Spirits. The great Reinforcement which is Every day Arriving & the Scandelous Retreat of the Rebels from Quebec has quite chang'd the face of Affairs in this Country, (which by the by had but a very pale Aspect about three months ago). The *Mercury* Packett is Arrived & we hourly expect the Arrival of Lord Howe & the Hessians. And no one doubt[s] the least of our finishing this Bussiness before Christmas, tho I expect we shall meet a warm Reception. It is not yet Anounced where the Attack is to be made but most people think it will be at New York. We are all fitting out in the

Greatest Hurry, and if the Wind permitts shall sail to Morrow. The Packett which brings this Sails with us, only out of the Harbour. In order to inform you at home how soon we begin. And if Lord Howe does not come in to Morrow we shall certainly meet on the Way which will prevent a delay in time. Transports with the 42d [Regiment] is now coming in which I believe was part of the great fleet. I had a letter Yesterday of my brother William who is at Brunswick North Carolina, he mentions that things are going very well & that Genl: Clinton was preparing to Attack the Rebels, & that they had strong assurances of many people joining them.⁵ The *Swan* Sloop of War is to sail as soon as we Arrive at the place we are destin'd for. And I shall write to your Lordship by her, & every Oppertunity that offers. Your Lordship will excuse the Incorrectness as well as the shortness of my letters as the Hurry of duty takes up our whole time & it is not an uncommon speach to say here, that we might imploy ourselves better than Scribling. But I who am rather lawless will both think of my friends & write to them.

P:S I direct this to your Lordship in the Country, tho I think it is contrary to Orders, but I shall have the Pleasure of writing the name of Newnham twice, And also to request your Lordship to say every thing that is civil for me to two fair Ladies, that I hope are now under your Roof. This is being too good if you cou'd see the wretch'd place I am in and the Company I am Obliged to Keep.

1. Not entered in the letter book.
2. Two of these letters were not entered in the letter book.
3. The ordnance storeship *Hope* was captured on May 17, 1776, off Massachusetts by the American armed schooner *Franklin*.
4. Newburyport, Massachusetts.
5. Bowater is referring to the ill-fated Loyalist uprising which was crushed at the Battle of Moores Bridge on February 27, 1776, and to the Clinton-Parker expedition to the Southern Colonies.

56. To Lord Barrington

Newnham June 30th 1776

My Dear Lord

By the Inclosed you will find my friend Mr. Buckley has Compleatly fulfilled his Engagement I therefore flatter myself, his Commission will now be signed immediately, & if it can be antidated a few months, which is about the time he first began Recruiting, I think he is intitled to it, as the Raising the Men has been a great expence to him. I first talked this matter over about Feby or March last. It is very indifferent to Mr. Buckley into what part of the World he goes or into what Corp you place him, but I continue to think it will be for the good of Service, if he is left at home Recruiting this Summer.

57. From Lord Barrington

Cavendish Square July 5th 1776

Lord Barrington presents his complements to Lord Denbigh and having yesterday received a Certificate from General Evelyn[1] of the delivery of 25 Recruits for the 29th Regiment, will take the Very first oppertunity of laying the same before the King, when he is persuaded a Commission will be immediately ordered for Mr. Buckley. Lord Barrington will propose that the date shall be as early as possible; but it cannot be anterior to the Vacancy.

1. Lieutenant General William Evelyn, Colonel of the 29th Regiment of Foot.

58. From Captain John Bowater

On board his Majesty's Ship *Centurion*
Staten Island New York July 7th. 1776

My Lord

I had the Honor of writing to Your Lordship by the Packett which saild from Halifax the 10th. of June [No. 55], at which time we all got under sail for this place, and arrived safe here the 1st of July without the loss of any one Ship under our Convoy, & from the finest Weather I have seen in this Country & the Sperrits the Troops have keept up we have not a sick man. On the 3d the Troops landed on Staten Island without Opposition. A Body of five Hundred [American] Rifle men & one Troop of light Horse, who was Employ'd in destroying & driving off the Cattle, Stock, &c. Retreated very precipitally. The Inhabitants receiv'd our people with the Utmost Joy, having been long oppress'd for their Attachment to Government. They sell their things to the Soldiers at the most Reasonable Terms & they kept up their stock in spite of the Rebels. Governor Tryon landed & has Summoned the Millitia who had sent their Arms to him on Board[1] least they should fall into the Hands of the Rebels. And they are now Embodied, & in high Spirrits 600 in number. We are every Minute expecting Lord Howe with the Fleet & Troops and we shall then land on Long Island, and Attack the Heights call[ed] Red Hook which commands the Town of New York—more than Dorchester hill did Boston. We are at Anchor with the Men of War & transports at the North End of Staten Island & abreast of the Town of [New] York and we see all their Movements in the Town, which is Turn'd in to Barracks & they have several Encampments Batteries & Entrenchments without number but I believe they have not half Cannon Enough to Supply them. They are said to have forty Thousand men in Arms here but I dont give Credit to more than half that Number. They Desert to us hourly & what is still better they bring their Arms with them, as Genl. Howe has let them Know that we give ten Dollars reward for Rifle Guns. All the Principal People are with us, five Gentlemen & sixty private men & a Stand of Colours Came over in a Vessel from the Jersey's Yesterday.

General Washingtons Guards made a bold Attempt to put him into our hands a few days ago, but the Plot was discover'd and one of them hanged.[2] I Wonder they dont Bombard us as we are so Close to them, they Entertain us with some Shot in the narrows coming up but did no mischief & since that did a good deal of fireing has been kept up on the side next to Elizabeth Town & Muskett balls reach a Cross [the] River & they get behind trees and steal a Shot at the Centries, they kild one man and Wounded four on board one of our Arm'd Sloops Yesterday morning, since which we have got some field pieces & scowerd the Woods which has made them Retreat. We have Very good Accounts from Canada, and don't doubt but shall soon hear that Generl: Burgoyne has got into Albany. General Clinton goes on Well at South Carolina and is in Possession of Charleston.[3] General Lee is gone after him with ten Thousand men, but the Rebels have Very little hopes of success in that Quarter, & he is very much disliked for his Severity. The only bad news we have heard is that four Transports with five Hundred Highlanders on Board went into Boston and fell into the Hands of the Rebels[4] they stood a good fight Major [blank][5] and several other Officers and men were Kill'd. The Rebels treat them horridly, Shew them about as Monsters & beat the Rogues March before them. I am Very sorry Coll. [Archibald] Campbell is taken as he is an Excelent Engineer & its a great loss. I've not seen Major Stuart since he landed he is now Major to the Granadier Battalion, and Major Maitland of the Marines has a light Infantry Battalion. Its Very late for to begin a Campaigne, this Reinforcement shou'd have been here two months ago. Tho I have not the least doubt of our Reduceing this Place in a few Weeks. But we shall not be able to follow the blow so well as if we had begun sooner and the Weather is exceeding hot. We landed upwards of Eight Thousand fighting Men in this Island and there is fresh Provisions & Vegetables Enough for them for six Weeks without distressing the Inhabitants who like our Gold & Silver better than the Congress paper money. I wish'd to inclose your Lordship the *New York Gazette* but cou'd not prevail on the Gentleman who brought it away, to part with it. It contains the most Impudent Resolves of the Congress I ever saw pened—a full Declaration of Independence, and Coppies of all the Lying Paragraphs out of the London papers the Duke of Richmond & that Scoundrel Barre's[6] Speaches. We flatter our selves with the pleasing prospect of seeing their Heads ornament Temple Barr when we Return, for they Certainly have led these poor wretches into their present unhappy situation. My paper & subject obliges me to Conclude this dull scroll but I hope to make amends in my next & add the overcome.

1. General William Tryon, the last Royal Governor of New York. Tryon passed the winter of 1775-6 aboard the transport *Duchess of Gordon* in New York Harbor.
2. This was not a plot against Washington, rather it was a scheme set in motion by Tryon to recruit secretly a number of Americans at New York into the King's forces and to obtain arms from New York City. In the third week of June 1776, this plot was uncovered by a special secret committee of

the New York Provincial Congress, and in the course of the investigation it was found that three members of Washington's headquarters guard were involved. One of them, Thomas Hickey, was tried by a court martial, found guilty of mutiny and sedition, among other things; and on June 28, before a crowd of almost 20,000, he was hung at New York City.

3. This was a rumor, for Clinton's attack on Charleston was repulsed.

4. The Americans captured six transports carrying Highlanders—two in Boston Harbor and four others off the coast of Massachusetts. A total of 571 Scots soldiers were captured.

5. Major Robert Menzies of the 71st Regiment was killed in Boston Harbor.

6. Charles Lennox, 3rd Duke of Richmond, and Lieutenant Colonel Issac Barré, M.P. for Chipping Wycombe, were opposition politicians and outspoken critics of the government's American policy.

59.   From Lord Barrington

Cavendish square July 10th. 1776

Lord Barrington presents his Complements to Lord Denbigh, and has the Honor to acquaint him that Mr. Buckley is appointed an Ensign in the 29th Regiment. General Evelyn may Employ him either at home or a Broad as he thinks proper.

60.   From Lieutenant William Feilding

Halifax July 10th. 1776

My Lord

The Fleet with the Troops under Genl. Howe said the 10th *Ultimo*, & no Account of their destination has yet been Receiv'd. Lord Howe Arrived off the Harbour about a fortnight since, and after Receiving information where the fleet was gone, saild the same Evening. His Lordship spoke with Capn: [Francis] Banks in the *Renown* coming from Nantasket Road Boston—with sixteen Sail of Transports, with Hessians and Highlanders. His Lordship seem'd much surpriz'd when Capn. B.[anks] told him the Rebels had Erected a Battery on long Island [in Boston Bay] which Oblig'd him to leave his Station, leaving the *Milford* Frigate in the Bay to pick up the stragling Transports, which Frigate was Oblig'd to leave her station, a few days after, for want of Provisions. A Report prevails and not without foundation, that the Rebels as soon as Comodore Banks left Nantasket, sent a large Ship to lay there, with a large Red broad pendant, to decoy our Ships. And that they have met with too much success, as five Ships with Highlanders have fallen into their hands, some say more. One Ship in particular it is said, saild thro Nantasket Road up to Boston and Anchor'd off the Town imagining the British Troops were there. And the Rebels like Cowards fired at her the Whole way up. Kiled an Officer by name McKenzie[1] and twenty men, such conduct of Mr. B.[anks] has Occasiond *much Talk*.[2] The *Renown* sailed the 2d Instant with twenty sail of Hessian, Guards and Highlanders to join Genl. Howe. The fifth Inst. Arrived sixteen sail more of Hessians and Guards, with Genl. Heister,[3] and Lieut. Col: [Thomas] Cox of the Guards, which Transports saild the next day for the Army under Convoy of two Sloops, several more are expected here daily. It has often been Reported and sometimes Asserted for fact, that two Thousand Rebels had passd Fort Cumberland and enter'd this Province. I shou'd be Glad to see them here exposed to the two Batallions of Marines Only in Open field. I think we shoud be able to Give a very good Account of them. General Carleton has been Very successfull with his Army in Canada, and I make no doubt but he has Totally destroy'd the Rebel Army in that province. By a Schooner who Arrived last week from Canada, we have an Account of a Glorious Attack made by Capn. [George] Forster with his light Company of the 8th Regiment some Canadians and about two hundred Indians, on an intrench'd Post of the Rebels on the main, Call'd the Cedars, the particulars of which I send your Lordship in the news papers publish'd by Authority, with some curious accounts of the Congress &c. I make no doubt but General Howe of whome I have (as well as Other Officers & Soldiers) the highest Opinion of, will where Ever he lands be as successful as his Brother General in Canada. As the Americans mean to declare independance he will have a large Force to Attack, particularly if it is at New York, as they have Drawn most of the Troops to that Place. The Torey's in that provence has been Used extreamly Ill, by the Rebels, and will when ever an Opertunity offers fly to the Kings Standard. The *Milford* has taken and brought in here a privateer Brigg with twelve Carriage Guns and some swivels, Call'd the *Yankee Hero* Commanded by a Capn. [James] Tracy; which privateer engaged the *Milford* an Hour and half: The Shot she had on board were Round six pounders, double headed, and chaine Shot, with a Vast number pieces of Ragg'd Iron as Grape. The *Milford* has likewise taken several small Vessels with Provisions. For Continental news I Refer your Lordship to the Inclos'd papers. I have sent your Lordship in Another Packet, a Curious Journal of Occurrences, which happen'd to a detachment of about 1000 men that march'd last Summer from Roxbury and Cambridge to Canada, which Journal I got a Copy of from a Mr. Meigs[4] a major in that Detachment who was taken Prisoner at Quebec, and sent here in the *Cerberus*, he is since gone on his parole to his Family. Comodore [William] Hotham Appear'd off this Harbour the 8th Inst. with about 50 sail of Transports the Remainder of the Hessians and Guards, he was imediately acquainted from the General and Governor where the Fleet was. Bowater is gone with the Fleet, so that it will be some time before I see him.

[P.S.] This goes by Major [John] Tupper of Marines who has got the Generals leave to go to Bath for his health.

1. Major Robert Menzies.
2. On the night of June 16, 1776, in the absence of Banks' blockading squadron, two British transports entered Boston Harbor believing that Boston was still held by the British. After an engagement in which eight British soldiers were killed and twelve others wounded, the two transports were overpowered by the Americans. No convincing reason has emerged to explain why Banks' squadron withdrew from its station off Boston.
3. Lieutenant General Philip von Heister, commander of the Hessian contingent in the British army in America.
4. Major Return Jonathan Meigs' journal describing the march of Arnold's army through the wilderness of Maine to Quebec. This journal has been published by Kenneth Roberts in *March to Quebec: Journals of the Members of Arnold's Expedition* (New York, 1938).

61.   From Ensign William Buckley

Leicester July 13th. 1776

My Lord

I am this Morning honor'd with your Lordships Note,[1] acquainting me I am appointed an Ensign in the 29th. Regiment. I beg leave to Return your Lordship many thanks for the same. There being a Common Hall to morrow shall have a publick oppertunity of laying before my friends of the Corporation your Lordships favour. It will Require some little time to get some Nessisarys done at Leicester, will make a point of being as strict to my orders as possable.

P S Before I leave I will do myself the Honor personally to pay my Respect to your Lordship.

1. Not entered in the letter book.

62. To General William Evelyn

Newnham July 13th. 1776

Dear Sir

I am this Morning acquainted by a letter[1] from the War Office that Mr. William Buckley is appointed an Ensign in your Regiment. I have recommended to him to join your Companies immediately, which are gone into Hants, where Captain Richards[2] will put him in a Way of taking up his Commission having his Uniform made, & teach him his duty before he goes to America, wish therefore you would be kind enough to send him these orders down to Leicester.

1. Not entered in the letter book.
2. In 1776 the only officer in the British army named Richards is Lieutenant William Richards of the 65th Regiment, which was stationed in America. The only name in the 29th Regiment at this time which resembles Richards is Lieutenant Isaac Riches.

63. From General William Evelyn

Send Grove July 22d: 1776

My Lord

I am very glad to find by your Lordships letter of the 13th: Inst. [No. 62] which I shou'd have Answerd immediately had I been at home, that Mr. Buckley has got his Recruiting Reward in my Regiment. I propose continuing him at Leicester on that Service, and have wrote to him as your Lordship desired by this post.

64. To Captain John Bowater

Newnham July 24th. 1776

Dear Bow

I Receivd three of your letters, the last dated Halifax June the 8th [Nos. 48, 49, 55], by which I am Glad to find that all the Army has Embark'd in such good sperits. I hope & trust that you will prove in the right, & that all your American disturbances may be finished this Campagne. I have Receiv'd a malancholly letter [No. 60] from Adjutant Feilding Complaining Greveously at being left behind at Halifax. When you see him Assure him that Nothing shall be wanting on my part, either for his or Your promotion. Wonder not nor be Astonish'd, but behold my Eldest Daugter Hester Mundy, is maried to Sr. Roger Newdigate, the[y] seem Extreamly happy, but I fear her Comforts of matrimony will be in a Very narrow compass. You know Sr. Roger was but a Very bad hand when he was Young, what must he be now. Nelly[1] is perfectly well, tho still a Vergin, & like a fool means to die so. Doctor Marriott[2] who is here, thinner than Ever is making his prop at Nenny Cave[3] & with the Assitance of the Newnham Ladies, I think he will Succeed, tho Sr. Thomas wont give him a half a Crown at present, he is Crosser than Ever & I wish he was gone to the D---l. The two Boys[4] are Exceedingly well & desires to be Remember'd to you. Charles is Droller than Ever.

I most strongly Recommended your Brother the Seamen[5] to Admiral Montague,[6] under whose Command he now is, before he sail'd to Newfoundland, who promised he would do every thing in his power for him. My wife and Every body here desires their best wishes to you.

P.S. Inclose Your letters to me under Cover to Ld George Germain

1. Nelly Mundy, daughter of Edward Miller Mundy of Shipley Hall, Derbyshire.
2. Dr. Thomas Marriott, Prebend of Westminster and Rector of St. Michael Bashshare. He was Denbigh's cousin.
3. Daughter of Sir Thomas Cave, 5th Bart., M.P. for Leicestershire, 1714-1747, 1762-1774.
4. Denbigh's two sons.
5. Lieutenant Edward Bowater, R.N.
6. Vice-Admiral John Montagu, Governor of Newfoundland and commander-in-chief of the squadron there.

65. To General William Evelyn

Newnham July 27th: 1776

Dear Sir

I have Receivd yours of the 22d. Instant [No. 63], and am afraid you have Mistaken my letter, neither my self nor Mr. Buckley's Relations wish that he should continue any longer at Leicester for the present, but that you would be so good as to order him to join your Companies in Hampshire, where we wish him to stay a few Months with Capn. Richards, as well in order that he may learn his duty, as to keep him out of some very unnessisary expences, which he is at present got. He is a Spirited young Chap, & wants to see Service therefore the sooner you send him abroad the better. But if this last plan does not suite you, and you wish to send him back to Leicester a Recruiting in the Winter, I will then give him all the Assistance in my Power.

66.   From Captain John Bowater

On board the *Centurion* Staten Island
New York Road Augt. 15th. 1776

My Lord

I was in hopes before this to have been able to have given your Lordship an Account of a Victory obtained by our Troops, but we have been only looking at one another for this last Month and waiting for the Arrival of Commodore Hotham with the Hessians, Guards &c. &c. I've now the Pleasure of informing you of their safe Arrival & all very healthy, did not lose one Ship of their Convoy. We have also been Reinforced with seven Regiments with General Clinton, Lord Cornwallis & Commodore Sr. Peter Parker from South Carolina; where they Met with a severe Rebuff, and very wisely left that unhealthy Country which would have destroyd the whole Army & for little purpose. We have now about three & twenty Thousand well disciplin'd troops, and twenty Men of War, and about three hundred Transports; the fleet & Camp made the finest Appearance I ever saw. Tomorrow or the day After we expect to make a landing & it's said will be in three difrent places. The Hessians are landed this day on Staten Island in order to stretch their legs after their long confinement on board, and the British Troops are Embarking. The Rebels are said to be forty Thousand. They seem by their Movement to be in great Confusion, as they don't know where to expect us. They are very sickly at New York, the small pox has made great havock amongst them. We hear they intend burning the Town. They treated the declaration of the Commissioners with great contempt.[1] The Bayonet is the only thing to convince them and I think in the Course of this week a great Number will know the grand secret. We expect another Packet to sail next week and I shall give your Lordship a line. I've Receivd but one letter from your Lordship and never a one form Lord Wentworth. Please to present my best Respects to Lady Denbigh.

1. On the afternoon of July 12, 1776, Lord Howe sent Lieutenant Samuel Reeve to Perth Amboy, N.J. with dispatches to the governors of the colonies to the south of New York asking their assistance in making peace. Reeve also carried a number of private letters and a declaration dated June 20 stating that the Howes had been appointed Commissioners with the power to grant pardons to persons who returned to their allegiance and to declare at peace any region which permitted royal government to be restored. The Continental Congress published Lord Howe's declaration and letters along with a number of comments stating the American terms for ending hostilities.

67. From Lieutenant William Feilding

Halifax Augt. 17th. 1776

My Lord

About 10 days since the *Liverpool* Arrived here from the Southward, with four prizes, two of them Retaken West Indiamen, the other two bound to the Rebels. By her we learn that she left the fleet three weeks before at New York; that Genl. Howe was encamp'd on Staten Island, and that the Foreigners were expected daily. As soon as the General landed two thousand New Yorkers came off with Major Rogers,[1] and join'd him, and many more were expected, but the General was afraid the want of Boats would prevent them. A Flag of truce with a letter from Lord Howe was sent up to New York, directed to Geo. Washington Esq: which letter was Return'd the next day (unopen'd) by a Flag, (because it was not directed to his Excellency Genl. Washington Commanding the American Forces) with a letter to Genl: Howe, who with his Brother told the Officer the Contents

were such than an Answer cou'd not be given immediately.² Two
Ships of War was sent to lay one at each side of New York Neck: in
going up above 100 Shot were fired at them from the Forts, none of
which did any damage. Two shot only was Returned, which made
some of them Run. I suppose long before this, the General is in Possession of the Town, after giving them a severe thrashing. The *Milford* has brought in a very Valueable Jamaicaman which she Retook
close to the Rocks of Cape Anne: the Rebels made their escape in
boats, leaveing some sailors belonging to the Ship, a Lady & family
with her Effects going home, on board, which Lady had been used
very Ill by their Officers. This Ship with two others were taken off
Bermudas. By Accounts from Fort Cumberland, we hear, that 800
Indians have cut a Road from St. Johns [New Brunswick] towards
that place, and that they were waiting with some Cannon for the
Rebels to join them, to Attack the Fort and Carry this province if this
is true we shall have something to do this Campaigne. I last week saw
a Rebel paper of New Hampshire, in which was a letter from Lieut:
Coll: Campbell of the 71st: Regiment, to General Howe, giving an
Account of his being taken prisoner. As I was not able to get a Copy
of it, have indevoured to Recollect the particulars. Coll: Campbell
with 96 Highlanders in a Transport with six small Carriage Guns, in
Company with an other, with the same number of Highlanders, with
only 2 guns and some swivels, Standing in for Boston the 17th: June:
was Attack'd by four Arm'd Schooners with 40 men each, that from
the brisk fire of his Men, and the few Guns, beat them off. They then
went into a Port near Salem for more force. Upon which the Colonel
sail'd into Nantasket, where he expected to find the Army or some
Men of War to Releave him; but to his great Astonishment was fired
at very briskly from a Battery on long Island. He then intended to Attack this Battery with his two Transports, but unfortunately the
Transport with the two Guns got aground. Soon afterwards the four
Armed schooners with an Arm'd Brig of 16 Guns came into the
Road, and laid upon the Quarters, and Bows of the Transports, upon
which a very smart Attack ensued, in which Majr. Menzies and 7
private[s] were Kill'd, besides several wounded. The Coll: finding it
impossable to make his Escape, it being quite Calm, thought it most
prudent to strike, and not Sacrifice the lives of so many Gallant Soldiers. On his Arrival at Boston he found two Companies more of the
Highlanders, which had been taken nearly in the same manner, such

was the Consequence of the *Renown* leaving that place. Majr. Menzies was Buried in Boston with the Honors of War.[3]

1. Major Robert Rogers, who led the ranger unit which bore his name during the Seven Years War.
2. On July 14, 1776, Colonel Joseph Reed, one of Washington's aides-decamp, met with Lieutenant Philip Brown, R.N. under a flag of truce off Governor's Island. Brown informed Reed that he had a letter from Lord Howe for Washington. When Reed asked how the letter was addressed, Brown answered, "To George Washington, Esq., etc., etc., etc." Reed thereupon refused to accept the letter; and when Brown asked how Washington should be addressed, Reed replied that Washington's situation was public knowledge. Then without further exchange of words or documents, Brown and Reed departed for their respective headquarters. The following day, Washington wrote to the Howes complaining about British treatment of American prisoners.
3. See above, Nos. 58, 60.

68.   To General Sir John Irwine[1]

Newnham Sepr. 2d. 1776

Dear Sir

I find you are now got back to your Command in Ireland, & am much Mortified you did not find it convenient to honour me with your Company here for a few days as you pass'd Bye. I have in my Neighbourhood a Young Gentleman of good family & fortune, who is very desireous of going into the Army, and particularly of being Employ'd in America. If I could get a pair of Colours for him by your means in an Irish Corps, I should be extreamly happy but I will by no means owe the Obligation to the Lord Lieutenant, whose treatment of me upon a former Application, which I explained to you, I shall not easily forget. The Young Gentlemans Name is [Edward] Shuttleworth & all his family are very much my friends in this Country. I hope your Irish Affairs will go on so prosperously as to permit me to have the pleasure of meeting you in London this Winter.

1. Commander-in-Chief in Ireland.

69. **From Napthali Franks**[1]

Brighthelmstone Sepr. 6th. 1776

My Lord

I Receiv'd a letter yesterday from my Neighbour Mr. [Abraham] Guyot, he is Very anctious to know what Answer your Lordship has Received from Lord Sandwich on his Application for preferment in the Navy as he has some Reason to hope for Success your Lordships Answer will be very Obliging as I shall communicate the same to him. I have been at this place about three weeks & hope to be at Misterton the beginning of next month.

1. A London merchant and partner in the firm of Nesbitt, Drummond and Franks.

70. **From General Sir John Irwine**

Royal Hostpital Septr. 8th: 1776

My Lord

I had the Honor to Receive your Lordships letter [No. 68] yesterday. It was my full intention to make my Bow to your Lordship on my way hither but a Circumstance happen'd which obliged me to set out not only much sooner than I intended, but also to travel night & day till I got to the Waterside. Nothing would give me more pleasure than to obey any Commands of your Lordship or to facilitate a wish of yours, this I entreat your Lordship to be persuaded of: now with Respect to Mr. Shuttleworth, I will tell you Exactly how I stand. There are at present lying before my Lord Leiutenant two Recommendations of mine, for two Young Gentlemen to be Ensigns, Neither of which are yet done, & untill they are, it will not be possable for me to Recommend any other person: when they are disposed of, I shall most certainly Ask for Mr. Shuttleworth; but give me leave to observe to your Lordship that this may be a Work of time, for Added to the two Gentlemen who are before Mr. Shuttleworth, there is another circumstance which is, that we have so few Regiments here, that Vacancies happen very seldom. Therefore if I might presume to advise your Lordship, I should think your better way is to write to Genl:

Howe, who has the disposal of more Commissions by many than any other Servant of the Crown, & who I cannot doubt will be glad to Shew his Respect for your Lordship, and as the Gentleman in question is desireous of going to America, I cannot hesitate in saying in my opinion that is your Lordships best Method, especially as I do not yet see how it is possable to part with more Regiments from hence, unless some means are fallen upon to supply their places which I have not yet heard of. I submit this to your Lordships Consideration and After Repeating Assuranccs of my earnest desire to do any thing that will be agreable to your Lordship, and desiring my Respects to my Lady Denbigh, I shall conclude.

71. To Napthali Franks

Newnham Septr. 24th. 1776

Dear Sir

The Reason why you have not heard from me sooner, is because I have not been able as yet to get any satisfactory Answer about your friend Mr: Guyot, but by what I can learn it will not be possable for him to be made Master and Commander at home; The only method for his promotion will be to go out to Sea a Leiutenant, recommended to some flag Officer. Nothing shall be wanting on my part to promote this Matter, and when I come to Town, I will converse with you more fully on the Subject.

72. From Captain John Bowater

On Board the *Centurion* New York
Septr. 26th: 1776

My Lord

This is the twelfth letter I have wrote your Lordship since I have been in this Country, and have only Receiv'd one in Return [No. 64], which makes me suspect that people of the post office, or them in the packetts never deliver them. In my last [No. 66] I inform'd your Lordship of the troops landing on Long Island, and on the 27th: of last month I was an Eye Witness to the Compleatest Victory over the

Rebels, that has happen'd in America. Their loss 2000 Kill'd and wounded and near the same number taken Prisoners, the loss on our side was not more than two Hundred kill'd wounded & taken prisoners.[1] Two days after they quited the Island and left cannon & stores to a Considerable amount, & Works so strong that if they had had Courage might have been defended against fifty Thousand men. We continued Approaching and on the 15th: of this Month the Army Landed on New York Island under Cover of the Men of War; which kept up a most tremendious Cannonade, by which means the troops did not loose a man, the Rebels lost 200 killed and 800 taken prisoners[2] & they Evacuated the City in the Utmost precipitation, leaving behind them Cannon Stores &c. &c &c. &c., & taking nothing with them but their fears. A few days after a set of wretches who had conceald themselves & was hired by Washington set fire to the Town,[3] & it was with the utmost difficulty got under [control], with the loss of about one fourth of it (& them the best Houses in the Place). The Inhabitants hung & burnt eight upon the spot, And about three hundred are taken up & are to be try'd for this Crime. The Rebels are now at their strong hold at Kings bridge nine mile from the Town which they say is impregnable, but I think Generl Howe will very soon convince them of the Contrary. We are very impatient for the Arrival of the troops of the second division,[4] as it takes up great part of our Army to garrison the places taken. The fleet & Army are both very healthy and in exceeding high sperrits from their success, great plenty of provisions, fruits, &c. &c.

I dined a few days ago with Major Stuart, he is Well & I met with Parry. The Packett going in a Hurry Obliges me to Conclude, tho I must Request your Lordship to present my Respectful Complements to Lady Denbigh and family, my good wishes always Attend the house of Newnham.

P:S. I have not had one line from Lord Wentworth. My Marine Brother[5] is here & well. I lately heard from the other from Newfoundland.[6]

1. The American losses have been estimated to be 1,400 men from all causes; British casualties were 61 killed, 31 missing, and 257 wounded.
2. American casualties are not known, but the British captured 320 men. British losses were 3 killed, 16 or 18 wounded.
3. At the time, the British and the Americans blamed each other for the destruction of New York City.

4. The 16th Light Dragoons, 4,200 Hessians, and 680 Waldeckers.
5. Lieutenant William Bowater.
6. Lieutenant Edward Bowater, R.N.

73. To Lieutenant William Feilding

Newnham Octr: 14th: 1776

Dear Feilding

I have Receiv'd yours dated Halifax the 17th. of Augt. [No. 67]. By which I am glad to find you are Well and in good Spirits. I do not give much Credit to what you say of the Rebels intending to Attack Your Quarters, for by All their Actions particularly on long Island, fighting does not Appear to me to be their Choice: however if they do I dare say you will give a Very good Account of them. You may be Assured, I always have your interest most Sincerely at Heart. I take every oppertunity of bouring Lord S:[andwich] about you. He is very well disposed, and I flatter my self you will soon have a promotion. The whole House of Newnham is in perfect good Health. Dr. Marriott, is soon to be Married to Miss Cave, and Miss Noel to Sr. Ralph Milbank's[1] Eldest[2] Son. The operation is already preform'd on Miss Dixcy with George Pochin.[3]

1. Sir Ralph Milbank, 5th Bart., Sheriff of Yorkshire, 1753-1754; M.P. for Scarborough, 1754-1761, and for Richmond, 1761-1768.
2. Ralph Milbank, later 6th Bart.
3. George Pochin of Barkby, Leicestershire. Commissioned on July 25, 1778, Lieutenant Colonel of Leicestershire militia.

74. From Captain John Bowater

New York Novr. 5th. 1776

My Lord

I was honourd with a letter [No. 64] from your Lordship yesterday dated ye. 24th. of July, which is the second since I arrived in this Country. In my Last letter [No. 72] to your Lordship I inform'd you of our possessing New York. Since which many Actions have happened between our forces & the Rebels both by sea & land, in all of which the King's troops have been most Successfull. And on Tuesday last Mr. Washington & his whole Army Retreated from Kings Bridge. A place which they had made as Strong as possable it had every Advantage that Nature or Art could give it, but their fears from being surrounded made them quit this post which they boasted years could not force them to Evacuate besides a Considerable quantity of Cannon, Amunition & provision which they have left behind they Sustaining a great loss of men Kill'd & Wounded, the second Brigade of British Infantry Charged them, seconded by Baron de Heister with the Hessians. Our loss is very inconsiderable, only twelve Officers & 150 Men.[1] Great numbers of People are daily coming in and the province of New York have petitioned the Commissioners to be Restored to the Kings favour. And as we now have Connecticut open to us, I hope the Northern Provinces will follow the same Example. We have Accounts of very late date from Genl. Burgoyne who has crossd the Lakes, destroy'd all the Rebel fleet upon them & is with his Army, Canadians & Indians we hope near Albany in his way to this Country. I am afraid the Southern provinces will not be very Easily Subdued, as the Climate is so much in their favour, and they seem more United in their Oposition to Government. Tho the Luxurious style of living which all this Country had adopted I think will soon tire them of a Millitary life. I can best give your Lordship an Idea of their want of Covering at this Season of the Year by an Article from the Resolves of the Congress which directs a blanket off each bed, to be sent to the Camp to keep their Soldiers from starving. The Wisdom of Administration in sending out Lord Howe is every day more applauded. The Amazing difficulties which they have Surmounted by the Union of the fleet and army Requires a Better pen than mine to describe. And tho they have exerted themselves in the Utmost to Subdue & bring back these obstinate People to Reason, They have never Countenanced any kind of cruelty, but on the Contrary many of them who have been taken in Arms & almost Naked have been Clothed & treated with the greatest Humanity. Major Stuart was well a few days ago enquires much After Your Lordship, Capn Feilding[2] is here & in the *Diamond* and is indisposed with the Gout. I have not seen him. I had a letter from the Granidier [William Feilding] dated Halifax Octor. ye 10th: he is well but exceedingly tired of Nova Scotia. I think he had better Reconcile himself to it as there is very little probability of his leaving it for some time. As to my self I am very far from being in a happy situation Yet I every day see people in a much worse, so that with Comparison & a great deal of snuff, I'm a tollerable good philosopher *and for my Sins*, I expect to be here at least a twelve month longer. Your Lordship made me exceeding happy by saying that Lady Denbigh, Lord Feilding, Charles, Lady Newdigate & Miss Mundy were well, & did me the Honor to Remember me. I must beg your Lordship to present my most Respectfull Compliments to them and Assure them how Sincerely I wish them every happiness this World can afford them.

P.S. I have drawn a very Rough Sketch on the Cover to give your Lordship some Idea of the Situation of our fleet & army at present but you must not Compare it with a Regular draught as it is by no means perfect as to the points of the Compass.

1. Bowater is describing the Battle of White Plains, which was fought on October 28, 1778. American casualties have been estimated at between 400 and 500. The British accounting to the Deputy Adjutant General was: "about one Hundred and eighty Men Killed and Wounded."
2. Captain Charles Feilding, R.N., second son of Charles Feilding, who in turn was the third son of Basil Feilding, 4th Earl of Denbigh.

75. From Lieutenant William Feilding

Halifax Novr. 19th. 1776

My Lord

Since my last [No. 67] I have heard of no Operations on Either side of the Armies at New York. The disaffected in this Town have intelligence that Rebels made a stand at Kings bridge, and that a Vigorous & Spiritted Attack was made by the Royal Army, in which Vast Numbers were slain on both sides particularly the provincials, and that Genl: Howe gain'd the Victory. We have great Reason to believe it, as the Rebels seldom propagate any News to their disadvantage. We have just Receivd intelligence that the Rebels are before fort Cumberland, about 600 in Number, (headed by Jon. Eddy, Saml. Rogers, Wm. Howe & John Allen of Cumberland)[1] in Consequence of which a Detachment Consisting of the two Light Companies of Marines, Granadiers and light Company of M:Leans[2] and a party of the Windsor Malitia in all about 300, Embark'd Yesterday morning

at Windsor and Sailed Immediately under the Command of Major
[Thomas] Batt to Reinforce Col. Graham³ who has about 200 of his
Corps in the Fort. If they get there time Enough, I make no doubt but
they [the enemy] will be cut to pieces. The people in this province at
least the greatest part of them are Ripe for Rebellion, and have erected a Liberty Pole at Cobequid, how this will End is hard for me to
judge but it seems to be the General Opinion that we shall have much
severer duty this Winter then the last as the Rebels certainly mean to
Attack this place, the Dock Yard being a place of Consequence. The
Tryal will be desperate as what works are Raised, are capable of a
tollerable defence particularly a Redoubt & Block house on Citadel
Hill, with 300 men in it, will defend it against two or three Thousand
at least. Another Redoubt on the left of the lines but not quite so
strong owing to its Situation. The Lines which are for the defence of
the Yard and lays between the above Redoubts are not very strong, as
they are Composed of three Bastions in Front with a Stockade Cur-
tains for small Arms, and a Stockade leading to each side of the Yard,
Where Block Houses are Erected for Flanking in the Carrying of
which the enemy would loose Vast Numbers. The Country they have
to come thro' is very bad: And [they] will meet with many inconve-
niences and impediments from small [illegible] before they get to
Halifax, particularly if they bring Cannon, without which they will
not be able to Act. The Troops in this Garrison Consist of two Battalions of Marines, two compleat Company's of the 14th. Regiment 127
of the 37th. Regt: under the Command of Capn. M: Kinzie,⁴ upwards of two Hundred Invalids, and about 300 of McLeans Corps,
besides the Town Malitia. The Inhabitants are in dread of the Town
being set on fire. The party that Embark'd for Liverpool and Mala-
gash, as I inform'd your Lordship, was countermanded, it being too
late in the year. Many Retaken Vessels have been sent in Particularly
a Snow bound from Leghorn to Dublin, who was taken by a Rebel
privateer schooner of[f] Cape Finisterre, and Retaken a few leagues
from Marble head by the *Hope* Brig. I beg leave to Acquaint your
Lordship that Leiut. [Walter] Nugent who was Wounded at Long
Island is dead, and who I suppose (as being the oldest Leiut. in the
two Battalions of Marines) was promoted in the Room of Capn.
[George] Logan kill'd in the same Action. I therefore hope your
Lordship will remind Lord S.[andwich] of his promise to give me a
lift as there are but two senior to myself, and both from the half pay

since my present Commission, which I hope will be some little plea: and as I am inform'd his Lordship means to give promotions in future agreable to the Usial plan, Seniority of the last Commissions in which Case I am first, and flatter my self with your Lordships influence I shall Succeed. Since my last I was favour'd with your Lordships to Bowater [No. 64] and self by Way of New York with the Account of Miss Mundy being Married to whom I beg my Congratulations. Bowater is to the Southward.

P.S. Novr. 20th: two Vessels are just Arrived one from Quebec with the News of the Rebels being defeated on Lake Champlain, the other from New York, in 21 days, with the Account of Genl. Howe's Surrounding the Rebels at Kings bridge. The Enclosed is just printed.

1. Pro-American farmers from the Cumberland region of Nova Scotia who went to Machias, Maine to join the rebels. Aided by the Americans they returned to Nova Scotia with 72 men, and en route to Fort Cumberland were joined by a number of New Englanders and Scots-Irish. This force laid siege to Fort Cumberland until dispersed by loyal troops.
2. 84th Regiment.
3. Lieutenant Colonel Joseph Gorham.
4. Captain Kenneth MacKenzie.

76. From Lieutenant Edward Bowater

New Exchange Coffee house Strand
Novr. 20th: 1776

My Lord

The Vessel I commanded at Newfoundland being Rendered unfit for service, Admiral Montagu has thought proper to bring me home in his Ship, and I did myself the honor of calling on your Lordship in Audley Street to Return you many thanks for your Lordship's Recommendations, to which I owe my present Preferment and to which I must also impute the very great civility and Attention I Received from Admiral Montagu, this circumstance has for the present left me unemploy'd, but I should think myself very little deserving your Lordships obliging Patronage had I the most distant wish to be inactive when there is so great a Call for every Officer in each department. But I hope your Lordship will not look upon it as an unlaudable anxiety in a Young Man, wishing to go out in that line which will give him some prospect of preferment in his profession; The only one that at present presents itself is Mr Kepple's[1] being Appointed to the Command of a Fleet, and could I beg your Lordships Recommendation be appointed one of his Leiutenants, I Apprehend I should be a little in the line, your Lordships complyance with this Request will add to the Obligations already confered on your Lordships much Obliged and most Obedient humble Servant.

1. Admiral Hon. Augustus Keppel, commander-in-chief of the Channel Fleet, November 18, 1776, to March 21, 1779; in 1783 created 1st Viscount Keppel. He served as First Lord of the Admiralty from March 1782 to January 1783, and from April to December 1783.

77. From Lieutenant William Feilding

Halifax Novr: 25th. 1776

My Lord

By a Vessel just Arrived from New York in seven days we are informed that Genl: Howe has surrounded the Rebels in such a manner at Kings bridge, that it's impossable for them to Escape, that several Boats full attempted to get across to the Connecticut side, but were all destroy'd by the Men of War, likewise two Pennsylvania Regiments endevouring to get off was intercepted and cut to pieces, and that the General has offered them six days to lay down their Arms and give up their Leaders or he shall attack them and put every man to the Sword. I am likewise inform'd that his Situation is such that he can easily put his threats into Execution. General Howe has likewise taken Fort Washington with seventy pieces of Cannon and fourteen months provisions.

78. From Captain John Bowater

On board the *Centurion* New York
Novr: 25th: 1776

My Lord

I did my self the honor of writing [No. 74] to your Lordship by the last Packet & in which my Intelligence was not so perfect as it generally is, for the distance we lay from the grand Army, Occasions our often Receiving misinformation. In my last I inform'd your Lordship, that Fort Washington was taken, but it Really did not surrender till ten days after the date of my letter. It stood a fierce Attack by Genl: Howe on the Right, Lord Percy on the left, & Genl: Kniphausen[1] in the front, the latter succeeded with the Loss of four hundred kill'd & wounded, the Rebels sustain'd a great loss both in Men Provisions & Amunition & we took three Thousand prisoners.[2] Lord Cornwallis with five thousand troops was Immediately landed in East Jersey, and took fort Lee without any loss since which he has penetrated in to the Middle of that province & taken Immense Quantity's of Cannon Stores &c. by all the Account[s] I can Collect the Rebels Appear to be Retreating on every point of the Compass and I Really believe they will never stand another Attack. We have a great many friends join us every day, but I believe they are such as we cannot depend upon as its supposed they only wait to go with the strongest. Another Expedition is going forward in a few days. Sr. Peter Parker Commands by sea and General Clinton & Lord Percy by land. It is either to Boston or Rhode Island, most people Immagine the latter & we expect to sail on Thursday. The Ships will have a great deal to do at either as they have such a Number of Battery's in all their Harbours. The Men of War cannot Winter at New York so that we are Obliged to fight for a Harbour. The weather is uncommonly fine & I do not think the troops will go into Winter Quarters untill the middle of December.

P S Excuse hast[e]. Lord Winchelsea[3] comes home by this Conveyance. Capn. [Charles] Feilding laid up with the Gout. General Washington Commanded at Fort Washington till the day it was Attacked & left the Command to General [Nathanael] Green, who left it to Coll: McGaw,[4] who surrendered Immediately. It is now Call'd Fort Kniphausen and Major Maitland is Govenor of it. The Commissioners have not yet Restored the Civil Power of this province, nor Establish'd any Courts of the Vice Admiralty &c. All the Meeting houses belonging to the Quakers, Annabaptist, Presbyterians & other Rascally Sects are made into prisons. We have now seven Thousand on the stool of Repentance, in the very places where this horrid Rebellion was hatched. I shall write to your Lordship again soon as I do suppose an express will go with an Account of the Success of the Next Expedition. The Army will certainly pay the Congress a Visit at

Philadelphia early in the Spring if not before. Lord Cornwallis is not above fifty miles from it now. I hear that some of those wise heads are preparing for Switzerland.

1. Lieutenant General Wilhelm von Knyphausen, commander of the 2nd Division of Hessians and later commander-in-chief of the Hessian contingent.
2. There were 2,818 Americans captured at Fort Washington.
3. George Finch, 9th Earl of Winchelsea. His mother was Lady Frances Feilding, daughter of the 4th Earl of Denbigh.
4. Colonel Robert Magaw.

79.   To Lord Sandwich

Newnham Novr: 25th: 1776

Dear Sandwich

I find Admiral Montagu has brought my little Friend Leiut: Edward Bowater home in his Ship from Newfoundland the sooner he goes back the better he will like it, therefore if he does not continue with the Admiral, I wish you would place him as soon as you can on board some line of Battle ship. If Bickerton[1] or Edwards[2] have not their full Compliment of Leiuts. I dare say they will be glad of him for I hear he is a good Officer, and a Spirited Young fellow. My Compliments to Miss R:[3]

1. Captain Sir Richard Bickerton of the *Terrible.*
2. Captain Richard Edwards of the *Sandwich.*
3. Martha Ray, Sandwich's mistress.

80.   To Lieutenant Edward Bowater

Newnham Novr: 25th: 1776

Sir

I am sorry I had left Town when you Call'd at South Street, as to Applying for your being Appointed on Board Admiral Keppel's Ship, that is impossible for I have not the least connection with him and he will certainly Name his own Officers, besides you are by far too Young a Leiut. to think of promotion as Yet, but when Ever a proper time comes leave that matter to me. If you are not to Continue on board Admiral Montagu's Ship go immediately On the Receipt of this to the Admiralty Enquire for Mr Stephens with my Compliments and desire you may be appointed a Leiut. on board some line of Battle Ship, but do not on any Consideration Name the Word promotion. Make my best Compliments to Admil. Montagu with my thanks to him for the Civility shown you on my Account, and if he can Continue you on Board his Ship, I shall take it as an additional favour, write to me again as soon as you have seen Mr Stephens, and desire him to mention the Above Request to Lord Sandwich in my name.

P:S: Show this to Admiral Montagu. I am sure he will tell you I advice you well for no young man should Remain Idle on Shore one minute such times as these and if you deserve it (which I dare say you do) I hope the Admiral will say a good word for you to Lord Sandwich.

81. From Lord Sandwich

Admiralty Novr: 28th: 1776

My dear Lord

According to your desire, Mr. Bowater is Appointed one of the Lieutenants on Board Sir Richard Bickertons Ship.

82. To Lord Barrington

Newnham Novr: 28th: 1776

Lord Denbigh's Compliments to Lord Barrington, begs leave to Acquaint him that by a letter he has this day Received from Lord Feilding he finds there are two Vacant Cornices [cornets] in Mostyn's Draggoons,[1] if they should not both be by purchase Lord D: hopes Lord Barrington will Remind his Majesty of Lord Feilding.

1. General John Mostyn, Colonel of the lst Dragoon Guards.

83.   **From Lieutenant Edward Bowater**

New Exchange Coffee house, Strand
Novr. 29th: 1776

My Lord

I Received the honor of your Lordship's letter of ye. 25th: [No. 80] and according to your directions waited on Mr. Stephens and mentioned what you desired me to him; but found I have been Appointed the day before to be one of the Lieutenants of the *Terrible*, Commanded by Sir Richard Bickerton. I am Sorry at the seeming displeasure of your Lordship on my Requesting for preferment, my having been Thirteen Years in the Service (twelve of which in the Capacity of a Midshipman) will I hope in some measure apologize for my Request.

I yesterday waited upon Admiral Montagu, who desires his Compliments to your Lordship and that I would inform you, that if he had it in his Power, he would serve me with pleasure, but at present he has not; I am to Acquaint your Lordship that I have attained Sr. Richd Bickertons leave of absence till the 12th: of next month on account of a tryal that I have coming on at the Admiralty Respecting a Vessel I took from the Americans when on a Cruze at Newfoundland.

84.   **From Lord Barrington**

Cavendish Square Decr. 2d. 1776

Lord Barrington presents his Compliments to Lord Denbigh, has heard of no Vacancy of Cornet, of any kind in any Regiment, but will Remind the King of Lord Feilding on every proper Occasion which presents itself.

85.   **From Captain John Bowater**

Centurion, Rhode Island Decemr. 9th 1776

My Lord

I wrote to Your Lordship the 24th. of Novr: [No. 78] acquainting you that an Expedition was going forward but its destination kept a secret. On Sunday the 1st of Decemr: we sailed with the fleet under the Command of Sr. Peter Parker and seven Thousand troops under the Command of Genl: Clinton & Lord Percy. On the 7th. we arrived at Rhode Island. The Rebels made a precipitate Retreat as soon as the troops Landed leaving Cannon, Baggage &c. &c. to a Considerable amount. The Rebel Admiral Hopkins, with three of their largest privateers from twenty to thirty Guns, Run away as soon as the fleet Appear'd, throwed their Guns &c. over board & went up a River to a place called Providence, where they was blocked up by two of our Men of War. I can with Pleasure Congratulate your Lordship on our Regaining another province to Government without any loss. This has been a very Extraordinary Effort at this season of the Year.

The Capitol Town is call'd Newport, is large & well built & has excellent Harbour for Shipping, besides Rhode Island, many others of its dependences have fell Conanicut, Hope & block Islands &c. &c. We have found the Country well stocked with Sheep & Cattle & it abounds with fish & wild fowl. I expect we shall stay the Winter here, as it will be too late to attempt anything Else. Early in the Spring I hope to Revisit Boston, we are now only fifty miles from it by land tho it is long passage by Water.

P.S. I've Received but two letters from your Lordship.

86.   From Samuel Jordan[1]

Leicester Decemr. 23d: 1776

My Lord

I have been strongly Solicited by many of Your Lordships friends to Recommend to Your Lordship the bearer: Young [Robert] Bruce[2] of this Place for the Ensigncy Mr. Gamble[3] Refused for his Son, if tis not engaged, he is Reckoned a very sober Young Man, his Relations well Attached to your Lordships Interest and have been steady Voters with the Majority of the Corporation upon every Occasion, his father will find the Money for Raising the Seventy Men and Allow him what your Lordship thinks Nessisary as far as his Ability will go, which he says will not admit of more than 30 £ per Ann: he has a Recommendation signed by most of the Majority Aldermen, the Rest I intirely submit to your Lordships pleasure.

1. Mayor of Leicester.
2. Robert Bruce appears never to have obtained a commission either in the army or the marines.
3. John Gamble, an alderman of the Borough of Leicester.

87.   From the Mayor and Corporation of Leicester

Leicester Decemr: 28th. 1776

May it please Your Lordship

We the Mayor and Aldermen of the Borough of Leicester Whose Names are here unto Subscribed, beg leave to Recommend Henry Norton Gamble,[1] of the Borough aforesaid, seventeen Years of Age to your Lordships Notice and humbly solicit your Lordships Interest to procure him a Commission, in the Marines Service, will be esteamed a favour as if done.

1. Son of Alderman John Gamble.

88.   From Lieutenant William Feilding

Halifax Decr. 29th. 1776

My Lord

By the *Lark* who arrived here the 23rd. inst: from New York We are informed that Genl: Howe was (when she saild) within 24 hours march of Philadelphia, & make no doubt but he has gaind it with his usual success, the Congress upon hearing the Genl. was so near the Town, ordered the Shops to be Shut & every Man in the Town to take up Arms for its defence, & retire them selves to Maryland. I was in great hopes Genl. Howe would have been able to take the Congress, as I some time since was informd the Rebels was determined he should not have Philadelphia. Genl Clinton & Lord Percy with 10,000 Men & all the two deck Ships except the *Eagle*, was gone to Rhode Island & after Reducing it G: Clinton was to go to England with the News, leaving Ld. Percy, to Command who it is said is to proceed Early in the spring to Boston, the distance but 60 miles. Genl. Carleton is expected to penitrate into New England, as soon as the Frost breaks up. Lord Cornwallis Commands in the Jerseys, & Genl. [James] Robinson at New York. I hear the Rebels works near New York are immense, & which they had not Courage to defend. I think their Game is almost over, haveing lost most of their strong posts, they intend to make a stand at Providence, which lays between Rhode Island & Boston, a place where most of their Arm'd Vessels have fitted out & prizes Carried to: the depth of Water not being Sufficient for our Men of War.

I acquainted your Lordship in my last that the Rebels had invested Fort Cumberland [No. 75]. I have now the pleasure to inform you, that soon after the Arrival our two Light Companys under the Command of Majr. Batt, Royal F. Americans, they Salied out at 5 oClock in the morning the 29th Nov and surprised the Banditty, Rebels, & Indians in the Camp. Majr. Batt's account of it, I send your Lordship in this Weeks Paper. It is Reported that they mean to prosecute their design in the Spring of invading this province but I believe they Know better. I beg leave to send your Lordship a copy of a letter from an Officer on Board the *Emerald* a friend of mine.

Emerald New York Novr: 20th. *76*

"The *Emerald* has been stationd some time up the North, or Hudsons River very near a Rebel Fort called Constitution. Our Situation afforded us a sight of the Engagement the 16th: Inst: let it Suffice to Remark that the Rebels flew on all sides from Redoubt, to Redoubt, (till they were drove into Fort Washington) like so many Sheep, & was soon Oblig'd to surrender themselves prisoners of War. This mighty, & indeed strong place, with Real Military Men, could have held out a two month seige, was Reduced by our brave Troops in six or seven hours; out of Curiosity I went the next day to the Fort. It was erected on an Exceeding lofty Hill, & Contained 23 pieces of Cannon, and ten large pieces before it as a breast work; with a great quantity of Arms & Amunition and upwards of 3.000 prisoners. I am informed the Hessians behaved extraordinary well in forcing the Rebel lines, which was also Erected on the Very summit of a Hill with entrenchments behind exceeding deep. I was astonish'd to think it was forced, without great Slaughter. My self and an Other Gentleman with all our agility could hardly Clamber up unopposed. The number of Redoubts between their lines and last Resource, Fort Washington, was surprising. I counted seventeen in the space of 3½ or 4 miles. Washington either was not in the Action or Else made his Escape privately. Our Bussiness was to cut off the Rebels Retreat over to the Jersey shore which we did very Easy. Our Troops crossed the River two days afterwards & took Fort Constitution (so annoying to our Ships). As soon as they knew our Troops had landed they immediately decamp'd, leaving several pieces of Cannon behind. We are now Masters of Hudsons River, Whereby a Communication is open'd to Albany & the Lakes."

P:S: By a Retaken Ship from Newbury, we are inform'd that our Troops from Rhode Island have taken Providence. If this [is] true Should Suppose Lord Percy will Winter in Boston 40 miles distance & a fine Road.

89.   To Lord Sandwich

Newnham Decr: 31st: 1776

My dear Lord

When I had the pleasure of seeing you last in Town you was so Obliging as to promise me a Second Lieutenancy of Marines for the Raising of Twenty Men, which I now think I shall be very easily able to do in a very short time, with the Interest and Assistance of the family & friends of the Young Gentleman for whom I now solicit the Commission, his Name is Henry Norton Gamble. He is a very Genteel pretty Man Aged just Seventeen. There is a Recruiting party of Marines now at Leicester, into whose hands the men shall be turned over as fast as enlisted, to Convince you the young Gentlemans friends are not only in earnest, but able to Raise the Men. I do not desire his Commission to be sign'd untill 14 men be Actually Raised & approved of by the party, and when he is once in I am sure He will be abe by his Interest to Raise even more than the twenty Stipulated for.

III

January 1777-June 1777

The British emerged from the campaign of 1776 the apparent victors, for they had beaten the Americans in every battle. Yet in a political and military conflict as complex as the American Revolution, victory can be elusive; and while the British seemed to be winning the war in America, they were in fact entering a strategic trap. On December 25, 1976, Washington's army crossed the Delaware River and in a surprise attack destroyed the Hessian garrison at Trenton. Several days later at Princeton, the Americans foiled a British counterattack when they cut up a British infantry brigade. The surprise American winter offensive of 1776-77 forced the British to withdraw from the line of the Delaware River, thereby surrendering control of most of the New Jersey countryside to the Americans, and to concentrate the King's forces in a few well-defined and easily defended regions such as New York City.

The abandonment of New Jersey was a political and logistical catastrophe for the British. Politically, the loss of New Jersey showed that the British were unable to protect American supporters of the crown. When the British invaded New Jersey in the autumn of 1776, the Loyalists of the region had come forward and begun the task of regaining political control of the province from the rebels. However, the evacuation of New Jersey left the Loyalists with a harsh choice: flee with the British army to New York, or face political retribution at the hands of the American rebels. This bitter decision had confronted the Loyalists of Boston and was to be faced repeatedly by Loyalists not only in New Jersey but in Pennsylvania and the American South as well. Logistically, the loss of New Jersey denied the British an area in America from which to draw supplies of food, fuel, and forage. From the beginning of 1777 until the end of the war, not only munitions but everything required by the King's forces in America including food had to be supplied from the British Isles. The mere feeding of the British forces in America required the employment of scores of warships and thousands of tons of merchant shipping, and by 1782 rations for 72,000 men in North America were being drawn from Britain and Ireland. This logistical problem might have been tolerable if the British had been able to maintain control of the North Atlantic; however, the Americans, at the same time that they launched the winter campaign in New Jersey, also began a cruiser offensive in Europe and the West Indies against British seaborne trade. In 1777 alone, the British would lose over three hundred merchant ships to American cruisers; and the Royal Navy's strength was increasingly absorbed in protecting trade convoys and hunting for American cruisers.

Even before the beginning of the main British effort in 1777, the King's forces in America were confined to a few bridgeheads on the edge of the American continent and were logistically dependent on European sources of supply while British seaborne trade was being subjected to American attack. Very few of the British realized it at the time, but Trenton and Princeton showed that the war would continue and that it would be a war in which the mere winning of battles by the British would not necessarily result in the restoration of royal authority in America.

90. From Lord Sandwich

Hampton Court Jany 3d: 1777

My dear Lord

Tho I should very Readily have given You a marine Commission for a Young Gentleman of the proper Age, without Annexing a Condition to it, Yet I can't Refuse the offer you make; the Rather as it will give you an Oppertunity of disproving what the World (at least the female world) are apt to suspect you of, namely, promising more than you are able to perform. You may therefore depend upon a Commission for Mr. Gamble, as soon as the Recruiting officer at Leicester Certify's his having Supplied him with fourteen good Recruits.

91. From Captain John Bowater

Newport Rhode Island Jany. 9th. 1777

My Lord

I have wrote to your Lordship by every Oppertunity, & think I perseveer with little hopes as I've Receivd but two from your Lordship. We are now in Winter Quarters & the Motions made are so great a Secret that I can hardly tell you with Certainty what is done as they are so Variously Represented. Harcourts taking Lee[1] was Glorious, but we have met with some disasters, which the Publick prints will very much Magnify. I can now only add, that the Army & Navy are very Healthy & wish for the Spring. Lord Percy is the Commandent. I've not time to write to Lord Wentworth therefore must beg your Lordship to say that I meant to write to him.

1. On the morning of December 13, 1776, a party of light dragoons commanded by Lieutenant Colonel William Harcourt captured Major General Charles Lee outside the American lines at White's Tavern near Basking Ridge, N.J.

92. From John Gamble

Leicester March ye: 3d: 1777

My Lord

Your favour my Son Receivd. We are thankfull for your trouble in procuring his Commission, may depend on me & so far as in my power family, and friends, to make every Return, you'll please to Command. Surely Government will not desire any more men, it has Cost £71.17s.2d. including payment of their quarters in Leicester & to Plymouth, & yet have more to do, he will wait upon your Lordship this next week, he and his men lay at Hinkley this Night, from thence to Birmingham, to join Capn: [William] Lewis's Men, whom go with my Sons men to Plymouth when they come to Know my Son will not join them, there will be a strange destraction, as some of them went on his Account, upon every other I think it better. My Lord you shall at all times find me Blunt, honest & sincere in whatever I undertake.

P.S. I am Sorry to hear the mayor is Ill his family are Well.

93.   To Lord Barrington

South Street Wednes. Morning March y. 5th 1777

Lord Denbighs best Respect to Lord Barrington is a sham'd he has not sent him an Answer sooner, he now desires that his best duty may be presented to his Majesty Acquainting him that Lord Feilding will with the Greatest Gratitude Accept of the Commission which his Majesty has been most Graciously Pleased to Offer him in the 7th Regiment. Lord D: very much fears he shall not be able to place Lord Feilding about Genl Clinton, he must therefore be Satisfy'd with staying at home this Year, but hopes he may be indulged with leave to be at Mr Lochie's Academy till he joins the Army.

94.   From Lord Barrington

March 8th. 1777

Lord Barrington presents his Compliments to the Earl of Denbigh, and has the Honor to inform him, that Lord Feildings notification to a Lieutenancy in the Royal Fuzileers,[1] is issued from the War Office.

1. 7th Regiment of Foot.

95.   From George Buckley

Thornton March 18th: 1777

My Lord

I am informd my Son Wm. Buckley is coming into the Country to Recruit, which if he does he will certainly get into a Prison, and their he shall Remain. I therefore humbly beg that your Lordship will be pleased to get him order'd to America as soon as Convenient, for he'll make all the excuses as possable to evade going. I am a shamed troubleing your Lordship about him, for if I could have known what trouble it would have given your Lordship I never would have made any Application [Nos. 35, 46] for him.

96.   From Captain William Feilding

Halifax March 31st. 1777

My Lord

I have the pleasure to Acquaint your Lordship that the Rebellious disturbances in this province are at present at an End. The Banditty that invested Fort Cumberland had no authority from Congress, are intirely dispersed and the Troops who have an open Country are often sent out in parties, for two or three days some miles into the woods, and find every thing quiet. Two Indians who lately Arrived at the Fort from St. Johns brings Account that the Rebels are forming a Magazine there in Order to Carry on a Campaigne in the Spring, against this province; ' but that I give little Credit to; as they have Enough to do, to the So[uth]ward to get an Army together without Attempting to Raise one to the No[rth]ward, particularly as the whole Continent seems to think they have the worst of it. An Armd Cutter was sent to Marblehead about a month ago as a Cartel for Exchange of prisoners and Arrived here last Week; by the New England papers they are Raising an Emence Army; the greatest part of which are destind for Ticonderoga and Crown point. Genl. Carleton not leaving a Garrison at the above places Surprises them much. They are so distress'd for Volunteers, as to be obliged to pass a law to make it death for any man, (residing in and Claiming the protection of the Laws) to Refuse to take up Arms, and all Inlistments are for the War, and not for a terms of Months, as before. The Inhabitants of Boston are greatly distressed for fresh and Salt provisions, as the Country People will not bring any to Market owing to an Act of Congress, specifying the price of *all Kinds* of provisions. We have had no Accounts from New York since Christmas. The Winter has been much milder here, than has been known for Years, but the great Quantity of bad spirits which the Soldiers purchase Cheap, has made them Rather sickly, our Corps have lost since our Arrival above sixty Men, most of them good Soldiers and McLeans Corp's have lost as many. This place may well be Call'd (as it was by a Member in the House of Commons a few years ago) the dram shop of America. I hope we shall not see another Winter in it, for its the Ruin of a good Corps. I have at last heard of Mr. Farrel,¹ who is in this province, in a most miserable Condition, living on his Estate (called deer Island in the

Bay of Fundy) with a Woman he brought from England, by whom he has several Children. The Attorney Genl [W.] Nesbit to whom I happend to mention his name, told me he is a madman and is much Surprised he had not been hanged, As he has been guilty of the most Atrocious Acts of Madness. I am in great hopes this Winter which has been Severe to the Northward will put an End to the existance of such a Villian. Mr. Nesbit likewise told me the Island is Worth the £500 he gave Col. Gorham for it, provided this Rebellion was at an End, and has promised in Case of his death to enter a Caveat against all Attachments, for the good of his Family.

P:S: By a letter, I Receivd this day from my Mother, by way of New York, I was made happy with the News of my being promoted the 8th: of November, for which I Return your Lordship my most Sincere thanks. The Commanding Officer has Receivd directions from the Admiralty to form the two Battalions of Marines into one Consisting of six Companies of one hundred Men each; together with the following field & Staff Officers, Viz: two Majors one Adjutant, and one quarter Master, and to send the Commission'd Officers over and above the Number Nessisary to Compleat the Battalion, to England the first Oppertunity, in Consequence of which there will be 10 Supernumery Captains, two Adjutants and three or four Subalterns, among which Number, I have the Extreem Mortification to be one. Mr. Waller[2] the Senior Adjutant Chusing to Stay. I most Earnestly Wish to have stay'd with the Marines till the Rebellion was over, and to Return with them to England.

1. Thomas Farrell, ex-army officer and husband of William Feilding's sister Sarah, whom he had deserted.
2. Major John Waller, senior adjutant of the marine brigade at Halifax.

97. From Captain John Bowater

Rhode Island April 4th: 1777

My Lord

I am this day honord with a letter from your Lordship date[d] Novr. 10th:[1] and have Receivd every letter your Lordship names except one. I am sorry that my present Situation will not afford matter for an Amusing letter & that I can give your Lordship but little Intelligence at present, and we have Remain'd quite inactive, owing to the Severity of the Season. And the Army here under the Command of Lord Percy has had very little to do. A constant Cannonading has been kept up between our People & the Rebels on the Opposite Shore, particularly at Bristol, Fogland and Hereford Ferrys, but without doing them any matterial Damage, and our people have not lost a man since we Arrived. Some of the Rebels Row Galleys have been very daring & our Battery's have very severely Corrected them for it. Our Cruizers Continue very Successfull Seldom a day passes without their sending or bringing some prizes into this Harbour. I have inclosed to your Lordship the New York papers as it Contains the last proclamation of Sr. Wm: Howe:[2] which has been Attended with Wonderfull Effect. I hear that many hundreds have already taken the benifit of it: and as the Season is near the opening the Campaign, I am in hopes that these poor deluded wretches, will save our people the trouble of putting them to death by Accepting the offer that is made them. I am certain that our troops will act with less Humanity, this Campaign than they did in the last, as they have been very much Irritated by the most Wanton Crueltys Committed by the Rebels in the Jerseys by which we lost a number of very fine fellows, both Officers & Men, and in a manner too horrid to discribe. Major Stuart is here & well we are always together. He has made me spend the winter much more agreable than I thought was possable in such a place. The Natives are such a Levelling, underbred, Artfull, Race of people that we Cannot Associate with them. Void of principal, their whole Conversation is turn'd on their Interest, and as to gratitude they have no such word in their dictionary & either cant or wont understand what it means. (For instance as to levelling) I met a man of very good property a few days ago, who had a Complaint to make and I Refer'd him to Lord Percy. I heard him enquire at his Lordships door for Mr. Percy, thinking him Ignorant I stept up & told him again Lord Percy, he Replied to me, he knew no Lord but the Lord Jehovah. Thus it is throughout America and a sad set of presbyterian Rascals they are. I read Butler[3] every day, and I see it in every face I meet. Their dress is so formal, and their words come up so Slow, that I frequently long to Shove a Soup ladle down their throat, and it is not want of Conception that these people are so Slow in Delivery, But from a certain determind duplicity that Governs all their

Actions, and they think they are very Ill employ'd if they are not over Reaching you. I am exceeding happy in hearing the Granidier [William Feilding] has got a Captain Lieutenancy, and am much oblig'd to your Lordship for the expressions you make use of as to my self, being bred in the School of Adversity, I have learn'd to bear patiently with Evils which I could not prevent, and am now arrived at a Certain Age, which the Toy of Ambition does not so much allure, & I very soon shall persuade my self that a Company of Invalides is one of the Most Comfortable things belonging to our profession, as I think it most likely to be my Dernier resort. My best Respects & good wishes always attend on Lady Denbigh, Lord & Mr. Feilding, and your Lordship will be so good as to say every thing that is civil for me to all enquiring friends particularly the fair ones. I hope I Need not use many words to Assure your Lordship how much I feel myself honourd by your Lordships Correspondence & flatter my self that my Stupid, incorrect Epistles meet with every indulgence from your Lordship & that as soon read the fiery Ordeal is performd on them.

P.S. This was intended to go from Rhode Island the day after its date when we Receivd orders to join Lord Howe here in Order to man the flat boats &c. for Transporting the Troops. We arrived yesterday. No great Alternation. Numbers come in every day, & the betts Run here with odds, that there will be no Campaign, however the Troops cannot take the field at present for want of Forrage. Ld. P. goes home in the Packett, its given out that it is on Account of his family affairs, the true Reason is disgust, & I believe a little Jealousy of a Brother Peer in the Jerseys.[4] This Harbour is full of prizes, no Ships from England & two Packetts due.   New York April 21st 1777

1. Not entered in the letter book.
2. On March 15, 1777, General Howe issued a proclamation promising pardon and security of property to any soldier in the Continental Army who surrendered by May 1, 1777.
3. Samuel Butler, satirical poet and author of *Hudibras,* a mock-heroic poem satirizing the hypocrisy, pride, sophistry, and boorishness of the Presbyterians and Independents.
4. Lord Percy demanded and obtained his recall from America not because he was jealous of Lord Cornwallis, but because he was disgusted with General Howe's conduct of the war.

98.   From Captain John Bowater

New York May 4th: 1777

My Lord

I did my self the honor to Answer [No. 97] the last letter[1] I Receiv'd from your Lordship by the Packett which Sailed from hence the 25th of April, yours was dated the 11th[1] Novr: & nothing has Arrived here since, except some Victuallers and Private traders, so that your Lordship will observe by the date of this that I am six months in Arrier of English News. I believe I did not mention to your Lordsp. in my last an Expedition under the Command of Coll: [John] Bird, had been up the North River as far as Fish Kills & had destroyed a very Considerable Magazine of Arms Stores, & provision without any loss on our side. An other of the same kind has been Undertaken by Genll: Tryon, he had Detachments from six Regiments & five Hundred of our Provincials with some field pieces. Saild the 25th. of Aprile. They went through Hell Gate, and landed near Fairfield in Connecticut & March'd to Danbury a Small Town where they found a Very large Magazine for the Supply of the Rebel Army intended to Act against Genl Carleton. They Reduced the whole Town and all its Contents by fire—but on their Return, the Rebels had Collected about seven Thousand Men under the Command of Generals Wooster, & Arnold, and Knowing how much Fatigue our Men had gone thro' having March'd near Sixty Miles, & had been three days & Nights under Arms, without any Refreshment. The Rebels kept up a very brisk fire, which our People Return'd as long as their Amunition lasted & until they got within sight of their Boats. The Rebels prest very hard upon them and it was found Nessisary to prevent their firing upon the Boats on their Retreat, to give them a Charge which was Carried with such Spirit that they, Never Returned. No quarter was given on either side, we had Eight Officer Wounded but none of them Mortally & we had about Ninety kill'd, wounded and missing. The Rebels left between two & three hundred dead on the field, but what other loss they had cannot be Ascertain'd, both Arnold & Wooster was seen to be wounded, and Report says they are Dead.[2] Sr: Wm: Erskin[e][3] & Major Stuart have gaind great Credit by their Spirrited Conducts. This Bussiness of destroying their Magazines is the most Effectual method of distressing them, one article particularly, that of salt provision. There was 12,000 Barrels of Beef & pork, two large Stores of Medicines besides Tents entrenching tools, Rum, Molases, Sugar, Wine &c. &c. The Weather is now quite settled & the greatest preparations are making for taking the Field in a few days. The Plan of Opperation is kept a profound Secret. Great Numbers of People have come in with their Arms, &c. &c. We have now five Thousand of them in our pay, well arm'd & Clothed, & I have not the least doubt but they will Act with great Spirrit against their Rebellious Country Men. When any thing Material happens, & I've an Oppertunity of Conveyance, your Lordship may depend on hearing from me.

1. Not entered in the letter book.
2. During the raid on Danbury the British lost 154 men, killed and wounded; the American casualties were about 20 killed. Arnold had his horse shot out from under him; Wooster was mortally wounded.
3. Brigadier Sir William Erskine, appointed Quartermaster General of the British army in America on October 7, 1776.

99. **From Lord Barrington**

War Office May 8th 1777

Lord Barrington presents his Compliments to Lord Denbigh and has the Honour to Acquaint his Lordship that General Howe keeps the 7th Regmt: to serve as a Corps in North America.

100. **From Captain John Bowater**

New York May 22d. 1777

My Lord

I Receiv'd a short letter[1] from your Lordship dated Feby. 18th: by the *Augusta* in which your Lordship Requests an Account of the Surprize of the Hessians. This unfortunate Affair[2] cannot be easily described with a Pen, as so many Circumstances may be Urged, both for & against them. But what strikes me, is, that Lord Cornwallis should not have push'd his Conquest so far. The very few Towns there is in the Jerseys and those at a great distance made it next to impossable for one post to support an Other. The most Remarkable open Winter ever known in this Country, which favor'd the Enemy's Passing the Delaware at a Season which it has ever before known to be Block'd up with Ice. And going into Winter quarters so late as to make it impossable to entrench or throw up any works for the defence of small Vilages. Now as to the Hessians, they are the worst Troops I ever saw. Government has been Cheated by their sending one half Militia, and the greatest part of the others are Recruits, very few Viterons amongst them, they are Voted British pay, which their Prince Cheats them out of one half, they are Exceedingly dissatisfy'd at this, so that to make it up they turn their whole thoughts upon plunder. It was their attention to this Plunder, that made them fall a sacrifice to the Rebels at Trenton. They are Exceeding Slow, their mode of dicipline is not in the least Calculated for this Country and they are strictly enjoined by the Landgrave, not to alter it. They are so very dirty that they have always one half of their People in the Hostpitals, & I am well assured they have Burried almost a third of the Number they brought out, & they now put to Earth six or seven a day. The Bussiness was done if it had not been for this affair but the Rebels exposed their Prisoners & the Trophys of War. Many Orations was spoke at Philadelphia & other places to explain to the people, what a Contemptible Enemy they had to Cope with. By these & other artfull methods, they prevail'd on their People to Reinlist, and they have now got a very Considerable Army together, and you may depend upon it, they will beat the Hessians every time they meet (the Granadiers & Chassures only excepted). The British troops on the Contrary have been Remarkably healthy from the great Attention pay'd them. They Swim in the Sea most mornings & in the Evenings have foot Races & other manly Exercises, their Decipline is that of light Infantry, which is the only Method of proceeding in this Country. And I'm Convinced that they will gain as much Honor this Campaigne as they did last. The Rebels having destroyd the Forage all Round this Country, has prevented our people from taking the field so early as was expected, the Grass not yet being of Sufficient growth to Replace it. When any thing of Material happens your Lordship shall be inform'd of it.

P:S: I Receiv'd a long letter from Lord Wentworth which I have not time to Answer by this Ship. And as he expresses a desire of Knowing every thing Relative to the Hessians Bussiness, I should be glad your Lordship would Read him this letter.

1. Not entered in the letter book.
2. The Battle of Trenton.

IV

June 1777-December 1777

The 1777 campaign in America is one of the most appalling examples of strategic planning in all of British military history. In fact, there was no over-all plan, rather there were several contradictory ones. Because no one in authority in America, Canada, or London looked at the war as a whole in the early months of 1777, those responsible for planning the campaign of 1777 did not see that the Americans would have to be subdued in that campaign if the European powers were to be kept out of the war, nor did they perceive that to achieve this end they would have to destroy Washington's army. This lack of intellectual effort permitted two plans to be put into effect, neither of which would result in the destruction of the American army. One plan, which was accepted by the authorities in London, called for General John Burgoyne to march on Albany, New York with an army from Canada. What Burgoyne would do upon reaching Albany other than be, as he said, "on the high road to glory" will never be known. While Burgoyne was planning a march on Albany through the wilderness of upstate New York, General Sir William Howe, the commander of the British army at New York City, produced plan after plan for the 1777 campaign. Howe's first plan was to attack up the Hudson River towards Albany, next he decided upon an overland attack through New Jersey aimed at Philadelphia, and finally the British general resolved to leave a garrison to hold New York City and embark his army and attack Philadelphia from the sea. Howe knew that Burgoyne intended to march on Albany but did not see the need to support the force from Canada, and the authorities in London did not learn of Howe's scheme to proceed to Philadelphia by sea until it was too late to prevent the movement.

Compounding the lack of central planning for the campaign of 1777, which permitted Howe and Burgoyne each to make his own independent and isolated plan, was the fact that the authorities in London did not understand the war in America. The great fear in London was that while Howe's army went to Philadelphia by sea

Washington would take the opportunity to march north and overpower Burgoyne at Albany. What in fact happened was that Washington and his army moved south to defend Philadelphia as soon as Howe's objective became known; Burgoyne's army was overpowered in the woods of upstate New York by a hoard of American militia.

Howe's campaign for 1777 began on July 23 when his army sailed from Sandy Hook to attack Philadelphia from the sea. It was the height of the campaigning season, but for the next thirty-two days Howe's force was a strategic neuter as it slowly made its way along the American coast to the head of Chesapeake Bay, where it went ashore and began to march on Philadelphia from the south. Washington attempted to prevent the British from taking Philadelphia by fighting the battle at Brandywine Creek on September 9, but the Americans were not strong enough to prevent the British from occupying the city, which they did on September 26. At this point all offensive operations came to a halt as the British fought a bitter and costly battle lasting fifty-nine days in order to capture the American forts along the Delaware River, for the river was vital as a supply route for the King's forces at Philadelphia. While the invasion of Pennsylvania resulted in the occupation by the British of another American city, it did little to bring an end to the war, for the American army remained a powerful and threatening force.

While the British were battling to clear the Delaware River, the news arrived at Philadelphia that Burgoyne and his army had surrendered to the Americans at Saratoga. Burgoyne's march on Albany had started off well with the easy capture of Crown Point and Ticonderoga. But as Burgoyne's force of over five thousand men moved slowly south from Lake Champlain through a maze of hills, swamps, and forests, cutting a road as they went for their wagons and artillery, the Americans began to assemble in overpowering numbers to confront the British invaders. Perhaps the first sign that Burgoyne's army was in trouble came when his Indian allies deserted and the Americans began to destroy the road to Lake Champlain in the rear of the British army, cutting off the only avenue of retreat to Canada. By the end of September, Burgoyne's army was trapped in the wilderness north of Albany, cut off from the British forces in Canada and New York City, running out of supplies, and under heavy attack by the Americans. On October 7, at Freeman's Farm, Burgoyne was attacked and defeated by the Americans, and as the autumn rains began the British attempted to retreat northwards towards Canada. But the Americans, as a British sergeant put it, "Swarmed around the little adverse army like birds of prey." The end came on October 17 when, under constant attack, short of rations, and running out of munitions, Burgoyne was forced to surrender his whole army to the Americans at Saratoga. The loss of Burgoyne's army had a shattering effect on the morale of the British and made French intervention in the conflict inevitable.

101. **From Captain John Bowater**

My Lord   New York, June. 5th. & 11th: 1777

I was in hopes to have had it in my Power to inform'd your Lordship that some great stroke has been struck against the Rebels, but what has Occasioned the late opening of the Campaign, I cannot Account for. The troops have left Winter Quarters & are encampt both in the Jerseys & at New York & the places Adjacent, but no movement has been made & nothing material happend. Some slight Skirmishes in which our people have had the Advantage. Several Brigades are Embark'd & all the Generals Baggage, the Men of War & Arm'd Vessels all in high order, & every hour expect the final Orders, but the destination is kept a profound secret. Yesterday being the Kings Birth day was observd with the greatest demonstration of Joy, beyond any thing I ever saw in England. The same time Arrived the Reinforcements from Halifax, &c. &c. All the Camp Equipage & the Additional Officers, which makes me Immagin that very soon the Bussiness will begin & I have heard this day that Mr. Washington is Retreating to support Philadelphia. Yesterday when all this World was Rejoicing I was Order'd to take Mr. Genl. Lee under my charge who came on board the *Centurion* under a strong Guard at six oClock in the morning. Certainly all the plagues of Egypt Attends me and I now greatly lament, I was not bred a Chimney Sweeper. This is the second day and it appears to me a Year. It Requires a pen of a Littleton,¹ & the pencil of Hogarth,² to delineate the person & Character of this atrocious Monster, who (for my Sins, Another Bajazet³) is not only my Prisoner, but my Companion. He is as perfect in Treachery as if he had been an American born. And not with standing what Mr. Tryon says of the Numbers of friends to Government in this Country I should be very sorry to trust any one of them out of my sight. They swallow the Oaths of Allegience to the King, & Congress, Alternately, with as much ease as your Lordship does poached Eggs. And I think nothing but a total Exterpation of the Inhabitants of this Country, will ever make it a desirable object of any Prince or State.

June 11th: Finding the Packett cou'd not sail so soon as orderd, I left off writing in order to give your Lordship the latest Intelligence. Genl Howe & his aide de Camps &c., set out Yesterday for [New] Brunswick & the Transports with some troops on board fell down through the Narrows & out of Sight. By a Serjent & some deserters we have Accounts of the Approach of Genl. Carleton who is said to be within twelve miles of Albany but I am afraid they travel him Rather to fast. The lines & fort at Kingsbridge have been put in good Repair: two Brigades of Hessian one British & about two thousand of the New provincial Corps, all under the Command of Genl. Knyphausen are to Remain here for the Protection of this place, the Camp is form'd between Kings Bridge & fort Knyphausen. The Connecticut Rebels having Arnold at their head are about the White Plains & as near as New Rochelle, it is said the[y] Mean to Attack New York, but I want faith. Our Cruizers Continue to send in a Number of Prizes, the Delaware & Chesapeake are now Completely block'd up by our Men of War. The Rebels Complain greatly of the high price of Salt Provision, Dry goods, &c. &c. All their publications are full of New Regulations which have no Effect. A number of Galleys floating Batterys and Bridges of a different Construction are gone with the transports &c. &c. and I think my next must give an Account of something decisive. I must conclude this as I see the Vessels moving off.

1. George Lyttelton, 1st Baron Lyttelton of Frankley. Literary patron and author of a number of works, including *Dialogues of the Dead.*
2. William Hogarth, the savage pictorial satirist.
3. A sultan of the Ottoman Empire who strangled his younger brother.

102.   To Captain John Bowater

Newnham June 14th. 1777

Dear Bow

I have Received both yours, the first from Rhode Island dated April 4th: the other New York May the 4th: [Nos. 97, 98] for which I am much Oblig'd to you for, the last is a much more Accurate Account than has been Receiv'd by Government. God send you may finish the Bussiness this Campaigne or Else every body here will grow very Clamorous against the two Brothers,[1] for the Expence is Enormous, and very little probability of being able to hire more foreign Troops, or even of Recruiting our own Regiments. This Bussiness can never be Ended, but with the Bayonet. Proclamations & Lenity will have no Weight with them as soon as your backs are turned. I hartily wish those whom you have Cloathed & Armed may Remain Steady for I should not be in the least Surprised to hear that all the American troops now in our Service have deserted as soon as our Army shall have left New York. I have seen Your Brother the Tar,[2] often in London, his Capn. Sr. Richd. Bickerton is very fond of him and is gone now on another Cruize. Miss Betty & Miss Sophia Noel will both be married in the Course of this month. The first to a Mr. Burgess a very indifferent Match, the Second to Lord Scarsdales[3] Eldest Son,[4] a very great Match; Mr. Milbank who Married the Eldest, is very happy with her, but has not yet got her with Child, but Doctor Marriott, who I think I wrote you word, is married to Nenny Cave, has done his wife that favour. I sent you Word in my last that Lord Feilding is a Leiutenant in the Seventh, so that probably you will see him in America unless this Campaigne Ends the War.

1. The Howes.
2. Lieutenant Edward Bowater, R.N.
3. Nathaniel Curzon, 1st Baron Scarsdale.
4. Hon. Nathaniel Curzon, M.P. for Derbyshire, 1775-1784.

103.   From Captain William Feilding

Halifax June 15th: 1777

My Lord

In my last letter [No. 96] I acquainted your Lordship of the Kings Order for forming the two Battalions of Marines into one of 600 private[s] with Officers in proportion, and one Adjutant, and the Remainder of the Officers, over & above the Number for the Battalion to be sent to England the first Opportunity, amongst the latter I unfortunately was to have been one, Mr. Waller, the Senr. Adjutant, Claiming a Right to Stay, but his going to New York, with some dispatches from Genl: Massey to Genl. Howe and he having been strongly Recommended to the Commander in Chief some time ago, is now appointed Major Brigade[1] to the Provincials, under the Command of Genl. Tryon. I have therefore got Major [William] Souters (our Commanding Officers) Consent to Stay with the Battalion, if Lord Sandwich has no Objection to two Adjutants being in America, and as it is not my wish to go to England until the Corps I have the Honor to belong to does; or the Rebellion is at an End. I most earnestly Request your Lordship will obtain Lord Sandwich's permission for my Remaining with the Battalion. I Return your Lordship my most gratefull thanks for my promotion: your Lordships letter and a Marine list, sent to one of the Officers, has been the only Account Received of the Augmentation, tho several letters have been Receiv'd from the Admiralty, which takes no Notice of any Officer here being promoted, except a Mr. Willis[2] midshipman on board the *Tartar*, made Second Leiutenant and orderd to join the Battalion, which I presume has been mistake in Office, and a great loss to me of near £40 as the Batt and Forage to the Troops, for the Ensuing Campaigne is just paid, and myself only paid as Subaltern,[3] nor Can I be Acknowledg'd as Captain in the line, till a notification (of my Appointment) from the Admiralty Arrives, which is a little mortifying, As I am Oblig'd to Report to Junior Officers. I have the pleasure to Acquaint your Lordship that this province is at present free from any Rebellious disturbances, and that the Inhabitants and Indians of St. Johns River have taken the Oaths of Allegiance to his Majesty. I make no doubt but your Lordship has heard of a Large Magazine of Military Stores and provision being destroyd at Danbury, and the

Rebel Genl: Wooster was Kill'd. By a Vessel lately from [New] York, we hear the Army has taken the Field. I lament our Corp[s] is not with them as I am Convinced the Campaigne will be very Rapid and Successfull. Its a great grievance to the Officers to see so fine a Battalion of Men lay inactive. The Coast of America is now lined with Men of War, (which will put an End to their Navy this Summer) notwithstanding which they have several Ships of War, and privateers at Sea, and have Already sent into Boston some Valuable prizes. Our Ships have been pretty Successfull. The *Ambuscade* Capn. [Charles] Cartwright I hear has drove one of their large Frigates ashore, Capn. Feilding in the *Diamond*, and [Captain Archibald] Dixon in the *Greyhound* have taken Several prizes. And by a Cartel lately Arrived from Portsmouth Mentions those two Captains having sent to the Committee at Boston to send all their Ships of War and Privateers out that lay in the Harbour, (which Consisted of 18 of different sorts) and they would wait for them, which exaspirated the Congress so much, that they sent positive orders for their Vessels to be immediately Man'd and to go out and bring those two ships in. But I dont find those Orders have been Comply'd with.

1. Brigade Major.
2. Second Lieutenant Thomas Lake Wills.
3. Until official notification of his promotion arrived, Feilding was not to be permitted a captain's allowance of bat and forage money, which are payments to cover the feeding of an officer's horses and the transport of his baggage in the field.

104. From Captain John Bowater

New York July 15th: 1777

My Lord

I have not Receiv'd a letter from your Lordship of a later date then March. I have wrote by every oppertunity. Genl. Howe Continued pursuing Washington in the Jerseys & drove him back as far as the Blue Mountains a country quite impregnable from its height and strong defiles it was then Resolved to return to the Transports on which they detach'd two thousand Rebels to harras our Rear under the Command of Lord Sterling,[1] our people then Attackd them, Kill'd one hundred took seventy prisoners & four pieces of brass Cannon. The Rest set of[f] to there strong hold, our Loss was not more than ten or twelve men. We greatly lament on this occasion the loss of Capn. John Finch of the Guards, 4th: son of Lord Aylesford, his Company took the Cannon, he did not survive his Victory many hours. The troops imbark'd at [Perth] Amboy, landed on Staten Island and are now Refreshd & imbark't again in the Transports. But no one can judge the object some think Philadelphia, others Boston. They will sail tomorrow if the Weather permits I am afraid our troops will turn sickly if they go to the southward as the season is uncommonly hot. We have Accounts from Genl Burgoyne, he has taken Ticondcroga & is coming on very fast. Your hopes & expectations are Rather too sanguine at home. I dont doubt but the people have expected that we had killd & eat Washington & his whole Army long before this; But I must let you into one secret which is that they always beat us in *heels*, & in this Country there is no forcing people to fight against their Inclination. We are to Remain here to guard the Town &c. and I can asure your Lordship, that my prisoner Lee, is very safe on board.

[P.S.] Sr. Henry Clinton and Aid de Camps &c. &c. Arrived a few days ago he is to be left with Command of New York. Genl. de Heister is Recall'd & comes home by this Conveyance in the *Niger* Frigate.

1. Major General William Alexander, or Lord Stirling, an American who in 1775 undertook legal proceedings in England to attempt to gain the title Earl of Stirling, to which his father had been heir presumptive. Although he lost the suit, he was generally known as Lord Stirling.

105. From Sir John Palmer[1] and John Peach Hungerford

Leicester June 19th: 1777

My Lord

At the Request of many of our friends, we take the liberty to Recommend to your Lordship a Young Man, whose name is [John] Rippon, as a very diserving & proper Person for an Ensign's Commission in the Army. If it is agreable to your Lordship to obtain a Commission for him, it will not only lay a very great obligation on many of our friends, but on my Lord your Lordships, most obedient & very Humble Servant[s]

1. Sir John Palmer, M.P. for Leicestershire, 1765-1780.

106.   To Sir John Palmer

Newnham June 21st: 1777

Lord Denbigh's best Compliments to Sr. Jno: Palmer, Receivd his [No. 105] and Mr. Hungerfords letter by Mr. [illegible], Respecting a pair of Colours for Mr. Rippon, and is very sorry it is not in his power to serve him, as there are only 4 Regiments of Foot now at home, and no Commissions to be had without Raising 20 Men, in which Case Ld Denbigh stands already Engaged to another Gentleman first. But if, Mr. Rippon, can Comply with these Terms, Ld: D: will do his best Endeavours in his behalf.

107.   From Sir John Palmer

July 17th 1777

My Lord

I Receiv'd the honor of your letter [No. 106] by Mr [illegible], relative to the petition from Mr. Rippon for a pair of Colours, I trouble your Lordship`with a line at his Request who desires to be by these Means introduced to you, and is wiling and able to Comply with the Request Specify'd in your Lordships letter to me. His Heart seems to be quite set upon this Bussiness, and if you can procure it for him you will much Oblige your Obedient humble Servant.

108.   To Lord Sandwich

Newnham July 17th 1777

My dear Lord

I am afraid you'll think me a very Unreasonable Fellow in troubling you so often, for Commissions of Marines but I realy cannot resist the present Application in favour of Mr. John Rippon especially as he Engages to Raise fourteen good Recruits. He is a Young Gentleman of a Very good Family and in Every shape as well in point of Age person and good behav'our properly Qualified for that Service. If you can give him a Commission on the above Terms you will greatly Oblige my dear Lord yours sincerely.

P.S. Compliments to Miss R:--- [see No. 79]

109. **From Captain William Feilding**

Camp, near Halifax July 21st: 1777

My Lord

I have the pleasure to Acquaint your Lordship that on the 9th: Inst: His Majestys Ship *Flora* Captain [John] Brisbane Arrived here with the *Fox* Frigate of 28 Guns, which he took from the Rebels two days before in Company with two Rebel frigates, the *Hancock* & *Boston*, after a Smart Engagement. The Rebels took this Ship frigate on the Banks of Newfoundland, after a long & Warm Action in which she lost almost all her Yards, her Mast much damaged and her Riggin and shrouds shot to pieces, and from her Yards Riggin and sails falling on deck Rendered it impossable to fight her guns. In this situation Capt. [Patrick] Fotheringham [of the *Fox*] call'd all his Officers, and Ask'd their opinion what was to be done, a Ship laying a perfect wreck, and two Frigates Engaging, her without being able to return a Shot or to make their Escape, who thought it adviceable to strike and not sacrifice the lives of his Majesty's forces. During the *Flora*'s Engagement with the Rebel Squadron, the *Rainbow* of 40 guns, [Commodore] Sr. Geo:[rge] Collier, Appear'd in sight, upon which the three Ship seperated & stood difrent ways, the *Flora* pursuing the *Fox*, and the *Rainbow* the *Hancock*, Capn: [John] Manley, which she took the next morning without Receiving a shot and brought her in here the 11th. Instant. She is a very fine & well finishd Frigate of 32 Guns. The *Hancock* had several Men kild & wounded in the difrent Engagements with the *Fox* and *Flora*. The *Fox* had three men kill'd and 5 wounded, among the former was the Hon: Wm. Napier Lieut. of Marines. The *Flora* had not a man hurt. Mr. Manley (who is sent to New York) says in excuse for not Engaging the *Rainbow*, that he took her for the *Raisonnable* of 64 Guns. Capn. Fotheringham with 40 of his Men were on board the *Hancock*, his Officers & some of the men on board the *Boston*, and the Remainder, was put on Shore at Newfoundland. We have had no news from the grand Army for some time, it is Wisper'd in Town that Philadelphia was taken by Genl: Sr. Wm. Howe the 1st. of July, but there does not seem to be any foundation for this Report.

110. From Captain John Bowater

New York July 23d: 1777

My Lord

   I am afraid this letter will be of an old date before it comes to hand As the Ship that Convey's it is bound to Cork, with a Convoy of Irish Victualers, but it is the only oppertunity that has presented it self for some time as an Embargo was laid on all Vessels untill the grand Armiment sail'd (which left this place this very morning), And where bound nobody knows except the Brothers [Howe], As they took uncommon pains to disguise their designs by taking Pilots Draught Guides &c. &c. for every part of America. We have had Officers down from Genl. Burgoyne, who bring Accounts of the taking of Ticonderoga the 16th. Instant, and Fort Edward the 16th: and was on their March to Albany, which is only forty five miles from Fort Edward all in good health & Spirits. Sr. Henry Clinton is left at New York, with twelve Thousand Men, and it is supposed he will march forward & Endevour to joyn Mr. Burgoyne's Army. The Rebels are in the greatest Confusion. My Prisoner Lee, says it is all over with them and now is the time they should treat. But I'm in hopes the Commissioners[1] will cut them up a little in the Northern Colonies before the[y] admit them to do it, as they have been Foremost in this Rebellion, & as yet have felt none of the Horrors of War. I can not help saying this is the seventh letter I've wrote to your Lordship since I had the Honor of Receiveing one. I don't know where to lay the Charge, it must not be either Neglect, or Curiosity, I hope mine to your Lordship has been more successfull & I am sure they are quite Innocent, As I only Relate to your Lordship the Common Occurrences, and wish to Shew my Attention to your Lordship & Lady Denbigh.

1. The Howes.

111.   **From Captain John Bowater**

New York July 29th: 1777

My Lord

I begin to fear my letters are a very great Bore to your Lordship and its unfortunate at this distance, that its possable that I may persist in it for many Months before I can be Corrected at present I've a pretty decent hint, my last ten letters being as yet unanswer'd. I am tempted now by an old Acquaintance who has promised to put this in the Post Office, Capn. Parry, who is order'd home on the Recruiting service, tho I've some doubts of his taking a Nap & forgetting it. I think I inform'd your Lordship in my last [No. 110] of the Embarkation of the Troops, they saild with Lord & Genl Howe the 22d Instant, and Yesterday a small Vessell Arrived from them Acquainting us that they was arrived at the Entrance of the Delaware. The Ships can go up as far as Newcastle which is but a very few miles from Philadelphia it will be an Easy Conquest. I dont expect to hear of any Opposition as the Inhabitants of that Country have been long wishing for the Kings Troops. We have had in more Officers from Genl. Burgoyne with duplicates of the Account of his possessing himself of Ticonderoga the 6th: and of his being on his March towards Albany; his Army is Joyn'd by a Considerable Body of Canadians & Indians. I have also seen an Account publish'd by order of the Congress, in which Genl Schuyler[1] Acknowledges that he Retreated with the Utmost precipitation leaving behind him all his Cannon, Baggage Stores &c. &c. he also informs them that he does not know what Route he shall take as he fears he may fall in with the Enemy. Major Hamilton[2] with some Regular[s] & a body of Indians came Round by Oswego, & has destroy'd their grand Magazine near Carlisle. This is said to be a very Capital Bussiness. Sr. Heny. Clinton Commands at this place & at Kings bridge he has about 10 Thousand Men with him & is prepairing to Enter Connecticut, so that we shall have three

Considerable Armys in motion, & my next I hope will inform your Lordship of *Provinces Subdued.* Mr. Washington Remains at his strong Post at Morris Town with the long Range of blue Mountains in his Rear, it appears to me as if he means to Remain there on the defensive. We have had a great many deserters from him of late Chiefly from their light Horse a Reward of fifteen pounds has been given them with horse & Accoutrements, & five & twenty Shillings to their Infantry bringing in their Arms. I shall not be Surprized if they bring in their Generall, tho no price is as yet fixt upon him. We shall Certainly Come home this Winter, but my hopes are to Visit Boston first, the Retreat from that place sticks in my Stomach, (like Sr. John Falstaff, I hate to do any thing by Compultion). I thirst for Revenge on that place & nothing can pacify it but fire, the Harbour can be very easily destroy'd & the name should be Changed, it is said here that the presbiterian Clergy at Boston (after some pains have been taken with them) are to be made a present to the Managers of the Opera, the Reverend Colonels, Majors & Captains with their white Wiggs & Red Sashes over long black Coats will make a very pretty figure on the stage.

July 30*th*   I am this Instant told that Lord Feilding is appointed a Leiutenant in ye Royal Fuziliers & that he is Coming to joyn his Regiment. If true I hope he will Arrive before I move from this place as I'm Acquainted with the Officers of that Corps & should do my Utmost by introduceing him to the people worthy his Acquaintance & Endeavour to point out the line to him which has Recommended the most Amiable to preferment. We have been exceeding well Supply'd here with provisions and the·moving off of near sixteen thousand Mouths during the last week to Pennsylvania, has lowered the price of Every Article. The beef is not half so good as in Old England & I'm glad of it, as the natives are ten times Worse, great plenty & Variety of Vegetables & fruits, but they do not Rejoyce in high flavour. Fish in Abundance, & good, & we have been well supply'd with Turtle, & pine[apple]s, from the West Indies. The Water very bad but our Liquors are perfect. The Rebels having by stratagem, stole away General [Richard] Prescott, the Commandant at Rhode Island, has put our prisoner Mr. Lee, in high Spirrits thinking he should be Exchanged, but he has just now been told, that he is in a very diffrent predicament & that no such thing will happen. The former is very much condemn'd for being at a lonely House four miles from his Camp with only one Centinal & a Corporals guard at a great distance. They took him & his aid de camp, [Lieutenant William] Barrington, out of their Beds with nothing but their shirts on, lapped them up in Blankets & Carried them to Providence. This happened at 12 oClock at Night & it was three in the Morning before it was discovered which prevented a pursuit. He was frequently told of the impropriety of his Situation, but despised Advice. He treated the Inhabitants with great severity & I shall not be Surprized to hear the Rebels have hanged him. We have had some small Men of War here lately from St. Augustine, the Rebels of Georgia & south Carolina have made two Attacks on that place & have been Repulsed with great loss the last time we let off the Creek Indians, who Kill'd & Scalpt one hundred & sixty of them, they do not expect another Visit. I've kept this letter unsealed to the last minute in hopes of getting some more Intelligence, but now I conclude in a hurry & Request your Lordship to make my best Respects to Lady Denbigh & Family. This will arrive, I expect at the time your Lordship is amusing your self with the destruction of the partridges, our Shooting is rather more serious. John Ladbrook³ wou'd be puzzled to bring in the game and I think your Lordship would not have so much Curiosity, if you was here.

1. Major General Philip Schuyler, commander of the American forces in upstate New York.
2. Lieutenant Governor Henry Hamilton of Canada. Known to the Americans as "the hair buyer" because he was suspected of paying Indians for American scalps.
3. Denbigh's gamekeeper.

112. To Charles Wright¹

Newnham August 4th: 1777

Lord Denbighs Compliments to Mr Wright acquaints him he has Receiv'd a letter [No. 103] from Adjutant Feilding dated Halifax June 15th, 77. Where in he Ardently Wishes to Remain with the Marines till they Come home, as (Mr. Waller) the Senior Adjutant is gone to New York & is promoted there under the Command of Genl. Tryon Adjutant Feilding has got the Consent of Major Souter, (his

Commanding Officer) to stay with the Battalion, provided Lord Sandwich has no objection to two Adjutants being in America. He also Complains of the Neglect of the pay Master of Marines in not sending the Notification of his promotion, tho letters have been Receiv'd from the Admiralty, since the time of his promotion, by which Neglect Adjutant Feilding has lost near £40 of the Batt & forage money & pay. Therefore Ld: D: will be Obligd to Mr. Wright, if he will Acquaint Mr. Stephens with the Contents & if should be any Neglect of the Agent for the Marines about it, begs he will make Enquiry & have it set to Rights as soon as possable. When Lord Denbigh Receives Mr Wrights Answer will immediately Acquaint Adjutant Feilding of the Same. If Lord Sandwich is in Town is desired to send an Answer as soon as possable to Lord Denbighs letter [No. 108], wherein he Offers fourteen Recruits for a Second Lieutenancy of Marines for Mr John Rippon whom Ld. D: finds to be of a proper Age & every way Qualify'd for such Commission, be so good as to let Lord Sandwich see the Whole of this letter.

1. Sandwich's secretary.

113. **From Lord Sandwich**

Hampton Court August 26th: 1777

My dear Lord

When I cannot Answer the letters of my friends in a Satisfactory Manner, I am very Apt not to Answer them at all. Marine Commissions are now much more difficult to be got at than before the Augmentation was Compleated, and I have a very long list of Previous Applications. Vacancies now Seldom happend but by death, and you will Conceive that does not occasion above 12 Vacancies in a Year. As to the 14 Men it is no object and is a Mode of giving Commissions, to which there are many objections, after haveing said all this I have only to add, that I will put your Young Man on my list with a disposition to serve him when I can do it Consistant with previous Engagements. Now the *Fox* is again in our possession you see my Spirrits are so far Recover'd, as to Allow me to write.

[P.S.] It is Nessisary I should know Mr Rippons precise Age.

114.   **To Captain John Bowater**

Newnham Augt: 30th: 1777

Dear Bow:

Your two last of the 23d & 30th of July [Nos. 110, 111] I Receiv'd yesterday morning & am extreemly obliged to you for them, and I must most Earnestly Request that you do Continue to write by every oppertunity. How it comes to pass that my letters do not come to Your hands I cannot understand for I always sent them in the Admiralty Packett, as the safest Conveyance. I shall inclose this to Mr Stephens, and scould him most abominably: I wrote you word in my two last that Lord Feilding was appointed Leiutenant in the Seventh, but he will not join his Regiment till next spring, His Majesty thinking it proper that he should remain some time at Lochie's Military Academy. I perfectly agree with you wishing to give due Correction to the Bostonians before any Accomodations and I hope this will be the Case. Lord Wentworth and I are just Return'd from a Wedding Visit to Lord Scarsdale, who's son, is just married to little Sophy [Noel]. Your friend Charles[1] Chuses to be a Bishop. I believe he would be the first that ever was of the Feilding family. He is now here in perfect health & desires jointly his best Compliments with my Wife Lady Newdigate Miss Mundy &c. &c. We all hope to see you Return in the Winter with a deal of prize money.

1. Hon. Charles Feilding.

115.   **From Captain John Bowater**

New York Augt. 23d. 1777

My Lord

I have such Attention to your Lordships first Request of wrighting at least two lines by every opportunity that I can not Resist the present, as we just had a skirmish which I was an Eye Witness to. One [John] Sullivan a General in the Rebel Service, landed with about twelve Hundred Men in order to Burn a small Magazine of Hay, which the[y] Accomplish'd, but was Attack'd in the Rear, by Genl: [Archibald] Campbell with the 52d Regiment, one of Waldeck &

some of our Provincials. Our people kil'd two hundred on the spot & took, upwards of three hundred prisoners,[1] our loss not twenty, & the Hay not worth a Hundred pounds. Genl: Burgoyne is Certainly in possession of Albany. We have no Account from Lord or Genl. Howe, their destination is still a Secret. The *Bristol* & Convoy are every day Expected [by] Genl. Clinton, for them to Garrison New York, before he can possably move as the Rebels keep a strong force in his front.

1. According to General Sir Henry Clinton, the Americans lost 259 men captured and and unknown number killed.

116. From Captain William Feilding

Camp near Halifax Septr: 21st: 1777

My Lord

No Accounts has been Receiv'd from Lord or Genl: Howes destination with the Army. Among the Various & Extraordinary Reports here, one is that the Brothers, after Cruizing off the Capes of the Delaware, were Return'd to New York & since went up the North River to Endevour a Junction with Burgoynes Army at Albany. And that the Troops going to the Southward was only meant to Harrass the Rebels, & draw off their Attention from Ticonderoga. I suppose your Lordship has heard ere this of Genl: Burgoynes Crossing the lakes, his movements has been publishd in this Province['s] Gazette which with some other News papers I enclose for your Lordship. Sr: Geo: Collier saild some time ago on a Cruizè to the bay of Fundy & has destroy'd the Boom & some store Houses in the Harbour of Machias, with the loss of seventeen Marines wounded & three kill'd besides some sea men taken in a boat. Major Small[1] with the Marine light Company, the Grenadiers and light Company of the Royal Highland Emigrants and a detachment of Gorham's Corps[2] Sail'd about a month ago for St. Johns River in order to proceed to Machias by land & destroy that place but on their Arrival at St. Johns, were inform'd, that about 1200 Rebels were strongly intrenchd at the above place, and that it was impossable with so small a number as three Hundred to Attempt an attack of that sort without having Succour at hand. Genl. Massey has therefore Recall'd them. The *Diamond Flora* & *Lark*, saild about three weeks ago from Rhode Island on a Cruize to Boston Bay, the latter has since Come into this Harbour, the *Flora* having sprung her main & fore masts, the *Lark* having lost her main mast, & sprung her mizin mast in a Gale of Wind. The *Diamond* Received no damage & was well a few days ago, by the Intelligence of her Prize. I expect to see Charles[2] here soon. Of the three Hundred Rebels taken in the *Fox* & *Hancock*, upwards of sixty of them have died of the Goal distemper, & Small Pox, the surgeon of the *Hancock* having Enoculated most of the Ships Company before they were Landed, to prevent them from Entering into the Service.

1. Major John Small, Commandant of the Royal Highland Emigrants.
2. Royal Fencible Americans.
3. Captain Charles Feilding, R.N., of the *Diamond.*

117. **To Major John Bowater**

Newnham Octr: 2d. 1777

Dear Bow:

I have But just time to wish you joy of your promotion, which everybody here joins with me in doing most sincerely. We are all on this side [of] the Water in the utmost Astonishment at not having had the least Intelligence of the two Howe's since they sail'd with the grand fleet from New York; Variety of Reports are spread, but that which seems to prevail the most, is that they have fail'd in making their landing good in the Delaware, which they had been obliged to quit and were saild to the North. Not one word of this do I believe; Everybody is Charmed with the Conduct of Genl: Burgoyne, I think he & he only will do the Bussiness yet. Parliament meets the 28th. of next month, before which time I hope we shall have some good news from your side of the Atlantic or Else we shall have a Warm Political Campaign and much Ill humour.

P:S: I hope you have by this time Receiv'd some of my letters for I have wrote to you very often, this Comes by the Admiralty Packett.

118.   **To Rear Admiral Robert Duff**

Newnham Octr: 9th 1777

Dear Admiral

As I find you are Appointed to the Command of the fleet in the Mediterranean I should take it as a particular favour if you will take my friend Leiutenant Edward Bowater, on Board the *Terrible*, which is an inactive life, & he very much Wishes to go along with you his Old friend.

P.S. I understand your ship is the *Panther* & that there is a Vacant Leiutenancy.

119.   **From Rear Admiral Robert Duff**

Craven Street Octr. 11th. 1777

My Lord

This Afternoon I had the Honor to Receive your Lordships letter [No. 118] Concerning Mr. Edward Bowaters going with me in the *Panther*. When Lord Sandwich Appointed me to the Mediterranean Command, agreable to the promise I made your Lordship when last I had the Honor to see you, I askd his Lordship to appoint Mr. Bowater third Lieut. of the *Panther* his Lordships Answer was, that he could not grant my Request, having promised it to an Other. A Commission had been made out, near three weeks for Lieut. [David] Graves who is daily Expected from Ireland. I call'd at your Lordships House in Town, to Acquaint you of what I had done, & to see if your Lordship would think proper to speak to Lord Sandwich to get Mr. Bowater into the *Panther* before Mr. Graves's Commission was made out.

120.   **From Lieutenant Edward Bowater**

Portsmouth Octr. 26th. 1777

My Lord

I Receivd the Honor of your Lordships letter,[1] and should think myself wanting of that Gratitude Which I owe to your Lordship, was

I not to take the Earliest Oppertunity of Returning you my most greatfull thanks for the Trouble you have had on my Account, and although I have been so unfortunate as not to Succeed in this point, I shall ever Retain a just Sense of the Obligations I am under to your Lordship. I have wrote to Admiral Duff by this days post, to thank him for his enteresting himself so much in my behalf.

1. Not entered in the letter book.

121. From Major John Bowater

New York Novr. 17th. 1777

My Lord

A Long Ceries of Illness has prevented my paying my Respects to your Lordship, And I think I should congratulate your Lordship on the Occassion, as it has prevented you hearing a great deal of Very bad news from a very bad penman.[1] I am now much Recoverd, tho' far from Well, my mind more than my body is now most distress'd, as I have of late lost a great many of my most intimate friends. Indeed there seems to be such a fatality with my friendships, that it looks like Cruelty my ever Adding one to my stock. I hope it is not so with my old friends in England, but from my not hearing from any of them makes me suspect the worst, indeed if there is any thing worse than death, it must be the being Neglected by those we thought most Attached to us. The late unfortunate Events which I am afraid will put many of the most Respectable Families in England into Sable is not so Melancholly as the objects every day exibbited here. I have ever thought death a Smaller misfortune than a miserable object alive. The Numbers of fine young men from fifteen to five and twenty with loss of limbs &c. hurts me beyond conception, And I every day curse Columbus and all the discoverers of this Diabolical Country, which no Earthly Compensation can put me in Charity with. It is so long since I wrote to your Lordship on the Subject of Intelligence & News, that I neither know where I left off or where to begin, so think your Lordship had best trust to the publick prints which Relate things with more Authenticity than I can, as they Come more from the scene of Action, from which I have been long detach'd. As to Opinions they are rather dangerous, particularly on Paper but thus far I will Venture, as I am certain I am not Singular, that the want of Spirits in the foreign troops has been the principal cause of all our misfortunes and that we should have been much stronger without them. The provincial troops in our Service (contrary to the Opinion form'd at home) have behaved like Heroes, upon Every Occassion. I flatter myself that I should have had it in my Power to Relate Personally to your Lordship, my knowledge of this Country and People before Christmas, but the times are so Changed that it is very uncertain where or when we shall go, As no Arrangement of either fleet or Army as yet is mentioned tho the Season is Already set in very severe. In what manner the Parliament will Act on this Occassion we cannot Conceive, our hopes are that they will either take it up with a very high hand, or let it drop entirely. A Reinforcement of seven Regiments went from here last week to Philadelphia, the 7th: was of the number. The young M----[2] is I think, no Acquisition to the Army, as he seems to be the most disipated Young Man I ever Met with, *not to say worse*, but I am very happy Lord Feilding did not come out with him, as I am sure he is a very dangerous Companion. If Lord Feilding comes to this Country whilst I Remain in it you may be assured he will Command my best Services. Poor as I am I must tell your Lordship that I am very desirous to Repay back some part of your Lordships favours tho they will fall very short on those which have been Conferr'd. I will not tresspass any longer on your Lordships patience, but to Request you will present my best Respects to Lady Denbigh Lord Feilding & Charles, my hopes are that both they and you enjoy that health & happiness which is to me denied (and indeed which I should not doubt) as they so much better deserve.

1. The Battle of Saratoga.
2. See below, p. 152.

122. To Lord Buckinghamshire[1]

South Street Decr: 5th: 1777

My dear Lord

Knowing the load of Bussiness which you Naturally must have upon your hands this season of the Year, I shall not presume to trouble you with a long letter, but shall come to my point at once, and from our long Acquaintance I hope you will not think my Request Unreasonable. Lord Feilding is in the Army and very high up amongst the Lieutenants, of the 7th. Regiment. Rank is always the object of a Soldier, and the favour I have to Ask of your Lordship is to permit him to Purchase the Rank of Captain, either in the Horse, [or] foot, on the Irish Establishment, which ever can be most Conveniently done. I shall trouble your Lordship with this by the Advice of my old Friend Sr. John Irwine, who is so obliging, as to tell me, if I was to Attain your Approbation he will Assist Lord Feilding in this Bussiness as much as lies in his Power. My best Respects to Lady Buckinghamshire.

1. John Hobart, 2nd Earl of Buckinghamshire, Lord Lieutenant of Ireland, December 18, 1776-May 23, 1780.

123. From Lord Barrington

Cavendish Square Decr: 12th: 1777

My dear Lord

A week ago I offerd by the Kings Order the Leiutenancy in the Horse Granadier Guards to a Young Man of Quality, who has been some years in the Service, and it was Accepted. When the Appointment comes out it will give general Satisfaction; but I am Concern'd there is not another Commission of the same kind for Lord Feilding.[1]

1. It is noted in the letter book that this letter is "in Answer to one Requesting an Exchange for Lord Feilding."

124. From Lord Buckinghamshire

Dublin Castle Decr. 15th. 1777

My Lord

I have Receivd the favour of your Lordships letter of the 5th. Inst. [No. 122] desireing that Lord Feilding whom your Lordship Mentions to be Very high amongst the Leiuts. of the 7th. Regt. of Foot, may be permitted to purchase a troop, or Company in Any of his Majestys Regiment of Horse Draggoons or Foot on this Establishment. It would give me very Particular pleasure, if it were in my Power to Comply with your Lordships Recommendation, but in my Situation I have so many Applications of the like kind from persons of Rank & distinction in this Kingdom whose Support of Government makes it Nessissary they should be Obligd, that I cannot hold out to your Lordship any probable expectation of my being able to serve Lord Feilding; but your Lordship may be Assured that I should with great pleasure lay hold of any Oppertunity that might enable me to do it.

125.   To Lord Barrington

Newnham Decr: 27th: 1777

My dear Lord

I never was more disappointed than on having applied too late for an Exchange for Lord Feilding into the Horse Granediers; His Majesty very well Knows that my original wish for him was the Cavalry. And that his Mother (who is now one of the most Miserable Women in the World) gave her consent to his going into the Army on no Other terms. Permit me therefore my dear Lord to intreat you to find out some method either by purchase or Exchange, to Remove Lord Feilding out of the Foot. Perhaps the Person who you Mention'd to have the Leiutenancy of the Grenadiers may be Equally Satisfy'd with Lord Feildings Commission in the 7th: as it is Equal Rank, but if these difficulties cannot be Surmounted, I still flatter my self that neither his Majesty, nor your Lordship will think me Unreasonable in desireing he may have leave to Raise a Company either as an Independant one, or in Any New Regiment that may be levied. I will engage to Raise Eighty or even a Hundred Men in a very short time, on these terms. Viz: Lord Feilding to be Captain, and to have the Recommendation of the Ensign. This will make Lady Denbigh very happy for the present as it will probably Remove her Anxieties for some time. I trust to your Lordships friendship and Judgement, whether you will shew the whole of this letter to my Royal Master at present, or whether you would think it to be more Advisable to wait till I come to Town to Ask it in Person; which will be by the Birth day in the mean time, I beg a favour of a line, which I hope will give some Comfort to my Lady Denbigh.

126. From Lord Barrington

Mistley Decr. 30th: 1777

My dear Lord

I am this moment honor'd by your Lordships letter of the 27th Inst: [No. 125] And I think I cannot do better, than lay it before the King, as soon as I Return to London, for which place I shall set out tomorrow.

127. To Major John Bowater

Newnham Decr: 31st: 1777

I can assure you Dear Bow, I never was more Concernd, then I was at the Receipt of your Malencholly letter dated New York Novr. 17th: [No. 121] but as I know you are now & then apt to be Nervous I flatter my self matters are not so bad as you Represent them. As to Your own Concerns, what ever friends you have lost in America, you will never loose my friendship in great Brittain. The Advice I give you at present since you have got your promotion, is to plead your bad health, and apply to Lord Howe to give you leave to come home, which I dare say he will not Refuse you. As to publick Matters you Represent the foreign troops in a very diffrent light from what we look upon them here, for the Attack which the Hessians made upon Red bank (tho the Expedition was very injudiciously orderd, as the[y] had neither Cannon nor Scaling ladders) tells very much in their favour.[1] I was not a little disappointed at your making no Mention of what became of the Expedition up the North River under Col: [John] Vaughan,[2] for we are under great anxiety here lest he should have been Surrounded and under gone the Same fate as poor Burgoyne. We are also in great Anxiety about New York, since so large a detachment has been sent from You to Reinforce Howe at Philadelphia. All this Country is much prejudiced in favour of Burgoyne, although he has been unfortunate We are not in the least dejected and you may be Assured that the Parliament will exert all it's Power to make good the loss: Although the Scoundrels in Opposition exult very much and leave no stone unturn'd to Embarrass our measures. I am very much Astonished that you still Complain at not hearing from me, for I have wrote by every oppertunity and my letters have always been sent in the Admiralty Packett directed to you on board the *Centurion*, New York. Be pleased to be more explicit in your next as well of your own Opinion as of Events, for as you do not sign Your Name you need be under no Apprehensions. We are all Exceedingly Well here, and your Friend Charles is now my Secretary. Ld. F.[eilding] I take it for granted will join his Regt: early in the Spring. And he is Sufficently Apprized of the Character of the Marquess,³ not to be misled by him. Indeed I can say with great pleasure that I beleave him incapable of being corrupted by him.

[P.S.] So far from my father, and now in Propria Persona, I am exceedingly Sorry for your Ill health, but advice you not to indulge your Spleen, And Return to us your Sincere friends, who Ardently long to see you, and none so particular as my self—Charles

1. A reckless, bloody, and unsuccessful attack undertaken on October 22, 1777, against the American-held Fort Mercer at Red Bank, N.J. in which the Hessians lost 371 men.
2. An attempt to rescue Burgoyne's trapped army by forcing a passage through the Hudson Highlands.
3. No marquis appears in the army lists as an officer of the 7th Regiment at this time. See also above, p. 148.

V

January 1778-December 1778

The British defeat at Saratoga and the signing of the Franco-American alliance made war with France in 1778 inescapable. What had begun as a British attempt to suppress a rebellion in America had blown up into a world-wide maritime war in which Britain would face not only the naval power of France and America but ultimately that of Spain and Holland as well. When the news of the loss of Burgoyne's army reached London, it was clear that the entire conduct of the war would have to be changed, for measures would have to be taken to meet the French challenge not only in America but also in Europe, the West Indies, and India. However, in the first months of 1778, nobody in London knew where the French would attack. Would they attempt to gain control of the English Channel and invade Britain, or would they send ships and troops to America or the West Indies? Another question that bedevilled British war planners at the beginning of 1778 was how the war in America should be conducted now that the conflict was about to become a European maritime war.

In hindsight, the best policy for Britain after Saratoga would have been to give America independence before a Franco-American alliance could be signed, and then make the best of a bad bargain. But in the best of times policy making is not a very logical process, and in 1778 the British government was neither politically nor morally strong enough to grant American independence. So in the first months of 1778, it was decided to mobilize the Royal Navy to hold the English Channel and when necessary make detachments from this force to counter any French move in America or the West Indies. At the same time plans were made to recast the entire conduct of the war in America.

The new policy called first for a commission headed by Lord Carlisle to be sent to America in an attempt to end the fighting by granting every one of the American demands short of independence, which would prove to be the only condition the Americans would accept for ending the war. Secondly, the new British commander-in-chief in America, General Sir Henry Clinton, was authorized to evacuate every British-held position in America if it became necessary. Moreover, Clinton was directed to send detachments to Florida to invade the American South—a policy which would end in catastrophe three years later at Yorktown; he was to send another detachment from the army in America to the West Indies to capture the French island of St. Lucia, which was to be used as a naval base in the Lesser Antilles. The British policy thus became one of holding the English Channel and writing off America north of the Mason-Dixon Line, shifting the main theater of the war to the American South and the West Indies.

The first fighting between the British and the French began on June 17 when ships of the Channel Fleet fought several engagements with some French frigates which were "reconnoitering" the British force. Throughout the summer and fall of 1778, the Channel Fleet under the command of Vice-Admiral Augustus Keppel made several cruises in the English Channel, the Western Approaches, and the Bay of Biscay. Except for an indecisive battle off Ushant on July 27, however, these cruises were for the most part uneventful. The great danger lay in America.

On April 13, 1778, several months before the beginning of actual fighting between the British and the French, the Comte d'Estaing sailed from Toulon with twelve ships-of-the-line. When news of the departure of this squadron reached London, the British government was deeply split over whether or not to send reinforcements at once to America or wait for certain intelligence to reach England of d'Estaing's destination. It was not until June 2 that news arrived in England that d'Estaing was indeed proceeding to America, and several days later a squadron under the command of Vice-Admiral John Byron was detached from the Channel Fleet and sent to reinforce the Royal Navy in America.

In the spring of 1778, the first dispatches arrived in Philadelphia telling of the impending French entry into the war and outlining the government's new policy. Their contents forced Clinton to decide to abandon Philadelphia and concentrate his army at New York. On June 18 the British army left Philadelphia, crossed the Delaware into New Jersey, marching for New York. They fought a bloody rear guard action at Monmouth Court House on June 28; and as they approached Sandy Hook heard of the impending arrival of d'Estaing's strong squadron. Believing that they did not have the strength to beat the French in a naval battle, the British decided that the only thing they could do was barricade themselves in New York. On July 11 d'Estaing's squadron appeared off Sandy Hook but made no attempt to enter New York Harbor, deterred by British fortifications and the fear of running aground. After several days of indecision, the French sailed to Rhode Island to attempt to capture, in conjunction with the Americans, the British post at Newport.

D'Estaing's squadron arrived at Newport on July 29, and shortly afterwards American troops began to invest the British positions there. Although outnumbered by the French and without hope of reinforcements from England, Byron's squadron having been damaged and dispersed by a storm, the British at New York nonetheless were determined to prevent the capture of Newport. On the evening of August 9, a British squadron from New York arrived off Point Judith, and the next morning d'Estaing sailed from Newport to drive away the British ships. Before the two fleets could come to battle, however, they were dispersed and badly damaged by a storm. The French returned briefly to Rhode Island and then broke off the siege of Newport and went to Boston to repair their storm-damaged ships before proceeding to the West Indies. The Franco-American attack on Newport having failed, Clinton, as was called for in his instructions, dispatched three thousand troops to the Floridas and another five thousand to the West Indies to attack St. Lucia. With the departure of the expeditions to the Floridas and St. Lucia, the New York region, with the exception of the disastrous Yorktown campaign, became a strategic backwater, for the center of the conflict had shifted away from the Northern Colonies.

128.   To Lord Barrington

Newnham Jany: 4th: 1778

Lord Denbighs Compliments to Lord Barrington, has Receiv'd his Obliging Note [No. 126], dated Decr. 30th, but wishes (if he has not done it already) that he would not lay his last letter before the King untill he has the Honour of Seeing Lord Barrington in Town; but in case he has already done it, Lord D. desires he will send the Answer to South Street, from whence it will be transmitted to him, to Lord Mount Stuarts¹ in Herefordshire to which place he setts out for to morrow.

1. John Stuart, Lord Mountstuart, Lord Lieutenant of Glamorganshire, 1773-1793.

129.   From Major John Bowater

New York Jany. 4th. 1778

My Lord

I was Yesterday honor'd with the Receipt of two of your letters, one dated in Augt. [No. 114] the other the 2d: Septr:¹ From the tenor of the last I cannot help thinking how much you will be Surprised at the fate of Gen: Burgoyne, and how much you have been Mistaken in your Conjectures concerning him. We are Anxious to hear how it is Receiv'd in England as well by the Parliament as the Mobility, who are in general very Violently agitated with a Reverse of fortune. We Military people Reconcile ourselves to Misfortunes with hopes of Succeeding better another time, & quote [precedents], as Closter seven² &c. &c.

Experience with years has long Convinced me, that no Rank of Men are worth Contending for, and that Admirals & Generals have Errors in Common with other Men. But the fable of Frogs³ have been but too often exhibbited in this Country. I think I can yet say from good Authority that things are not yet so bad as some people may wish them on your side of the Water. Altho the Army have not cut so many throats as was expected or indeed they wish'd to do; I still think a more powerful Engine is at work & which will be more Effectual, they will most Certainly be starved into Compliance. It is impossable to discribe their distress for want of Shoes, stockings & warm Covering, And which has already drove great numbers to the Royal Army.

Mr. Washington has Retreated across the Schuylkill twenty six miles South of Philadelphia & has Hutted upon Inaccessable Mountains.⁴ They have threaten'd to Attack this place, & have held out what great plunders may be Attained if Successful, our only fear is that they will not attempt it as we have Receivd a Considerable Reinforcement. I did flatter my self with the hopes of Relateing personally to your Lordship this History, but am now told it will not be untill the Spring, & then very possable another delay. The Situation of Affairs in this Country should convince us that we have no Right to set our hearts on any thing. I cannot think your Lordship Serious when you wish me Joy in being a Brevet Major.[5] I Received it in a different light. It appears to Me only to Mark the Unfortunate, those like me who have had a Company upwards of seventeen Years, are included by Sign Manual to take a different title.[6] Implies only that they was destitute of both *Friends* & *Merit* or they would have been *Really* preferd many years before. If Lord Feilding comes to this Country in the Spring you will be so good as to point out how far I can be of service to him, and you may depend upon my Fidelity in every thing that will in the best conduce to his or your Lordships happiness. Be pleased to present my most Respectful Compliments to Lady Denbigh, Lord & Mr. Feilding.

I am much flatterd with the Enquiries of Lady Newdigate & Miss Mundy after me, & in Return Request your Lordship to present my best Respects with many thanks for their Civilities. Col. Cosmo Gordon[7] is here & joins me in every good wish to your Lordships Health & Happiness.

1. October 2, 1777. See No. 117.
2. The Convention of Kloster-Zeven, signed by the Duke of Cumberland on September 8, 1757, after being defeated by the French at Hastenbeck.
3. Aesop's fable of "The Frogs Desiring a King."
4. Valley Forge.
5. Promotion by brevet confers nominal rank but allows only a limited exercise of that higher rank. John Bowater was commissioned a brevet major in the army on August 27, 1777; he did not become a major in the marines until August 24, 1779. See above, pp. 15-16.
6. A commission signed by the King.
7. Colonel Cosmo Gordon, M.P. for Nairnshire, 1774-1777; Baron of the Scottish Court of Exchequer, 1777-1800.

130.   **From Lord Barrington**

War Office Jany 14th. 1778

Lord Barrington presents his Compliments to Lord Denbigh and has the Honour to Acquaint his Lordship, that the King has Consented to Lord Feildings Raising a Company in Wales.

131.   **From Captain Alexander Campbell**

Carrington Street, Jany. 15th. 1778

Mr. Campbell presents his Compliments to Lord Denbigh he has just Receiv'd a Note from Lord Barrington informing him the King has Approved of Lord Feildings haveing a Company. Mr Campbell & Mr Johns will wait upon Lord Denbigh, they beg leave Lord Denbigh will permit them to bring with them Capn: [Hugh] Lord, who is to have the Direction & forming of the Companies.

132.   **To Major John Bowater**

South Street March 4th. 1778

Dear Bow

In my last [No. 127] which I hope you have Receiv'd, I advised you on Account of the bad state of your health to get leave to Come home, (as I do not conceive now you have got your Rank, you can[not] do yourself any good by staying in America) I heartily congratulate you on your having got Rid of the troublesom fellow *Lee.*[1] I dare say that has contributed to Restore you to good health. I dare to say you will see by this packett, that two very Extraordinary Concillitory Bills[2] which has just past Parliament. I shall give you no Opinion about them, only that thank god they had not the Sanction of my Vote. I dare say the Congress will not Accept them, and then our Ministers say the War is to be Carried on as Briskly as Ever. The new Levies fill very fast, Lord Feilding has got a Company in the Welch Volunteers,[3] so that probably you will not see him this Summer unless you come to England, where my self & all your friends most Sincerely desire to see You. My Wife, Miss Mundy & Charles desire their best love to you. Feilding is Recruiting in Wales. Your brother Ned still continues Leiutenant on board the *Terrible* Sr. R. Bickerton.

1. Lee was paroled and then on May 6, 1778, formally exchanged for Major General Richard Prescott.
2. Legislation setting up the Carlisle Commission, which was authorized to grant the Americans any concession except independence in an attempt to gain a settlement before the French entered the war.
3. 75th Regiment.

133. From Admiral Sir Thomas Pye[1]

Portsmouth March 15th: 1778

Admiral Pye presents his most Respectfull Compliments to Lord Denbigh, he might well be Surprised if he found *Adm: Pye* incapable of Serving Any body his Lordship Patronis'd, had his Lordship Signified his wish to his Humble Servant, either by letter or by Message A.P. would have strain'd a point in favour of Young Bowater, and should have done it as it was, had it been in his Power Consistant with the Nature of the Service. Sr. Richd. Bickerton was going upon not by the orders he is under. Adm. Pye judges Sr. Richd, has Reason to Expect, *Actual Service* And was at that time 3 Leiuts. Short of the Number Allow'd, it was therefore impossable for me to dispence with his Absence, as it was Adm. Pye has been obliged to take a Leiut. out of an Other Ship to Supply Sr Richd. with, and is now gone out without Lt. when his per No. is ---- Your Lordship will see How inca[pa]ble with my duty I was of Serving Lt. Bowater. Sr. Richard is gone a Short Cruize, and Admiral Gambier[2] Stop'd, so that its probable they may Meet, and now I know your Lordships inclinations I will do Every thing in my power as far as is Consistant with my duty these Very bussy times, but I should judge the best way would be for your Lordship to get his Commission sent down here against his Return, And should Admiral Gambier be Sail'd, there will be so many Oppertunity of following him in the Course of the Summer that it could not be long before he got to his Duty and as Admiral Gambier is not first in Command, Promotion through him must not be very Rapid more particularly as I understand he was to be fifth Leiutenant.

1. Admiral Sir Thomas Pye, commander-in-chief at Portsmouth.
2. Rear Admiral James Gambier. Soon after, Gambier left for America to become second in command of the squadron there.

134.   From Lord Sandwich

Admiralty March 20th. 1778

Lord Sandwich presents his Compliments to Lord Denbigh and Acquaints him that Mr. John Rippon, who his Lordship Recommended [No. 108] will be Appointed a Leiutenant of Marines on his Raising 14 Recruits as proposed.

135.   From General Sir John Irwine

Dublin 12th. May 1778

My Lord

General [Robert] Cunningham brought Me a Message from your Lordship, which was by no Means Nessisary, as I could not possably forget any Commands your Lordship was pleased to honour me with; But there has Offered no opportunity to Serve Mr. [Issac] Riches late of the 29th: Regiment, the Augmentation which has been Made to the troops on this Establishment having been of such a Nature as not to admit of it. All the Ensigns of the Regiments being to Succeed to Leiutenantcies on their Raising a Certain Number of Men, and so many Young Men Appointed Ensigns in their Room on their Raising also a given Number of Men. Should new Corps be Raised here, I shall not fail to Lay Mr. Riches's Name before my Lord Leiutenant, and shall acquaint his Excilency that he has the Honor of being protected by your Lordship.

136.   From Lord Percy

Northumberland House May 17th: 1778

My Dear Lord

   I have this Instant Receivd Lord Amherst['s] Approbation of Lord Feilding as my Aid de Camp which makes me very happy. The Universal good Character which his Lordship bears from Every body who Knows him, gives me the greatest pleasure & Convinces me that I shall Receive both Pleasure & advantage from having such a Young Nobleman in my Family. Your Lordship may now order an Aid de Camps Uniform, & the proper Horse furniture for Lord Feilding as soon as you please, and as our Stay in Town is uncertain, I should think the Sooner the better, my other aide de Camp, is Capn. [James] Johnson of the Marines, a worthy Experienced old Officer, who has served with Me during these troubles in America, & from whom Lord Feilding may learn much good, & I am sure can get no harm.

137.   From Lieutenant James Berkley

On Board the *Proserpine* at Falmouth
June 2d. 1778

My Lord

   I have done my self the honour of Addressing a few lines to you imagining your Lordship might be desireous of having as Early an Account as Possable of the Toulon Fleet; We sailed from Spithead the 20th: with sealed orders And Arrived at Gibraltar the 27th. of April with dispatches for the Governor and Admiral: since which, we have been Cruizing in the Gut, between Europa Point and Ceuta, to look out for the French fleet, which we discovered on the 16th: Ulto, Consisting of 13 Sail of the line and 7 Frigates; under the Command of the Count De Stang.[1] They Arrived opposite our Garrison, about 7 oClock in the Evening, but Kept more over on the Barbary, than the Spanish Shore, I suppose to prevent their being Known, as none of them wore a flag, or distinguishing Pendant, nor would they shew their Colours. Altho we hoisted ours to them. We follow'd them about 120 Leagues, West & by South, from the Mouth of the Gut, and parted Company with them about half past 5 oClock in the morning of the 18th. Ult: they then Steering about West, and we Shaped our Course for England where we this day Arrived, having had Contrary Winds most of the Passage. This my Lord is all I am able to inform You of the fleet, as it is impossible to Know their destination by the Course they Steered. I am particularly obliged to your Lordship for the Trouble you took in having me Removed to my old Division, and shall ever gratefully Remember the Many favours Your Lordship has Conferr'd on your most Obedient and most Obliged humble Servt.

P.S. Pray present my best Respects to Lady Denbigh. I beg your Lordship will not trouble your self in Answering this, as I am sensible how difficult a task writing is, to a person who has weak Eyes.

1. Vice-Admiral Charles Henri Théodat, Comte d'Estaing Du Saillans.

138. From Major John Bowater

Halifax June 2d. 1778

My Lord

In obedience to your Lordships Commands I send you two lines to inform you that my last [No. 129] was sent from New York which place we left about three months ago from thence to Rhode Island & stay'd ten days then we went to Cape Cod Bay near Boston, to send away the Transports as the Congress did not Chuse to let Genl. Burgoyne's Army Return to England. After which we had a Cruize on St. Georges Bank for six weeks, took two small prizes & Brought them into this place. And the Ship is orderd to Carreen & then to Sea again, which I suppose will be in about three weeks. I found my friend the Granadier Feilding in high health & Spirits. As he writes to your Lordship by this Oppertunity [No. 139] I shall not tresspass longer on your patience, than to Request your Lordship to present my best Respects to Lady Denbigh, Lord & Mr. Feilding. I have been severely Attackd with the Scurvy & which has settled its self in my Leg. I've wrote to be Releaved, but in these troublesome times I don't suppose they will pay any Attention to us small people.

139.   From Captain William Feilding

Halifax June 2d. 1778

My Lord

I have Nothing particular to Acquaint your Lordship of, Except some French Vessels taken by the Cruizers on this station, the *Duc de Choiseul* a Ship of 24 Guns Run on Shore the 20th of April last, at Liverpool in this province by the *Blonde;* her Cargo 5,000 Stand of Armes, 5,000 Suits of Cloathing 8 pieces of brass Cannon buried in Salt in her hold, and a Quantity of Bale Goods. The Ship is lost but the Cargo is Chiefly saved. This Ship when she left France was Valued at £50,000, Sterling. The *Cabbot* Armed Brig Lieut. [Edmund] Dod, about the same time took the *Doux Ames*, a snow, Cargo nearly the same, but no Cannon, both these Vessels sailed from Nantes in Company with 60 Sail intend'd for the Americans but Cleared for Cape Francois. The above Men of War fell in with them on the Coast of New England. The Snow had some french Officers on board, but of no Rank, who said they were going on a party of pleasure to St. Eustatia. The *Cabbot* at the same time took a french Ship from Martinique for Boston, with Rum & Molasses. The *Centurion*, Capn. [Richard] Braithwaite has likewise taken a French Brig, *Sophia*, Cargo Silks, Cordials, & Sweetmeats. Capn. Charles Feilding has the Command of the Ships on this Station; he is well, & saild about a fortnight ago on a Cruize in Company with the *Raisonnable.* The *Experiment*, Sr. Ja[me]s Wallace Arrived here about ten days since with the prisoners of the *Portsmouth* Privateer a Ship of 24 Guns which he took a few days before, and sent to New York. By the last Accounts from the Southward the Army was inactive, and that Genl. Clinton was gone to Philadelphia. Flying Reports in Town this day that the Congress had Refused the Terms offered them by Parliament and that Mr. Washington was defeated by Genl. Clinton. Bowater is here in the *Centurion* and joins with me in best Respects to Lady Denbigh and Family.

140.   **From Philip Stephens**

                                        Admiralty Office June 12th. 1778
My Lord

   I have Communicated to my Lords Commissioners of the Admiralty your Lordships letter of the 8th Instant[1] Respecting the Bounty
Money which You Apprehend Mr. Rippon is intitled to, for the
Recruits he has Raised; And in Return I am Commanded to Acquaint your Lordship that there is no instance of any Bounty money
being paid to Officers who have stipulated to Raise Recruits for their
Commissions in the Marine Service.

1. Not entered in the letter book.

141.   **From Lieutenant Edward Bowater**

                                        On board the *Terrible* Spithead
                                                   July 9th. 1778
My Lord

   I Receiv'd the Honor of your Lordships letter,[1] which I should have
Answerd immediately & have given you (as you desired) an Account
of what Ships we have here fit for Sea. I then was not Certain of the
numbers, but am now to inform your Lordship that Admiral Keppel
sail[ed] this morning from St. Helens with twenty five sail of the Line,
three Frigates two Fire Ships & a Cutter having been Reinforced with
the following Ships, the *Duke* & *Formidable* of 90 Guns each, *Ven-
geance* & *Thunderer* of 74 and *Defiance* of 64. The *Centaur* of 74
and *Worcester* of 64, are to join them tomorrow they are now at
Spithead the former waiting for a few more men, and the latter for
provisions. In the Harbour there is the *Vigilant* of 64 Ready for Sea
but wants men, the *Superb* and *Magnificent* of seventy four, with the
Burford and *Lyon*, are fitting for the East Indies and are almost
Ready but want men. I am sorry to inform your Lordship, that the
Terrible after haveing been in the Harbour for Six Weeks, and every
method taken to Eradicate the distemper on board is now much worse
than before, being obliged to send 20 men a day to the Hospital, and
we have now three Hundred there, this has put the Ship out of the

Line of being of any kind of service. We therefore Expect to be ordered into the Harbour again. I hope your Lordship will not think I make an improper Request, when I ask the favour of your getting me Removed into a more Active situation, as I am now, I can be of no Service to My Country or myself. I offered to Exchange duty with any Officer in Admiral Keppels fleet, but could find no one to Accept the offer.

P:S: I wish it was in my power to give your Lordship any information of my Brother the Major [John Bowater] but I have not heard of him these many Months. I enquired on Board of the Frigate that came from America but could not hear anything of him.

1. Not entered in the letter book.

142. **From Lieutenant Edward Bowater**

On Board the *Terrible* at Plymouth
July 31st: 1778

My Lord

I have the Honr: to inform your Lordship of our safe Arrival at this place, and think it my Duty to inform you what has been the fate of us in this ship. You must long before you Receive this been inform'd of the Action our fleet has had with the french, we were in Chaice of them for five days before we engaged, our Ship being far to Windward we passed through a very heavey fire from five & twenty of the Enemy's Ships which Shatter'd our Masts Riging and sails all to pieces. We have ten men killed and twenty one wounded we think ourselves very luckey in not having more, from the great fire we pass'd through we have but one Officer wounded who is Shot through the mouth but is in a fair way of Recovery. Most of our wounded have lost either their legs or Arms. We should have faired much worse had not Sir Hugh Palliser[1] in the *Formidable*, come in between the french Admiral[2] and us which being a three deck ship we found too heavy for us. I thank God I have Receiv'd no hurt. We expected to have had an other Attack in the morning, but found the Enemy gone when it was daylight. They managed their ships very well, had they not they must have Suffered very much, we had but few of our ships Engaged, the french Admiral must have suffered very much, as three of our three Deckers Attacked him one after the other. We are come in here to Refit, and expect to Sail again in a few days. There are many circumstances Relative to the Action that I could inform your Lordship of, but I have been so bad these two days past with the Rheumatism, from having Laid for several days on deck in my wett Cloathes that, I am oblig'd to sit up in bed to write this.

1. The senior professional Lord of the Admiralty and third in command of the Channel Fleet.
2. Lieutenant General Louis Guillouet, Comte d'Orvilliers.

143.   From Major John Bowater

> *Centurion* Sandy Hook near New York
> July 31st. 1778

My Lord

I have this day Receiv'd your Lordships letter dated March the 4th. [No. 132] & the former one I answered from Halifax [No. 138]. Your Lordship is Already Acquainted of the Count d'Estaings Arrival in America & with his intention of Blocking up both our Fleet & Army also of their Retreat from Philadelphia & Mr. Washington falling on the Rear of our Army, by which he lost above fourteen hundred Men[1] and some of our people say his loss would have been much more, if some of our people had not been Mistaken. And they lay the blame on Gen: Lee, who is now on his Trial for disobedience of Orders, & is thought by some to be exceeding Nervous. The Count finding that the Birds were flown came & Anchored off the light house at Sandy Hook to block up the Port of New York. Lord Howe collected his little fleet to the Entrance to guard the Passage, they also fortified the point & threw a small Garrison into it. In this Situation the two fleets lay at Anchor for ten days. The Count threatening to Come in and to destroy all before him & the Viscount [Howe] biding him defiance. The latter dispatchd his light frigates to the different Stations to call in the large Ships & warn the Others of the danger. Yesterday we Arrived with the *Raisonnable* from Halifax, & narrowly Escaped falling in with the french fleet. One of Mr. Byrons[2] Ships a 74 Gun Arrivd Yesterday & a 50 from the West Indies which has determind Lord Howe to Sail tomorrow morning After the french fleet which has been gone five days from here & was seen two days ago Steering for Rhode Island. Mr. Washington with his Army has cross'd the North River & is on his march for that place. And they mean to land under cover of the french Fleet, we have Reinforced the place with 3000 men it now consists of seven [thousand], Genl. [Robert] Pigot commanding there. The french Fleet is much heavier than ours, but we out Number them, so that I think it will be a very tight match. The Count—2 of 84 Guns—5 of 74—4 of 64—1 of 56—& six frigates—The British—1 of 74 Guns—7 of 64—5 of 50—2 of 44 —frigates innumerable. We may meet with some more of Mr. Byrons Squadron on our Passage, and we shall certainly be so well bred as to desire them to partake in our Amusements. All the Seamen belonging to the Transports, Victualers & Merchantmen are come on board as Volunteers & we have taken the [Royal] Welch Fuzeliers & some Companies of Granadiers in addition to the Marines. A better man'd fleet can not be & I think they will do their duty. The french Expected to have swept the whole Coast as they knew our ships was so much divided at present they have only taken two small Armed Sloops, Commanded by Leiutenants and the May Packet from Falmouth. We left at Halifax Capn. Charles Feilding as Commodore with some frigates. Genl. Massey had fortified the place expecting a visit from the Count. As to the Commissioners³ what shall I say a Contemptible—O—is the best description of them except the Governor,⁴ who is so black a Rascal that even the *Americans* have exposed & Ridiculed him. And now my Lord I must inform you of what has Surprised me more than if Tommy Sheldon⁵ had left off fretting at Cards or the Dowager Lady Cr---n⁶ transformed into Venus—The Presbyterian fanatic Clergy of New England praying publickly for their great Ally the french King, as the great protector of Civil and Religious Liberty. I must now conclude as I hear the Packett, is going away & indeed I have Related all I know, but hope my next will give you an Account of a Compleat Victory.

1. The Battle of Monmouth Courthouse. American casualties were 72 killed, 161 wounded, and 132 missing. The British listed 294 killed and wounded and 64 missing but this figure is too low, for the Americans buried 217 British soldiers at the site of the battle.
2. Vice-Admiral Hon. John Byron, commander of a squadron sent to reinforce the Royal Navy in America.
3. The Carlisle Commission.

4. Commodore George Johnstone, known as Governor Johnstone because he had once been Governor of West Florida.
5. Colonel Thomas Sheldon of the marines.
6. Jane Craven, Dowager Baroness Craven.

144.   From Lieutenant Edward Bowater

On board the *Terrible* Plymouth
Aug 2d: 1778

My Lord

When I did my self the honour of writing to Your Lordship the other day [No. 142] I did not expect so soon to trouble you with another letter. I hope you will pardon the Intrusion on Your Lordships time and not think me troublesom. I was Yesterday inform'd of Admiral [Robert] Mans being Appointed to the Mediterranean Command, and Admiral [Sir Edward] Hughes to the East Indias. I should think myself Very happy if your Lordship would get me appointed one of the Leiutenants of Either Ship, and more particularly so at present as they are going to a Warmer Climate as I find the Rheumatic Complaint which I am troubled with grow worse so much so I am afraid was this Ship to proceed to Sea, in a few days I should not be able to go with her. I have obtained Sr. Ricd: Bickertons permission to be on Shore for a few days for the Benifit of the Air. As I was uncertain whether your Lordship was in Town or Country I directed my last to Newnham, but hope you will have Receiv'd it before this. The Ships are fitting as fast as possable but find on Examination they are much more Shattered than expected, it is expected they will go to sea again in the Course of ten days or a fortnight.

145.   To Lord Sandwich

Newnham Augt. 8th: 1778

My Dear Lord

In this time of Hurry and Bussiness I shall not trouble you with one word more than Nessisary, which is most Earnestly to Request that you will Appoint my friend Leiut. Bowater (now in the *Terrible*) on Board Admiral Hughes' Ship who I find is to Command the fleet going to the East Indias. Lord Wentworth begs leave to join with me in this wish.

P.S. Should Admiral Hughes' Ship be full & he Can be put on Board the Admiral's Ship going to the Mediterranean, that will do as well.

146.   From Lieutenant Edward Bowater

Plymouth Augt. 16th: 1778

My Lord

I had the pleasure to Receive your Lordships letter of the 6th: Yesterday[1] am happy to find mine proved Acceptable, had my health permitted me, I should have then given you a more particular Account of the Action then I have. Your Lordship observes, that it was a drawn Battle, it seems to be understood so by most officers of the fleet as there was no particular Advantage gain'd on either Side, if anything we were sufferers, as severall of our ships was very much disabled, so much so, that had the Enemy Renewed the Attack, we should have fought under very great disadvantage, the want of a proper line being formd, made it a very confused fight on our side & some very serious consequences attending it. I mean that of our ships fireing into each other, which was the case in the *Egmont* Capn. [John] Allen, who Receiv'd a whole broadside from the *Thunderer* Capn. [Hon. Robert Boyle] Walsingham which did them great damage, and Kill'd & wounded several of their men. The want of Attention to the Signals that were made occassion'd all the Confusion that happend. The Capn. of the *Duke* [William Brereton] is much condemnd for not coming into Action, as its said he might have done, how far its true I know not as we were not in that division I could not make any observations on the occassion. The Number of Ships Engaged on our side from what I can learn was not more then twenty two but some of these at such a distance that it would have been of no consequence if they had never fired a shot. We were very much surprised in the morning to find the Enemy gone, except three Ships, which I apprehend had mistook the signal but made all the Sail they could when they saw us. Its a general observation of the Officers of the fleet, that no ships could be fought better or better managed than the Enemies Ships were, there line was formed very exact. I had in the Evening an Oppertunity (when they were to Leeward of us) of taking a good observation of them, they seemed most of them to be very fine Ships. We are now fit for sea, but there are several other ships that will not be Ready these some days, as there is a great scarcity of many Articles that the Ships are in want of. The *Valiant* & *Bienfaisant*, with the *Arethusa* frigate Arrived here on fryday have brought in three prizes & yesterday saild two [ships] in their Room, it is said we are to sail some time this week but I should suppose not till we have got a Reinforcement, as its very certain the French have of eight sail of the line. I hope my next to your Lordship will give you an Account of a decisive Battle on our side as I find they mean to meet us again, we expect some Ships from Portsmouth, at present we are but thirty altogether, the french had thirty two of the line when we engaged, we have one of Adml. Byron's fleet here (the *Russell*) that was obliged to come back, from Sickness & bad weather and most of the rest of Adml. Byrons Squadron are seperated in a gale of wind, some got to America, the others to Newfoundland & the West Indies. The people at this place seem disatisfied at our not bringing in with us some of the Enemy's Ships, we have only one thing in my opinion to brag of that they were certainly sick of the Bussiness or they would not have Run away in the night but I hope its a confidence we shall never place in them again. I hope your Lordship will not think me impertinent, in giving my opinion so freely in what I have now Related, and as its only my private opinion I flatter myself it will Rest so with your Lordship. My haveing been very Ill & still but very indifferent oblig'd me to be on Shore for some days but I yesterday Return'd on board, & am carrying on the duty of the Ship, as the first & second Leiutenants are Absent on leave, but I find my self very unequal to the task, as I am so very weak and am oblig'd to be on Deck from daylight till night. I took the liberty of writing to your Lordship two days following the letter [No. 144] I find you have Receiv'd. I hope you have Receivd it before this and will not think my request an improper one. I shall be happy in being favour'd with a line from your Lordship.

1. Not entered in the letter book.

147.   **From Lord Sandwich**

Admiralty Septr. 3d. 1778

My dear Lord

I find in my hurry I misunderstood you about Mr. Bowater [No. 145], imagining you had been writing to Me about the Marine, instead of the Sea Officer. Upon Sir Edward Hughes's being appointed to the Command in the East Indias, I gave him his Choice of All his Officers. I should have been very Glad if he had Recommended Mr. Bowater for one of them, but the Ship is now Compleat with Regard to Leiuts. & I do not foresee any Opportunity of Placeing him with any other Admiral where it would be of Use to him in the Way of Perferment. We are in hourly & anxious Expectation of news from Admiral Keppel, the french fleet is Certainly at Sea & I think is inferior to him in strength. Captain [William] Brereton has been dismised from the Command of his Ship by a Court Martial which he himself Asked for to Enquire into his Conduct; he is honourably Acquitted from any Charge of misbehavour on the day of Action; but is dismissed for having been intoxicated with Liquor on the Evenings of the 26th: & 27th: of July being the Evenings before & after the Battle. I direct this to Your own house Concluding that you could not be Absent for more than a Week.

148.   **From Captain William Feilding**

Halifax Septr. 7th: 1778

My Lord

Since Admiral Arbuthnot saild from here, I Receivd my Box of linnen by Govr Hughes,[1] for which I am greatly Obliged to your Lordship for this Singular mark of your Lordships friendship. I was in great hopes to have been in England soon After the Admiral, to Return your Lordship my Acknowledgements & thanks (for the many favours Receivd) in Person; but the *Ariel* Arrived yesterday (the day fixt for our Sailing) with a letter from Lord Howe to the Commander of his Majesty's forces in this province, Acquainting him, he had drove the French fleet into Boston and that he was gone to ye Reliefe of Rhode Island where (I hear) the Rebels have eighteen thousand men landed; and that if General Massey thought there was occassion to detain the Battalion of Marines, to do it, if not to send them to England as soon as possable, in consequence of which the Leiut. Govenor have Requested our being detained till we hear further News from the Southward, which is expected in a week or 10 days. I have great pleasure in acquainting your Lordship that Capn: [John] Raynor in the *Isis*, a 50 gun ship, fell in with the french Commodore in the *Caesar* of 74 guns, and engaged for some time at last parted The *Caesar* having about 200 men kil'd and wounded with the Captains Arm shot off, and otherwise much wounded. The *Isis*, had about 15 men killd & wounded, but the Riggin was so much cut, that she was incapable of following, therefore gave her three Chears at parting, in Return for three Chears the Commodore gave her before the Action, in hopes so small a ship as 50 guns would have struck without Engaging. The [*Cabbot*] Leiut. Dod sails immediately for England with this news and perhaps with more than I have heard.

[P.S.] Admiral Byron would come in here by himself last week, saild the 4th inst. with the *Diamond, Culloden, Dispatch,* and *Hope* for New York. The Admiral Singly fell in with the french fleet at Anchor out of sight of land 20 leagues to the Southward of [New] York, & was under the Nessesity of bearing away for Halifax.

1. Rear Admiral Sir Richard Hughes, Lieutenant Governor of Nova Scotia.

149. From Lieutenant Edward Bowater

On board the *Terrible* off Falmouth
Septr. 11th: 1778

My Lord

As an oppertunity offers of writing a few lines by a Vessel Admiral Keppel has dispatchd with his dispatches for Government, I would not miss the favourable Oppertunity of writing to your Lordship, informing you of our present Situation and what we have been doing after our departure from Plymouth we Cruized off the Lizard for two or three days waiting for one of our fleet, but finding she did not come up we went to Cruize off Ushant where we expected to have found the french fleet. After Cruizing there for some days and not meeting

them we Went forty leagues to ye West in expectation of seeing them
but was unsuccessfull but met with two of their large Ships which we
gave Chace to but the night coming on we lost sight of them. We now
Apprehend they are in detached Squadrons and do no[t] suppose they
will meet in force again part of them we believe are in Brest where
we suppose we shall go next. Our fleet now Consists of thirty two Sail
of the line being joined by two to day. We are all in great order and
Ready and Willing to meet the french when they please, but do not
Suppose they will give us an oppertunity. I hope your Lordship will
excuse the Abruptness of this Epistle as the Boats going.

150.   **From Major John Bowater**

New York Septr. 23d. 1778
My Lord

The news we have sent you from this Country these last two
months must have Alarm'd you very much at home. I wish it may
not have been productive of some more timid Resolutions [of] our unwise people in Power. Mr. Washington has Removed from the White
Plains, the greatest part of his Army gone to their Harvest. Lord
Cornwallis went yesterday morning to Reposses the Jerseys, & I have
heard of no force to oppose him. Sr. Henry Clinton, Knyphausen &c.
&c. with a very fine Army march'd out this morning & by the
preparations seem to be bound for the Northward, he has left a sufficient force here to prevent surprize. The Count d'Estaing Remains at
Boston Repairing his damage, & as soon as compleat I do suppose he
will Return to Europe, without Accomplishing any part of the treach-
erous plan he came out upon. The french & Americans are Violent in
condemning each other for their Ill success against Rhode Island,
much might now be done in Negociating. Lord Carlisle,[1] and his
friend [Anthony] Storer are too Ridiculous. This letter comes to your
Lordship by the *Tartar*, Governor Johnstone is a passenger in her.
After being struck out of the Commission by the congress, they Refus-
ing to have any thing to say to our Commissioners whilst such an In-
famous person Remain'd in it. An other Curious History—Genl. Lee
espoused by many great men here, then exchanged & now suspended
by a Court Martial of Rebel General Officers, for Cowardice disobedience &c. And I hear he means to be a Candidate for Middlesex,[2] at

the next Election, (I shall not be surprized to see the Garter upon him.) Lord Howe has Relinquish'd his Command & sail'd Yesterday Morning. I admire him as a Sea Officer. As a politician I dont understand him. His quiting at this time and throwing that department quite into confusion I think unpardonable. Mr. Gambiers Ill state of health makes him quite unfit for this Command.[3] Adml. Byron has not been able to get into this place, he is now at Rhode Island & part of the fleet will go to him. We are not yet inform'd if he is commander in Chief or whether he is only Waiting on the Count d'Estaing. I may come home this Winter if I please & am now less Anxious on that Account. I have not Receiv'd a letter from your Lordship of four months, I've wrote by every oppertunity, two very long ones by the last Packett. I dined yesterday with Col. Stuart, he is not so well as I could wish.

P.S. Eight of Adml. Byrons fleet are here but are very sickly, himself and one more at Rhode Island, three of his Ships still missing. It is said that Sir Hugh Palliser advised his coming by the northern passage, which is greatly condemn'd by the Gentlemen of the Navy here —it is the best way for a single Ship but the worst for a fleet, for if they [do not] make a Short Passage they generally come in sickly and out of Repair.

1. Frederick Howard, 5th Earl of Carlisle. In 1778 he headed the commission appointed to negotiate an end to the war in America.
2. The constituency which repeatedly returned John Wilkes to the House of Commons after his expulsion from Parliament in 1768.
3. It was believed by many that Gambier was made second in command of the squadron in America as a means of getting him to give up the Commissionership of Portsmouth Dockyard.

151. **From Lieutenant Edward Bowater**

On board the *Terrible* Spithead
Octr. 27th: 1778

My Lord

I have the pleasure to inform your Lordship of our Arrival here with Part of Admiral Keppel's fleet yesterday, most of our Ships in a Shatterd condition from the Very bad Wheather we have had the latter part of our Cruize, most of the Ships were seperated, but hope we shall soon hear of their safe Arrival. The *Ocean* of 90 Guns, was left at sea so leakey as to be Very near going down, and the *Sandwich* and *Ramillies* are Arrived in the same state. We saw Nothing of the French fleet Chased three or four of their large Ships, but the thick weather prevented our coming up with them, we have taken during our Cruize, eight sail of St. Domingo ships, supposed to be of the Value of one hundred & fifty Thousand pounds all together. We are fitting our Ships as fast as possable, and it is expected we shall sail again in the Course of a fortnight. By the *Eagle* which Arrived here the day before Yesterday with Lord Howe, I had the pleasure of hearing of my Brother John, who was very Well at New York and is coming home soon.

152. To Lieutenant Edward Bowater

Newnham Octr. 31st. 1778

Dear Ned

I have this Minute Receiv'd yours of the 27th: [No. 151] I am sorry to find the fleet is Returned in the bad condition you mention, but more so at its having done Nothing, for if its true that the french fleet has been out & saild so far as Cape Finisterre, how did your Admiral [Keppel] contrive to let it get back again into Brest unmolested, pray clear up this matter to me? Immediately on the Receipt of your former letter [No. 144], desireing to go to the East Indies I applied both to Lord Sandwich & Sr. Edwd. Hughes, the former Answered me [No. 147] that he did not interfere in naming the officers on board the Admirals ship, & the latter Returnd me the Inclosed Answer.[1] I shall be in Town at the Meeting of Parliament when I will leave no stone unturn'd, to get you placed in a more Advantagious Situation.

P S I have had a letter from your Brother the Major by this days post dated New York Septr. 23d: [No. 150] He is very well says he has leave to come home this winter but doubts whether he will make use of it.

1. A notation in the margin of the letter book says, "which was that he was sorry but that all his Leiuts. was all appointed."

153.   **To Major John Bowater**

Newnham Oct. 31st. 1778

Dear Bow

I Receivd your letter dated the 31st. of July, as also your last by the *Tartar* dated New York Septr. 23d. [Nos. 143, 150] I was in hopes by the good Spirits with which you wrote your first, your 2d: would have given an Account of a Victory over d'Estaings fleet particularly as some of Byrons ships had join'd you before the french got into Boston Harbour, but Alas, how are we all disappointed, when we see your Admiral [Howe] Return home and nothing done by him. I depend greatly on Sr. H: Clinton, and Lord Cornwallis, they are men of Spirit & if properly Supported from home may Recover America yet; as to the 3 Ships of Byrons which you say are still missing—The *Russell* is come home, the *Albion*, put into Lisbon, but has long since saild again to join you, & I think the *Invincible*, Capn. [Henry Francis] Evans which we have heard of at Newfoundland; If Lord Cornwallis can maintain himself in the Jerseys this winter, & Sr. H: Clinton penetrates as far as Albany it will give our Army a great deal of Elbow Room, but if they should suffer New York to be Surprised in doing this all is lost. I believe I told you in my last that Lord Feilding had got a Company & was Aid de Camp to Lord Percy, who speaks very highly of him, but if his Regiment, (the Welch Volunteers) should come to America he will most certainly not stay behind. Since you have got leave pray come home, for you can do yourself no good by staying in America any longer, & perhaps I may be of Use to you here. I am doing all in my power to get your Brother Ned promoted to a Sloop, & dont despair of Success. My two young Men, My Wife, Miss Mundy, & many other friends are all well & desired to be Remember'd to you.

154.   **To Lord Barrington**

Newnham Novr 2d: 1778

My dear Lord

I now address myself to you, not only as Secretary at War, but also as one of the oldest friends I have in the World, first for your Advice, next for your Assistance. I find the Welch Volunteers are likely to go to the East Indies a service where but little Honour is to be acquired; & perhaps no other Enemy to contend with but a bad Climet, this therefore cannot be an Eligable Situation for Lord Feilding to be placed in, but if Lord Pembroke,[1] (who's Son is in the same Corp) thinks it Right for Lord Herbert[2] to go; Lord Feilding shall most certainly not stay behind: on the other hand, if he is to be Exchanged into any other Regiment I flatter my self, I may depend on your friendship to procure the same Indulgence for Lord Feilding; the Mode I leave totally to You, but could Rather wish him in the Guards, or in the Dragoons tho only a Captain Leiutenancy, such an Exchange with your Assistance surely might be purchased, and the more so as I am told the East India Service will be a very Profitable one, and suit a Soldier of Fortune, but be no object to My Son. I hope that when your Lordship is so kind as to lay this my humble Request before his Majesty he will be Graciously pleased to Approve of it, as he will Remember my first Application was for a Cavalry Commission in order to Avoid my Eldest Son's being sent to fight against Climet only, if you think it is Nessisary for me to Come up to Town I will set out immediately on the Honour of a line from Your Lordship.

1. Henry Herbert, 10th Earl of Pembroke.
2. George Augustus Herbert, Lord Herbert.

155. From Lord Barrington

Cavendish Square Novr. 4th: 1778

My dear Lord

I am this moment Honour'd by your letter [No. 154], and will not loose a moment in Answering it. I hope to Your Lordships Satisfaction. I have never heard the least hint of an Intention to send the Welch Volunteers to India, and am Confident no Idea of the sort has been Entertain'd by Any body. When Your Lordship Comes to Town I shall be happy to Consult with You what can be most Advantagious to such an Heir of such a family as Lord Feilding.

156. From Lieutenant Edward Bowater

Spithead Novr. 4th: 1778

My Lord

Your Lordship is Surprised we did not intercept the french fleet Returning to Brest: it is Apprehended the Admirals Station was limitted, and as the french did not come within those bounds is the reason we saw nothing of them. We knew they were off Cape Finisterre but they did not Remain long at Sea after we was out, the[y] had the Precaution to go into Port, when they saw the Appearance of bad Weather, and the Equinoctial Gales of Winds coming on which proved so distrucfull to ours, indeed it is astonishing from circumstances and Situation, that we escaped so well, though there is not a Ship here, that has not some Defect in either Mast or Hull, and several in both. There has been several very Extraordinary Circumstances happen during our last Cruize. We have Reason to believe that one Night in a Gale of Wind we had several french Ships of War intermix'd with our fleet, and which we knew nothing of till our Arrival here, another night a line of Battle Ship was hail'd by the Admiral, they made no Answer, but Slipt away and was heard nothing further of. We have Reason to believe that at one time part of the french fleet were very Near and Seperated from part of the Squadron. We have several times had no more then fifteen or sixteen sail of our Ships together, having been Seperated by bad Weather and in this manner Returned to Spithead, having only with us fourteen Sail of the line, and two frigates; the Ships are now fitting with as much expedition as possable, but it will be some time before they are all Ready, as several of them have to Dock; most of our ships Rigging is in a bad state from the last Action, and we are oblig'd to make a shift with it, as they are not able to Supply us all with New. I fancy this Ship will be one of the first Ready for Sea as we have only one new Mast to get in; expect to be Ready for Sea in ten days or a fortnight. The Conduct of an Admiral third in Commission of a [fleet] is much talkd of here, with Respect to his conduct during the time of Actual Service; three letters which your Lordship must have seen in the papers address'd by an Honble. Captain Commanding a frigate have occassioned this, and it is said the matter will be very Serious, and go great lengths. Your Lordship will hear a great deal of this when you return to Town.[1] We have no particular News at this place at present, there are several Frigates Arrived from America and a Convoy going with Lord Seaforth['s] Regiment to Guernsey & Jersey it is said the french are determind to have these Islands. The success of our privateers has been Astonishing, in one french Convoy there has been forty out of forty two taken, we are in Expectation of three more of our Indiamen; I know of no other news and therefore must conclude.

1. Bowater is referring to the beginning of the Keppel-Palliser dispute. On October 15, 1778, an anonymous account of the action on July 27, 1778, between the British and French fleets appeared in a London newspaper. The article blamed Palliser, who was third in command, for the failure of the British to renew the action. Palliser attempted to obtain satisfaction from Keppel but failed; he then had his own signed account of the battle printed in at least six different London newspapers. This incident exploded into a major political battle over the conduct of the war. The government was violently attacked in Parliament, there was rioting in London, both Keppel and Palliser were court-martialed, and the officer corps of the Royal Navy was split into two hostile factions.

157.   From Major John Bowater

Pontivy Decer: 14th: 1778

My Lord

I did my self the Honour of writing to your Lordship from Brest but the frequent miscarriage of letters has induced me to trouble your Lordship with a second to inform you of my Situation, and also to Request your Assistance in getting me Exchanged or leave to Come to England on my Parole. The History of my self, I must begin from New York. The *Centurion* was order'd to the West Indies & I obtained six months leave of Absence from Admiral Gambier to go to England to settle my Private affairs, my self & four more Officers took a passage in a small Transport calld the *Fanny* with about twenty Wounded men on board & under Convoy of the *Leviathan.* We lost Company in a Storm of Wind, & Arrived within a days sail of England when we mett with a Squadron of French Men of War, Commanded by Monsr. de la Motte-Picquet who took us out of our Transport & Sunk her, as she was too old, empty & Rotten to send into port. I Remained ten days Prisoner on board the *St. Esprit*, And was then Removed on my Parole of Honour to this place (which if it did not incesantly Rain would not be a disagreable Town) I have been treated with great Politeness. We are limitted to six miles Round the Town and the Duke de Rhoan [Rouen] who has the Mannors & great property here abouts has given leave to all the English Officers to Shoot, Hunt, & Fish. The Town is very Ill built but the Country is Beautiful & plenty of Every thing. We have two Courses & a desert with Clarret & white wine for half a Crown, a Card Assembly every night & sometimes dancing. We found here the Officers of ye *Fox*, *Lively*, *Helina* &c. &c. about thirty in number. A Squadron of Draggoons are quartered here. The great disappointment to me was being so near my friends & stop'd just at the door. I enjoy exceeding good health & tho I am unfortunate I am not unhappy. The fortune of War makes us Millitary men submit with more ease to these little Reversé. We are still so unpolite as to drink toasts & the principal one is *Good Lord deliver us*. I request all my friends that go to Church to Remember me amongst the prisoners & Captives.

P.S. Please to direct A Monsieur Bowater Officer Anglais Pontivy en Bretagne France. I believe it nessisary to write a Single Sheet of paper & pay the postage and not one word about Politics which is a very severe Restriction to us Englishmen.

158. To Lord Amherst

South Street Decr. 20th. 1778

My dear Lord

As Mr. [Francis] Richardsons demands for an Exchange for my Son into the Guards are so Exorbitant, I find it impossable to Comply with them I hope your Lordship will not think me very unreasonable if I desire your Lordship to lay my humble Request before his Majesty for a Captain Leiutenancy of Draggoons which I hope cannot be very difficult, in the Additional Companies which are to be Raised for that Corp. I Request this the more as by a letter Receivd from his Mother to day she seems to Rest her happiness upon his being Removed into the Cavalry or the Guards Either of which will secure him from bad climates tho' at the same time nothing is more Lord Feildings Ambition than to see Real Service.

159. **From Lieutenant Edward Bowater**

Terrible at Spithead Decr. 22d: 1778

My Lord

I had the honour of Receiving your Lordships letter Yesterday & immediately waited upon Lord Shuldham with the inclosed;[1] his Lordship Receiv'd me with great politeness and desired I would inform you that he should have been happy to have obeyd your Commands by Receiving me into his Ship, as one of his Leiuts. but the Vacancies were all filled up which he was sorry for, as he was under the Necessity of Appointing officers which he knew very little of, Expecting he should go directly to Sea. I Return your Lordship many thanks for the trouble you have had upon this Occassion; but shall be still more obliged to your Lordship if you should hear any thing of my Brother [John] if you will honour me with a line. I am, and shall Remain very unhappy for the fate of my unfortunate Brother till I know what is become of him.

1. Not entered in the letter book.

160. **From Lord Amherst**

Whitehall Decr. 23d: 1778

My Lord

I am Honourd with the Receipt of your Lordships letter of ye 20th Inst: [No. 158] I will not fail to Remind the King of your Lordships Wish Respecting Lord Feilding when the proper Occassion offers.

161. **To Major John Bowater**

Newnham Decr. 30th: 1778

Dear Bow

I have this day Receivd yours dated Pontivy Decr. 14th: [No. 157] but none from Brest. I will use every Means in my Power to get you exchanged but in the mean time if you apply to the proper Officers under the plea of Health or Bussiness they will certainly give you your Parole.

We are all well here & Glad to hear you pass your time so merrily considering you are a prisoner. The family all join in Compliments.

VI

January 1779-March 1780

The American War, unlike other wars of the 18th century, deeply divided the ruling classes in England. By the end of 1778, London had been treated to the sight of defeated and disgruntled admirals and generals returning to Westminster to attempt to regain on the floor of the House of Commons what they had lost on the field of battle. All the frustration and rage produced by three years of futile war burst upon the London political world. It began with a heated and bitter exchange in the House of Commons over the battle off Ushant; the protagonists were Admiral Augustus Keppel, the commander of the Channel Fleet, and Admiral Sir Hugh Palliser, the third in command of the Fleet and the government's spokesman in the House on naval affairs. Opposition politicians joined the quarrel, demanding that Palliser be court-martialed and dismissed from office. Palliser in return demanded that Keppel be court-martialed. And the government found itself under sustained attack for mishandling the war. The result was a court-martial for Keppel, which was the biggest political trial in the Royal Navy since the one that condemned Admiral Byng to death, Palliser's career was ruined, and there was rioting in London. Even before the noise of the Keppel-Palliser affair had died down, Admiral Howe and his brother General Howe, joined by General Burgoyne, were demanding an inquiry into the conduct of the war in America; while a number of opposition politicians were demanding that Lord Sandwich be removed from the office of First Lord of the Admiralty for "misconduct, incapacity, and willful negligence."

While the politicians fought each other at Westminster, Britain was confronted with the greatest threat to her security to occur between the Armada and the Battle of Britain. France, in conjunction with Spain, who had entered the war, was planning to gain naval superiority in the English Channel with a fleet of sixty-six ships-of-the-line and then invade Britain. To oppose the French and Spanish, the Royal Navy could muster only thirty-five ships-of-the-line. This force was commanded by Admiral Sir Charles Hardy, who was appointed to the command of the faction-ridden Channel Fleet in the hopes that his great age and vast seniority would dampen the passions and hatreds generated in the Royal Navy by the Keppel-Palliser dispute. However, it was only Spanish and French ineptitude that saved the British from an invasion in 1779.

The invasion plan called for the French and Spanish fleets to meet in June at sea, gain control of the English Channel, and then cross a French army over to England. From the beginning, however, the scheme fell apart. The Spanish were late in leaving port, and while the French waited for their ally, provisions and water ran short and the ships' crews were ravaged by sickness. There were other delays and it was not until August 14 that the disease-ridden Franco-Spanish fleet appeared off the Lizard. On August 16, however, an easterly gale drove the French and Spanish out of the English Channel; and when they finally sighted the British Channel Fleet on August 29, they could not bring the British to battle. Short of provisions and water and with a rapidly increasing sick list, the French and Spanish had no choice but to put into Brest and call off the plan to send a French army to England in 1779. What saved England from invasion in 1779 was not the Royal Navy but rather luck, the weather, and the inability of the French and Spanish to carry out their plans.

It was clear after the Keppel-Palliser fight and the invasion scare of 1779 that what Britain needed above all was a victory and a fighting admiral. Oddly enough, it was in Paris that the Admiralty finally found an admiral who could win battles. At the end of 1779, Admiral Sir George Rodney, living in France to escape his English creditors, was appointed commander-in-chief of the Leeward Island squadron and given the task of resupplying the besieged garrison of Gibraltar while proceeding to his new command. On December 29, 1779, Rodney sailed from Plymouth with a force of twenty-two ships-of-the-line, fourteen smaller warships, and a convoy of merchant ships, transports, and storeships. On January 8, 1780, Rodney encountered, overpowered, and captured a Spanish convoy of fifteen storeships, six frigates, and a ship-of-the-line. Then on the night of January 16 off Cape St. Vincent, Rodney's fleet fought a night action with a Spanish squadron of eleven ships-of-the-line and two frigates. When the shooting stopped at 2 a.m. on the morning of the 17th, the British had destroyed one Spanish ship-of-the-line and captured six others. Rodney's fleet, the convoy, and the Spanish prizes arrived in triumph at Gibraltar on January 26. At last, in the fourth year of the war, the British had a tangible victory, for as Lord Sandwich wrote to Rodney, "You have taken more line-of-battle ships than had been captured in any one action in either of the two last preceding wars."

162. From Lord Amherst

Whitehall 16th Jany: 1779

My Lord

In compliance with your Lordships Wishes [No. 158] Respecting Lord Feilding I have made an Arrangement by which I shall be able to propose to the King, that Lord Feilding may be appointed to the light troop of the 10th: Regiment of Draggoons. As the Eldest Leiut. of that Regiment will be deprived of his Expected promotion to a troop on Lord Feildings Account I propose to Remove him to the Captain Leiutenantcy of an other Regiment, and that the Eldest Leiut there shall succeed to Lord Feildings Company in the 75th:. If it will be agreable to your Lordship to pay to this Officer the Regulated difference between a Company of foot and a Capn. Leiutenantcy of Draggoons. If your Lordship should agree to the proposition, Lord Feilding will be a Captain of a troop of Draggoons on paying 600 £ instead of £ 1,600 which is the Regulated difference between the Value of a Company of Foot and a troop of Draggoons.

163. To Lord Amherst

South Street Jany. 17th: 1779

Permit me my dear Lord, to Return you my most Sincere thanks for your very kind & obliging letter [No. 162] which I Receiv'd last night on my Arrival in Town the proposal containd in it, my Son most Joyfully Accepts of, and if there is any Pleasure in making a Whole family happy, your Lordship have made mine most compleatly so. The £600 shall be paid at a minutes Warning into any hands your Lordship shall think proper to direct.

164.   From Lord of Sandwich

Admiralty Feby: 1st: 1779

Lord Sandwich presents his Compliments to Lord Denbigh and has the Satisfaction to Acquaint him, that Leiut. Berkley who his Lordship Recommended, is appointed Adjutant to the Portsmouth Division of Marines.

165.   From Lieutenant James Berkley

Victory Spithead Feby. 2d. 1779

My Lord

I yesterday Evening was honourd with your Note,[1] informing me of my Appointment of Adjutant, and have took the Earliest oppertunity of Returning your Lordship my most grateful Acknowledgements for the honour & favour done me.

I cannot Sufficiently express my sense of Gratitude for the many obligations I am under to Your Lordship; I shall ever consider this, as one of the greatest conferred on me.

1. Not entered in the letter book.

166.   From Captain William Feilding

Portsmouth Feby 3d: 1779

My Lord

I have this day Embark'd on board the *Warwick* 50 Guns Capn. [Richard] Collins, who has orders for a warm Climate. I believe St. Helena for the East Indiamen and is to sail as soon as Ready by himself, which will be about ten days. I like my Captain much, & believe I shall live very happy with him, as he waited my Arrival before he made a demand. As it may not be impossable but that we may go to India from St: Helena I should be much obliged to your Lordship for letters to Sr Edwd: Hughes, Mr. & Mrs. Barton, and other of your friends in India. Miss Mundy will likewise make me very happy in Honouring me with letters to her sister. The Evidences that has been calld by Admiral Keppel, has been greatly in his favour, particularly that delivered this day by Sr. John Lindsay, which you will see in the papers to morrow much better than I can Relate & what pleased every body in Court.[1] I have not yet seen Bowater. Sr. Edwd. [Hughes] (it is imagined) will sail to morrow, if the wind permits.

1. The court-martial of Admiral Keppel was one of the most celebrated political trials of the decade. The proceedings were held on shore, permitting his supporters to pack the courtroom.

167. **From Major Robert Mason Lewis**

Leicester March 28th: 1779

My Lord

I make no doubt that before this your Lordship may have heard that I have Succeeded to the majority of the 10th: draggoons & that my name is given into the office for my Succession in the Regiment, I am sorry to Know that this will do nothing for Lord Feilding as the Capn: Leiutenant will purchase the Troop, & of course as a Senior Captain will be in the body of the Regiment. I had the honour to say to your Lordship in Town that I had Reason to immagin, the light Troops to the different Regiments would soon be Regimented. This opinion has now taken place, & which induces Me to lay before His Majesty; A Service of two & twenty Years, with being present at the whole German War, and Where the 10th. dragoons had more officers, & (I believe) men [killed] than the whole Brittish Cavalry, in the different Engagements, having my horse Shot under Me, not with standing which I brought off, the Kings Standard when the Regiment was attack'd by three Brigades of Infantry. This short Memorial I shall lay at his Majesty's feet, with every dutiful Respect, to know whether he thinks me worthy to Succeed to one of the Leiut. Collonels of the new formed Regiments of light dragoons, after being near two Years a Major by Brevet and fifteen Years a Captain. These Services my Friends mean to plead as I have Reason to conceive Officers will apply far Junior to my self in the army & some that never were abroad upon any Service. And if from some flattering Expressions of your Lordship I may take the liberty to Intreat your Intercession with the King, in my favour, and to obtain Lord Amherst's protection in this affair. You will at my promotion Secure Lord Feilding his troop in the 10th. Dragoons, and my Friends in Leicestershire & my self will Remember the Obligation when an oppertunity offers, to convince Lord Denbigh of the high sense We entertain of the favour.

168.   To Major Robert Mason Lewis

South Street April 3d. 1779

Dear Lewis

Nothing would have given me more pleasure, than to have had it in my Power to have Assisted in your promotion, but I much fear that cannot be accomplishd for the present; I had a Notification that Yesterday Capn: [Charles] Hinchman is appointed major to one of the New Regiments of light dragoons & that Ld. Feilding succeeds to his Troop by which means I have the Satisfaction to have him continue in the 10th: & to Remain under your Command. He means to join in a few days & march with the Regiment Down to Scotland, I wish you could get him quarter'd with, or as near you as possable, in order, that he may not only benifit by your Instructions to teach him his profession, but also by your Friendly advice & good Example in all other matters.

169.   From Leonard Morse[1]

Whitehall April 26th. 1779

Mr. Morse presents his Compliments to Lord Denbigh, and has the honour to inform his Lordship, that Lord Feilding is intended to be appointed to a Troop in the 3d Regiment of Dragoon Guards the Notification for which will be out immediately.

1. Lord Amherst's secretary.

170.   **To Lady Halford**[1]

South Street April 27th. 1779

Madam

I am extreamly happy to have the pleasure of informing You, that my friend Admiral Gambier, has made your Brother Leiut. [Thomas] Farnham, Captain of the *Nautilus* Sloop of War. I am not without hopes that he will soon be promoted to post—as I have strongly Recommended him to Admiral Arbuthnot who Succeeds to the Command of the Fleet in America. My best Compliments to Sr. Charles.

1. Sarah Farnham, daughter of Edward Farnham of Quorndon House, Leicestershire, and wife of Sir Charles Halford, Bart. Sir Charles died on July 21, 1780; the Countess of Denbigh died on October 14, 1782; and Lady Halford and Lord Denbigh were married on July 21, 1783.

171.   **From Captain William Bulkeley**[1]

London July ye. 13th 1779

My Lord

The Third Dragoon Guards are ordered to encamp the 21st. I have inquired after Lord Feilding's Camp Equipage & every thing is taken care of. People are most dreadfully alarmed at the Proclamation[2] and at Sr. Charles Hardy's[3] putting into Torbay. I understand that they are fortifying every Thing in the Neighbourhood of Plymouth, so that they have some fears of an Attack there. Four more Corps are ordered, Lord Winchelsea's,[4] Sr. Thos. Egerton,[5] Colon White's[6] of Fitzroys, & Mr. Leicester. The first is Infantry, & to be commanded by Lord Chewton[7] with half Pay & Rank; the second Infantry in the Style of Fencibles.[8] The third to be commanded by himself Infantry with half Pay and Rank, & the fourth light Cavalry with no Rank; many others are talked of. Lord Chatham[9] has bought a Company in an old American Regt.[10] previous it is say'd of his having a Majority in a new Corp. If your Lordship does not keep a look out at this Time you will have many of the young Nobility step over Ld. Feilding. I can propose to your Lordship a very good Plan for myself & no bad one for Ld. Feilding, which is for your Lordship to offer to rise a Corp, appoint me Lt. Collon: Commandant to which there would be no objection, & Ld. Feilding Majr.—for me to resign it in three months, or whenever it will suite your purpose to obtain the Succession for him: this was the Plan in the case of the Duke of Ancaster.[11]

[P.S.] London is now hotter than it was at Guadeloupe. Such a Corps as I have mentioned I would undertake to rise with little or no Expence to your Lordship and indeed such a Thing has been hinted to me as a matter that would meet with no objection. I beg to explain myself, that I would not propose to sell to Ld. Feilding but to resign to him at no Expence to your Lordship: & it gives me no Rank but what I am intitled to & might have to morrow & yet I am persuaded I could make it answer very well to myself & to your Lordship.[12]

1. Captain of the 2/42nd Regiment on the half-pay list, and appointed a captain of an Independent Company of Invalids at Plymouth on October 6, 1779.

2. On July 9, 1779, in response to the threat of impending entry into the English Channel by the combined fleets of France and Spain, a Royal Proclamation was issued directing that in the event of an invasion the inhabitants of the southern counties drive their cattle and horses away from the seacoast.

3. Admiral Sir Charles Hardy, commander of the Channel Fleet.

4. 87th Regiment.

5. Lieutenant Colonel Sir Thomas Egerton, Bart., commander of the Royal Lancashire Volunteers.

6. Colonel Richard Whyte of the 96th Regiment.

7. George Waldgrave, Viscount Chewton, M.P. for Newcastle-under-Lyme, 1774-1780; Lieutenant Colonel of the 87th Regiment.

8. A type of regiment raised only for home defense.

9. John Pitt, 2nd Earl of Chatham, a captain in the 82nd Regiment.

10. A regiment with a low number which had been serving in America since the beginning of the war.

11. Robert Bertie, 4th Duke of Ancaster. He had served in America as a volunteer, and died suddenly in London of scarlet fever on July 8, 1779.

12. Entered in the letter book following this letter is the notation: "Lord Denbigh declined this Plan thinking Lord Feilding too young."

172. **From Major John Bowater**

                     London Savile Row August the 3rd. 1779

My Lord

Lord Wentworth not having time this Evning to write to your
Lordship I have promised him to take up the Pen; & am sorry to
transmit bad news to you. We have just been acquainted with the
Capture of the Island of St. Vincent, by the Squadron of Monsr. De
La Motte-Picquet, & it is feared that he has since made an Attack
upon the Island of Grenada & the Grenadittos:[1] the Terms of Surren-
der has not yet been announced but the Fact is too true, an armed
Vessel called the *Botte Tour* arrived yesterday with the Express. The
Joy which the mercantile People had upon the safe arrival of the West
India Fleet has been very much loward upon this Event. Mr. Byron
& his Fleet went down to St. Kitts to see the merchantmen safe by
Martinique; they took this opportunity to attack: it is thought that it
may bring on a general Engagement; which is very much desired on
our Part, and if it proves succesfull, the Islands will very soon return
to their antient Masters. I had a Letter from my Brother the Sailor
[Edward] by the last Post. They were expecting to return in a few
hours to join Sr. Charles Hardys Fleet. I am sorry to tell you that
Mr. Perry a relation of my Lady Denbigh has been unfortunately
drowned in his return from India in a Dutch Ship. I cannot learn
where Ld. Feilding's Regt. is quartered I would pay him a Visit. Lord
Wentworth is not determin'd when he shall come down to the Countrey I mean to accompany him, If I can get a Letter saying that my
leave is renewed. A French Frigate called the *Prudente* is certainly
taken and carried into Jamaica. Govr. Wentworth[2] told me this morning that he was certain that Charleston had surrendered to General
[Augustine] Prevost.

P S. I saw Capn. [John] Ford this Day who is return'd from Commodore Johnstone's[3] Fleet which has now joined Sr. Charles Hardy;
they have visited all the French Ports, and say, the Preparations for an
Invasion are all a Bugbear; and the Countrey was in a dreadfull
Panick least we should invade them: fired at them five miles distant.
Byron is recall'd & comes home in the *Nonsuch*. The combined fleet[4]
was seen five Days ago between Cape Finisterre & Oporto, waiting
for the *Chatham*'s Convoy that had put into Lisbon. The Jamaica
Fleet hourly expected.

1. While the British squadron in the Lesser Antilles was concentrated around St. Kitts to protect the departure of the homeward-bound trade, the French under the command of d'Estaing attacked St. Vincent, which surrendered on June 18, 1779, and then Grenada in the Grenadines, which capitulated on July 14, 1779.
2. John Wentworth, last Royal Governor of New Hampshire.
3. Upon his return from America, Johnstone was given command of a detached squadron.
4. The combined fleets of France and Spain.

173.   To Captain William Bulkeley

Newnham August ye. 7th 1779

Dear Bulkeley

I agree with you that the Season of Invassion is over. As to the Numbers of new Regts. offerd & accepted, I am a good deal surprised at it since the Panick ought to have ceased. As to myself I am certain I could only have got the Rank of Majr. for Lord F :[eilding] & for that I would not give a Shilling. Ld. Pembroke is of my opinion, & will not accept of it for his Son.

174.   From Lieutenant Edward Bowater

Terrible at Spithead Sepbr. 3d 1779

My Lord

I should have long before this done myself the pleasure of writing to you could I have sent you any good News, but I have been so long waiting with expectation that I now give up the Idea, and am sorry to substitute bad news for good. I think I may make use of this Language when I am to inform your Lordship that we are drove into this Place, by the superior force of the Enemy: your Lordship must I suppose have receiv'd various Accounts of our Situation for this some time past. I shall as nearly as it's in my power explain it; after being joined by the *Formidable* & *Prudent*, making up the number of thirty six sail of the Line, we proceeded to the westward twenty Leagues keeping our Channel open; we cruized for some Days, not expecting to see the Enemy, who we supposed to be far to the Southward, when we were joined by the *Marlborough* & a Frigate who gave us The Information of the French Fleet being in the Channel. The wind being to the Eastward, prevented our proceeding to attack them immediately, which in the End proved a fortunate Circumstance as a Gale of wind coming on obliged the French to leave the Channel & at the same Time for us to enter it. We then did not know what their real force was, till we arrived off Scilly, & then found they were Sixty Six Sail of the Line, thirty Frigates, & as many fire Ships; I need not point out to your Lordship how fortunate we thought ourselves upon being between our own Port and the Enemy; particularly so, when we discovered the Enemy pursuing us. The next morning, we keep our Ships in a Collected Body & found that theirs could not come up with us. They therefore did not chuse to hazard their best sailing Ships. Three Frigates were very daring, often coming very near us. Captain [Gideon] Johnston often tryed to bring them to action by droping in the Rear but they allways made off. The most of the Enemy we ever had in Sight was sixty sail, nine or ten of which advanced very near. The Frigates in our sight took a Cutter. This we thought a mortifying Circumstance as we could not attempt to relieve Her. I little thought I should ever have to say that the british Fleet were obliged to retire before that of the Enemy's but so it was, and we thought ourselves fortunate in being able to do so, as they must from their Situation have had great Advantages over us. They persued us as far as Plymouth. We are now at Portsmouth, & whenever its in my Power, I shall give you every Information. I am at present but in an indifferent State of Health, & intend by your Lordship's permission, should the Fleet not go to sea directly, or on their return, to apply to the Lords of the Admiralty to go on half Pay. I should be happy to be favoured with a Line from your Lordship.[1]

1. Entered in the letter book following this letter is the notation: "The Earl of Denbigh's Answer to this Letter was that by no means that He should quit the Service & Retire on Half Pay."

175. From Lieutenant Edward Bowater

Portsmouth Octobr. ye 11th. 1779

My Lord

I have been waiting this some Days in expectations of sending you some good News, as its an unthankful Office to be the Author of bad

News however I shall only at present relate Circumstances as they are told me. Admiral Byron arrived here yesterday in the *Maidstone* Frigate by whom we have the disagreable News of Count d'Estaing having left Martinique (a few Days before he saild) with his fleet and fifty Sail of Transports for New York and it is much feared before this that place is in their Hands. Yesterday a Cutter arrived here who had been on a cruize with the *Quebec* Frigate. They fell in with a French forty gun Ship which the *Quebec* engaged & would have taken her had not Boats come from the Shore and towed her off. Some Minutes after this gallant behaviour (from the loose powder as it is supposed) the *Quebec* blew up & every soul perish'd except fifteen which were taken up by the Cutter that was with them. As to the Time of the Fleet sailing it seems from what I can learn to be very uncertain two Days since the signal was made for all Officers to repair on board and to bring the recover'd Men from the Hospital we then expected to sail next Morning but we have not moved as yet. I am this Morning inform'd by Keith Stuart[1] that Governor Johnstone with a small squadron are going on a cruize supposed to intercept a Fleet of St. Domingo Ships coming home. The Ships at Spithead remain in the same State as when I wrote last excepting the *Edgar* having joined us, and the *Monmouth* gone into Dock. The *Ajax* and *Sandwich* are getting ready fast and are expected will soon be at Spithead. The latter Sr. George Rodney[2] is to hoist his Flag on Board. We have still two or three of our Ships continue very sickley, so much so that I believe they would not be able to proceed to sea with us. The Spanish frigate taken by the *Pearl*, is a very fine one they behaved gallantly before the[y] struck. This morning a signal was made for the Fleet to sail, but the wind coming round to the westward has prevent their going & has the appearance of continuing in this Quarter this some Time.

P.S. I am not certain of the Number of Line of Battle Ships that go [to] Sea, as there are several from sickness that will be left behind, but suppose two or three & forty.

1. Captain Hon. Keith Stewart.
2. Admiral Sir George Bridges Rodney, Bart., commander-in-chief of the Leeward Islands squadron, 1780-1782.

176. **To Admiral Sir George Rodney**

Newnham Octobr. the 11th 1779

Dear Rodney

I most sincerely congratulate You on being appointed to the command of one of our Fleets & the more so as I am convinced an Officer of your abilities will bring Honour to the Crown, and render essential Services to the public: If you can without any inconveniency to yourself I should be particularly obliged to you if you would take Lieutenant Edward Bowater who is now in the *Terrible* on board your Ship. I have known him from a Child & am sure his own merit will recommend him to your favour & protection. He is a gallant young Fellow, has seen a great deal of Service, & will do me Credit, or I should not recommend him to you. I heartily wish you Success where ever you go.

P S. I hope there is no Truth in the Report of the *Ruby*'s & some [of] our Frigates being taken by d'Estaings Fleet.

177. **From Admiral Sir George Rodney**

London Octobr. ye. 13th. 1779

My dear Lord

No Person whatever has a greater Claim to command any thing in my Power than my old, & worthy Friend, Lord Denbigh, had your request [No. 176] been known to me before all my Officers had been commission'd which was on the first Day of this month, Mr. Bowater had certainly been appointed one of my Lieutenants, and whenever he sails in any Ship belonging to the Squadron which I command, I will take an Opportunity of shewing my regard to your Lordship by promoting him to a Command. Admiral Byron is arrived. D'Estaings is gone to New-York. No Truth in the *Ruby* being taken.

178. **From Lieutenant Edward Bowater**

Portsmouth Octobr. the 18th 1779

My Lord

As I should be very sorry to give your Lordship any unnecessary trouble on my account, I have been with Sr. George Rodney's Captain who informs me there is no vacancy for a Lieutenant: had I known your Lordship intended I should go abroad for preferment I could have inform'd you of several vacancy long since in the *Sandwich*. I had an offer of being one of Governor Johnstone['s] Lieut. who is going with a small squadron to cruize off Lisbon, but I declined it thinking your Lordship would not approve of my going, and that Vacancy is now filled up. The wind continuing to the westward prevents the fleet proceeding to sea, but several of the ships will be left behind on account of their being sickly more than I thought there would be, its said eight sail of the Line, so that our number will not amount to more than five or six and thirty. An armed Vessel is just arrived from Newfoundland having only fifteen day's Passage. That place in great distress for want of Provisions of every kind & the fishery almost ruin'd by the american privateers which have taken all their fishing Vessels. The day the ship sailed from Newfoundland a vessel arrived from New York they there knew nothing of Count d'Estaing coming to Pay them a visit and the report of the two line of Battle Ships and a Frigate of ours being taken was without foundation. It is said here the combined Fleets are to sail from Brest the twenty sixth of this month, several armed Ships some commanded by Captns. others by Lieuts. are fitting out at this and several of the Sea Ports & the promotion that daily takes place into them has been very great.

179. **From Lieutenant Edward Bowater**

Terrible off Gibraltar Bay
February ye 9th 1780

My Lord

I take the opportunity of writing a few Lines to your Lordship by the *Childers* armed Brigg, which carries the Dispatches from Sr. George Rodney, & will bring your Lordship such news as I am sure will give you pleasure, as it does me in the Relation of it. On the 16th of January we saw Cape St. Vincent and at noon the Signal was made for seeing the Enemy's Fleet in ye. S:E: Quarter. The Admiral made the Signal for a general Chaise, & as fast as the Ships came up with the Enemy the[y] began to engage; early in the Action, one of the Enemy's Ships blew up, a most horrid sight, and but one man saved; at nine, we in this Ship got up with one of the Enemy & began to engage, but another of our own Ships coming on the other side the Enemy, we quited her, & soon after came to action with another, which we engaged for two Hours & five Minuets, when having lost her fore-mast & all her rigging & Sails shot away, She struck her Colours; we took the Captn. & first Lieut. out of her, but two Days following, being seperated from the Fleet, & close in Shore near Cadiz, we were under the disagreable necessity of quitting our Prize, She being so unmanageable as not to be able to take her with us. They had thirty killed & sixty wounded, we only six killed and twelve wounded. The day following we jóined the Fleet which had been much dispersed from chaising different ways; we found on our joining, there were taken four Sail of the Line, one of them the Admiral's Ship, of eighty Guns the other three of seventy, they are now safe in Gibraltar Bay. The Spanish Fleet consisted of eight Sail of the Line, & four Frigates, out of which four of the Line are taken, one blown up, & one run on Shore after being taken, and entirely destroy'd; all our Convoy got safe to Gibraltar and very glad they were to see us as they were much in want of the Articles we brought them. We were so unfortunate in this Ship in going into Gibraltar in the Night, to drop close under the Spanish Battery's, from its falling little wind, to a strong current, they kept up a very heavy fire upon us for some Time, & threw several Shells, but tho several of their Shot hit us we were so fortunate as to have no Men killed, two other Ships were in the same Situation. We are just returned to Gibraltar in this Ship having been cruizing for a week off Malaga in order to intercept three Spanish Frigates which were expected to attempt running through the Straits in the night but we have seen nothing of them and are glad to return as the weather has been very bad. Three sail of the Line are gone with some transports to Minorca. Sr. Geo: Rodney has made six Captns. since he has been here, I intended waiting upon him but the Ship being ordered on the present Cruize prevented me. When we are to return, I know not, but I most heartily wish it as the daily Fatigue I have is more than I am equal to, have not known what it is to have my Cloaths off this Fortnight. Don Barcelo¹ with two Line of Battle Ships lays on the other side of Gibraltar Bay, but so covered by guns off the high hills round him that it is out of our Power to attempt any thing against him. Your Lordship must have been informed of our having taken a Convoy of Victualers with a sixty four Gun Ship. I do not expect much prize money as there are so many to share. I shall thank your Lordship to let some one inform my Friends, that I am well, likewise my Brother in the *Culloden*, as I have no Time to write at present, and which I hope will appologize for the hurry in which I am obliged to conclude.

[P.S.] We have been continually allarm'd with the Idea of the Enemy sending Fire ships amongst us, but we have keep a good look out, since I have wrote the above we are come to an Anchor in this place. I do not find there has any thing further happened since our Absence but hear we are to sail as soon as the Ships return from Minorca. The *Childers* being drove up the Mediterranean the *Hyena* goes to England, which brings your Lordship this.

1. Antonio Barceló, commander of the Spanish naval force before Gibraltar.

VII

April 1780-November 1783

For the British, the last two years of the American War were a grim struggle for national survival against ever increasing odds. There were many defeats, and the few British victories were rendered meaningless by the events which followed them. In 1780 it must have seemed to the British as if the whole world was turning against them. At the beginning of June 1780 London was ravaged by the Gordon riots, and for several days Britain's capital was to witness the worst rioting of the century as the poor of the city, drunk on gin, ran wild, looting, burning, and killing until the disorders were suppressed by the military. Hard on the heels of the Gordon riots came the news of the British capture of Charleston, South Carolina, and what appeared to be the beginning of the reconquest of the American South. But if the news was bright from America, the storm clouds were gathering in Europe. In August 1780, the French and Spanish fleets captured the combined outward-bound East and West India convoys; in one stroke sixty-one ships, three thousand men, and goods valued at one and a half million pounds were lost. Then at the end of 1780, Britain declared war on the Netherlands in order to prevent the formation of a league of armed neutrality which was designed to stop the Royal Navy from seizing naval stores bound to enemy ports in neutral ships.

At the beginning of 1781 Britain stood alone. At war with America, France, Spain, and Holland, the British were diplomatically isolated and without allies as they attempted to conquer the American South and fought to maintain naval control in such widely separated places as the Western Atlantic, the English Channel, the West Indies, and the Indian Ocean. In the American South, it appeared at first that the British were victorious; for after the capture of Charleston, the King's troops, under the command of Lord Cornwallis, rapidly overran most of South Carolina and then invaded North Carolina, beginning the disastrous campaign which would end on October 17, 1781, with the surrender of a British army to the Americans and French at Yorktown. When the news of the loss of Cornwallis' army at Yorktown reached London, the North government fell; and in March 1782, a new government was formed, headed by the Marquis of Rockingham. This government had pledged to end the war and began the negotiations which resulted in the signing of a preliminary treaty of peace with the Americans on November 30, 1782. Ironically, 1782 was also a year in which the British won a great victory. On April 12, 1782, Rodney decisively defeated the French fleet in the Battle of the Saints, culminating three years of almost continuous naval warfare in the Caribbean. What satisfaction the British might have gained from the Battle of the Saints must have been dampened by the terms of the peace, for the American colonies were lost forever. The last British troops were evacuated from America on November 25, 1783.

180.   From Lieutenant Edward Bowater

Alcide at Spithead March ye. 6th. 1780

My Lord

I did myself the pleasure of writing to your Lordship by the *Hyena* from Gibraltar [No. 179] which Letter I hope you received. I apprehend before this reaches you [you will] be informed of the particulars of our Voyage home, and the good Fortune we had in taking the *Prothee* a French 64 guns had we been fortunate enough to have fell in with them early in the morn we certainly should have taken the other line of Battle Ship & the rest of the Convoy. We left Gibraltar the 13th. of February & have had a fine Passage, but were in daily Expectations of being intercepted by a superior Fleet. We all came home weakly man'd on account of the number of Men we were obliged to put on Board our Spanish Prizes. Your Lordship will be surprised when I inform you of my being second Lieutenant of the *Alcide*, but my reasons I shall give for my being here will I hope meet with your Lordship's Approbation. After we returned from our cruize in the *Terrible* off Malaga, Sr. George Rodney thought proper to order the *Terrible* to proceed with him to the West Indies, as soon as we arrived I waited upon Sr. George who received me very politely but said it was not in his Power to do any thing for me at present though he had at this Time six vacancies for Lieut. in his Ship in consequence of the six he had promoted to be Captns. I therefore thought I could have very little Chance of promotion, when upon this Opportunity he would not take me into his Ship, though two Capts asked him to do it, they therefore advised me to get a Change into some Ship returning to England. I wish I had an Opportunity in Person of explaining the whole of this Business to your Lordship. I am returned very unwell and shall be very much obliged to your Lordship if you would get me superceeded from this Ship till I am better, this may be easily done at present as I have not yet an Admiralty Commission, but an Order to act from Sr. George Rodney, in the Room of Lord Robert Manners who was Lieut. of this Ship who is now promoted to the rank of Post Captn. I hope your Lordship will excuse the abrupt manner in which I am obliged to conclude but the Boat is just going & I am affraid will not be Time enough for the post.

181. From Lieutenant Edward Bowater

Alcide Plymth. May ye. 30th. 1780

My Lord

I intended doing myself the Honour of writing to your Lordship for some time past, but have been so ill, as to put it out of my power. I have no news to send your Lordship, except that of the Fleet which Mr. Walsingham having passed this Place yesterday, we are to follow them in this Ship in a few Days, having received Orders to go to the West Indies. I shall with pleasure execute any Commands you or Lady Denbigh may have to that Country.

182. To Admiral Sir George Rodney

South Street June ye. 2d. 1780

Dear Rodney

On the very polite Answer I received from you [No. 177] before you left England, in answer to my Application [No. 176], in favour of my Friend Ed: Bowater, I must confess I did flatter myself, you would have remembered him in the very large Promotion you made at Gibraltar or at least that you would have had the Goodness, to have taken him with you on board your own Ship to the West-Indies: He is now coming again under your Flag on board the *Alcide*; when I hope it will be in your power to promote him according to his Merit at the earnest request of One who ever was, still is, and ever will be, the very sincere Friend of Sr. George Rodney. I cannot conclude this Letter without joining in the common Voice of the Publick in thanking you for the great & emminent Services you have already done your King & Country; & at the same Time of assuring you that it is the Opinion of all Mankind here, that these Services would still have been greater if your Bravery & good Conduct had been properly supported on the 17th of April last. I heartily wish you all the Success & Happiness your Merit deserves.

183.   To Lord Sandwich

Newnham July ye. 24th. 1780

My dear Lord

I know you are allways ready to oblige your Friends when their Requests are not unreasonable ones: & I flatter myself you will not think mine at present so. It is to give me, when you can do it conveniently, a second Lieutenancy of Marines for a Son of a very particular Friend of mine; his name is Samuel Oliver. He is a very pretty Lad, has been well educated under his uncle Dr. [William] Langford the second master of Eaton School, he was designed by his Family for the Church, but he is a spirited Chap & chooses a red Coat rather than a black one: He is exactly of the right Age being sixteen next September. Lady Denbigh desires her Compts. to you & Lady Corke.[1]

P.S. I am sorry to find by a Letter received from Lord Wentworth to Day that an Account is come of the Junction of the Spanish & French Squadrons in the West Indies, which will render them so much superior to Sr. G: Rodney, but we flatter ourselves it is not exactly so as our Friend the Viscount is apt now & then to Croak.

1. Anne Kelland, Countess of Corke and Sandwich's niece.

184.   From Lord Sandwich

Admiralty July ye. 30th 1780

My dear Lord

I shall put Mr. Oliver on my list for a Commission in the Marines with a thorough Disposition to serve him, when I have got rid of two or three previous Engagements. It is certain that the Spanish Fleet joined Mr Guichen,[1] but there is reason to believe that they soon after went to their own Settlements; at all Events I think little Danger is to be apprehended at the Leeward Islands, as Sr. George Rodney must long ago be reinforced by several capital Ships; Commodore Walsingham was off Madeira the eleventh of June, & on the seventh had detached the *Centaur* and *Egmont* to make the best of their way, without further attending the Convoy.

1. Lieutenant-général Luc-Urbain Du Bouexic, Comte de Guichen.

185.   From Lord Pembroke

Wilton House Novr. ye. 21st: 1780

I trouble you with this my dear Lord, en qualité de Père, submitting to your Lordships better Judgement, whether it would not be adviseable for us to endeavour to get our Sons the rank of Major forthwith; By Brevet I should think it to be the easiest way. Lord Herbert is now second Captn. in the royal Dragoons, & probably will be the first very soon. Lord Feilding is nearly (if I mistake not) in the same Predicament in the Prince of Wales's Dragoon Guards. Formerly it was (I know) usual for young Men of Quality to pass over the rank of Major & to get Lieut. Colys. in the Guards from being Captains, but that seems to be no longer the Case, and should we now follow that Idea it may here after be plausibly answered to us, that our Sons have never been Majors. A son of Lord Dartmouth's is already one & has been so sometime though a younger Officer. A Patriot of all other Beings is the most unlikely to succeed in any Applications. None is likely as a Ministerialist. I must therefore my dear Lord beg leave to throw the labouring Oar on you (comme de raison) faithfully promising to try hard at it myself hereafter upon your account as well as my own, when all *Good* & *Bad* have met with their Deserts, & when my Friends are Ins, & your's are Out; which the Lord of his infinite mercy grant &c Adieu my dear Lord. Joking apart do think of this, & if you have any Commands for me be pleased to direct them to me at Wilton House Wilts.

186.   To Lord Pembroke

South Street Novbr. ye. 22d. 1780

Dear Peer

As to geting our Sons the Rank of Major by Brevet on present Occasion it is impossible as the Promotion will not reach them by near ten Years, I shall therefore most certainly not apply as I do not like a Refusal. If any new Corps are raised we may succeed by finding Men. As to my Friends going out & yours coming In, *God Forbid*, & they seem at present to be at a great distance. But no one has a greater Regard for the Earl of Pembroke than his most sincere Friend & humble Servt. the Earl of Denbigh.

187.   From Lord Pembroke

Wilton House 26 Novbr. 1780

I know my dear Lord that the promotions will not in their regular Course, come near our Sons; but I know also that, unless that regularity is got over their Fathers will die long before they are much advanced. As for their Advancement by raising Men for new Corps, I cannot expect it; for, accustomed as we are to the Folly & Inequity of the Times, I do not think that either can dream of such a Measure, whilst there is not perhaps a single old Regiment compleat, & many absolute Skeletons. But your Lordship having started that Idea, creates one in me, which might perhaps succeed, if you should think fit to espouse it. The difference between, a Captain's Commission of Foot, & a Major's, in Price is about £ 100. The encrease of Income about £ 85 annually a Brevet carrys no pecuniary advantage with it, and I should imagine that £ 500's worth in Men or the money paid down for recruiting, for Example one of the nominal Regts. for nominal they are, having no Men just return'd to Europe, would be a fair bargain on all sides, & by no means an improper Request for young Men of Quality who might remain as now Captains of Dragoons. Do turn this in your mind & we will talk it over more fully when next we meet over a bottle of Burgundy in Privy Gardens if you please, and I have some very good, as for my Cookery I cannot say much, but it may do if you do not breakfast the Day you favour me with your Company at dinner. Lord Feilding is not (I hear) with the Regiment in Dorsetshire. Before he returns to it pray put him in mind to Inn here & tell him I can shew him some good sport in the shooting way. I cannot conclude without desiring Leave: to change your *God forbid* into *God grant.* Of Course I wish to see my Friends in the Saddle; but rather than having no Alternation I will agree to the . . .[1] being thoroughly persuaded that we may get by any Change, and can lose by none. But let one who will be uppermost.

P.S. Men's flesh for the Army cost at present about £ 10 per head, I believe.

1. Illegible.

188.   **From Lord Onslow**[1]

Clandon House Novbr. ye. 26th. 1780

My dear Lord

The post before I received your Letter I had troubled you with one upon the same Subject, which I hope you received. I rejoice most exceedingly at what you tell me of Lord Feilding. I did suspect & hoped that, that was the Duke of Northumberland's Business with you. There cannot be enough of such young Men as Lord Feilding in the House of Commons. There are much too many of a very different Sort. The Duke of Newcastle[2] has done me the same favour with respect to my younger Son who he brings in for Aldborough in Yorkshire.[3] I promise you he thinks as we do. I wish you a merry Xtmas in Warwickshire. I am obliged to pass mine this year in London where I go next Monday and shall have the honour of representing your Lordship in the King's Bed Chamber the Monday following where, & every where else I shall be happy to obey your Commands.

P.S. You may depend on hearing from me of any thing happens worth your knowing.

1. George Onslow, 4th Earl of Onslow, Treasurer of His Majesty's Household.
2. Henry Fiennes Clinton, 2nd Duke of Newcastle.
3. The Hon. Edward Onslow, M.P. for Aldborough, November 28, 1780-May 1781.

189. From H. Carpenter[1]

Tavyton near Tavistock
Devon 3d Decbr. 1780

My Lord

I have the great pleasure to inform your Lordship that your Son Lord Feilding was yesterday unanimously chosen Member of Parliament for the Borough of Bere Alston in the room of Lord Algernon Percy,[2] on which I beg leave to congratulate you and his Lordship.

1. Election agent for the Duke of Northumberland.
2. M.P. for Bere Alston, September 9-December 2, 1780; Northumberland, 1774-September 1780, December 1780-1786.

190. To the Duke of Northumberland

South Street Decbr. ye. 7th. 1780

Lord Denbigh's best Respects to the Duke of Northumberland was very happy at the receipt of his Grace's note[1] last night, informing him that Lord Feilding's Election was over without any Difficulty. His Lordship had a Line from Mr. Carpenter [No. 189] himself to the same purpose last night. Lord D. will settle all the Business with Lord Algernon at his return to Town, which will most certainly be before the Expiration of the fourteen Day, after the meeting of Parliament, or sooner if required. Lord Denbigh hopes his Grace has had a better night & will soon be able to go to Bath.

1. Not entered in the letter book.

191.   From Captain William Feilding

Portsmouth Decbr. ye. 11th. 1780

My Lord

I was honoured with your Lordship's Letter last night, & am much surprised that you did not receive my Letter[1] of last Tuesday's date. I am sorry that your Lordship is prevented returning to Newnham by a return of your Complaint in your Bowels; but hope you will not be plagued with it long, as London must be disagreable to you after the Parliament is adjourned. The *St. Albans* & *Solebay* sailed on Saturday Morning with a Supply of Bread for the grand Fleet; as likewise did the *Portland, Monsieur* & another Frigate, and I believe in quest of the *Serapis* & *Ariel* under the Command of Paul Jones who was seen cruizing off the Lands End. The Wind being in the N:W: the grand Fleet is expected soon to arrive. I hear that a Frigate is arrived at Falmouth with an account that the combined Fleet was seen off Cape Finisterre, which I suppose is d'Estaing with the Trade for Brest. The *Royal George, Namur,* & *Ocean* are docked, and getting ready for Sea. The *Union* will be out of Dock in two or three Days. The *Raisonnable* & *Elizabeth* lately from the West Indies are to be paid off. Sr. Digby Dent with his Ship's Company from the *Raisonnable* to go on board the *Repulse* (64 g.) a new Ship just launched at Cowes. The *Monmouth* is fitting for the East Indies. The *Magnificent* & *Lyon* two of the Jamaica Ship are going to be docked & repaired. The Report of this place respecting our naval Loss in the Fleet (under Convoy of the *Ramillies*) captured by the Spanish Fleet is 24 setts of Masts & 24 suits of Sails for Rodney's Fleet in the West Indies; if that is true, it's a Loss not easily to be repaired. The General and Admiral have been very obliging in offering me their Assistance in getting on board any Ship I should like. I have fixed upon my old Ship, Captn. Keith Elphinston who is now on a cruize but expected in soon to take Money to America. I congratulate your Lordship on Lord Feilding's Return for Bere Alston; I make no doubt but his Lordship will make a good [Fusil] in the House. The navy here seem sorry for the revival of Palliser's Court Martial &c. as it may tend to make fresh Decentions in the Fleet which were pretty well subsided. Bowater left this place a Sunday [Sennight] went for Hampton Court. I am glad to hear our friend Yeo[2] is in good Spirits, I hope He & his Coleague will succeed. Admiral Pye is very well & sends his Compts. to your Lordship. If any News should arrive (at any Time) after Post, I will send it to your Lordship by the Diligence³ to Charing Cross.

1. Neither letter entered in the letter book.
2. Edward Roe Yeo, M.P. for Coventry, 1774-1780, February 1781-December 1782.
3. Stagecoach.

192.   From Captain William Feilding

Spithead Febry. ye. 20th. 1781

My Lord

I have just time to acquaint your Lordship the wind is fair & that we sail this Evening or to morrow morning. The Transports from the Downs are expected every Minuite for the Troops that go with G. Johnstone, & then I suppose the grand Fleet will sail, about 30 sail of the Line exclusive of Johnstone's Squadron, exceeding well manned; should the Spaniards & French endeavour to prevent Darby's¹ passing I think they will have a good Dressing.

1. Vice-Admiral George Darby, commander of the Channel Fleet.

193.   From Captain William Feilding

Cork March ye. 22d 1781

My Lord

I have the pleasure to acquaint your Lordship that we arrived here the 14th instant with the Transports for the Troops, who were all embarked by the 17th & now only waite for a fair Wind, which we are very anxious to have. The 16th the *St. Albans* sailed with seventy Sail of Victuallers to join the grand Fleet but the wind proving contrary the next day were oblige[d] to return with the whole of the Transports that sailed from Portsmouth under [convoy of] the *Medway* and three Frigates. The grand Fleet I am informed are cruizing of[f] Cape Clear. As soon as the wind come any thing fair, the whole of the Gibraltar Convoy will sail and join Admiral Darby. I am glad to hear Sr. George Rodney has been so successful in the West Indies; I hope Darby will be equally so off Cadiz.

194. From Captain William Feilding

New York June ye. 30th. 1781

My Lord

I have the pleasure to acquaint your Lordship that we arrived at Charleston the 4th. of June & landed the three Regiments the Day after, compleat & in good Health; & in our way to [New] York left the Guards at Portsmouth in Virginia. The Troops & Recruits were very healthy the whole passage but the *Warwick* was the reverse having buried 12 Men including the Surgeon's Mate & a Midshipman; & have sent on Shore to the Hospital since our arrival above a 100 sick; I am much affraid the Fever will go through the Ship. Nothing has happen'd in the Country since Lord Cornwallis's affair at Virginia. The French Fleet at Rhode Island, it is reported they mean to go to Boston to refit after the late action with Mr. Arbuthnot. I have just heard that the Admiral sails to morrow for England, & his coming up to [New] York gives me this opportunity.

P.S. In our Passage we took two small Prizes from the West Indies for Boston, for which I expect £ 50.

195. From Captain Edward Bowater[1]

Salamander, in Carlisle Bay, Barbados
July ye. 1st 1781

My Lord

It is some time since I did myself the pleasure of writing to you but ever since I have been appointed to the command of this Ship, I have not been more than a Day in one place; that, & the very few Opportunities I have of writing, will I hope apologize for my seeming neglect. The last Time I had the Honour of writing to your Lordship, I was at St. Eustatius, various have been our Situation since that Time. The Arrival of a French Fleet of twenty five sail of the Line, and an Action between them and eighteen of our's, under the Command of Sr. Samuel Hood, very soon changed the Situation of things in this Country. Till that Time, our whole care and attention was taken up on the Arraingement of our Spoils at St. Eustatius. Various have been the opinions of the Action between the two Fleets, one Thing seems not to admit of a Doubt, that the French from their Superiority in Numbers & Situation might have done more than they did; I do not believe there was an Idea of so superior a Fleet of the Enemy's, coming to this Country, it was the Cause of a general Confusion. After the Action we collected our ships together, & made the best of our Way to this Island, & intended going from hence to the Relief of St. Lucia, which the French had attacked, with their whole force, by Sea & Land. The number of Soldiers, landed, were I believe four thousand, they effected nothing, & after being on Shore three or four Days, reimbarked in a very precipitate manner, so much so, that the Marquise de Bouille,[2] the Commander in Chief, left part of his Camp Equipage behind him. There is no certain Reason known for their precipitate retreat some say it was in Consequence of their observing some Men, landing from two of our Frigates, which they took for a strong reinforcement, others say, it was from their bad Information of the Strength of the place. I do not believe we had more than fifteen hundred Men on the Island, but the Fortifications are very strong, in consequence of their Retreat, we remained at this Island, till we heard of a Detachment of the Enemy being sent to take Tobago, a Squadron of six sail of the Line, three frigates & some few Troops, under the Command of Admiral [Sir Francis Samuel] Drake, was sent in order to relieve that place (I was on this Expedition by the Request of Admiral Drake, acting as 2d. Captain of his Ship) but on our making the Island, we fell in with the whole French Fleet; we were very near them, & I was apprehensive for some Time that they would have taken us, however we found we had the Heels of them, they chaised us all Day, we returned with our Squadron to this place where we joined Sr. George Rodney, & the next Day sailed again for Tobago with our whole force, consisting of twenty Sail of the Line, one fire Ship & five Frigates with some Troops; on our making the Island, in the Evening, the Admiral sent an Officer in a small Vessel on Shore, in order to learn the Situation our Troops were in, this Vessel returned in the Morn, with information of the place being captured by the Enemy, at this Time we discovered the

French Fleet to Leeward of us, under a press of sail, without any Line being formed, & in a very unconected Situation. Both Fleets kept by the wind with all their Sails set, in this state we continued sailing nearly Paralel to each other, the whole Day, in the Eve the Van of the Enemy, had got well to windward we could see the Hulls of most of them, our Admiral made the Signal to prepare for Action in the morning, on our seeing the Enemy, & I fully believed there was to be one. The next morning we saw nothing of the Enemy; three Days after we made this Island where we have been ever since. Some Days after our return to this place, we were informed that, the Island of Tobago had not surrendered when we were there, nor did it till seven Days afterwards, how to account for this I know not. The Reasons for our not engaging the Enemy (from my own Conjecture) were, from our inferiority of our Fleet to theirs, our's being very sickly, Short of Numbers, & many of the Ships in bad Condition, had we risk[ed] an Action, without commanding Success our Fleet must have gone to leeward, which would have left all our Islands to the mercy of the Enemy, not that we are much better situated at present, for it is impossible for us to do any thing with an Enemy of so superior force as they are, but we wait in hopes of a strong reinforcement from England soon, one thing indeed, we must soon all leave this Country for a Time, as the hurricane Seasons will soon set in. The Enemy's fleet are at present, in Fort Royal Bay Martinique, but I do not think they will remain long there inactive whilst they remain Masters of these Seas. We hear there are four sail of the Line of St. Eustatius, & that the whole force of the Enemy is now twenty eight sail of the Line, some think they will, soon depart from this Country for either St. Domingo with a Convoy or for America. I think myself for both. The internal strength of our Islands in this Country, is so bad, that they soon become an easy conquest. The Inhabitants ever resting an implicit Faith in the Superiority of our force by Sea, will never raise a six-pence, to build any kind of fortification, I think I never met with a set of more disloyal people in my Life, one half are of the strongest American Principles, particularly so at this Island from whence the Enemy get all their information of our movements. I think I have now given your Lordship all the News I know in this part of the world; I most earnestly wish to be out of this Country, where I have had not one moments health. I have taken so much Medicine that it has lost all its Effects; I was nearly tempted to change with the Captn.

of the *Scourge*, who brings the Admiral's Dispatches, & by which I send this, but not knowing your Lordship's Sentiments on that Head, I shall remain in this Country till I hear from you. The many People Sr. George has to make Post will put me out of any manner of Chance, though I am upon very good Terms with him; but we have daily some one or other coming out with strong recommendations for preferment.

1. Rodney appointed Edward Bowater Master and Commander on February 13, 1781.
2. Marquis de Bouillé, Governor General of the French Windward Islands.

196. From Captain Thomas Farnham

Kite, Sheerness July ye. 4th. 1781

My Lord

I had the Honour to wait on your Lordship on my being appointed to the Command of the *Kite* Sloop to return my most gratefull acknowledgment for all Favours, but your Lordship being then out of Town, Ld. Feilding was pleased to say he would acquaint you, for fear it should be ommitted, permit me most humbly to assure your Lordship, I shall all ways retain a full sense of the many Obligations I am under & endeavour to merit your future favours by an upright & uniform Conduct in the Service that I hope will do honour to your Recommendation & establish my Character. The *Kite* will be ready by the middle of this Month having gone through a small Repair for Channel Service, if that should be my Station with the grand Fleet permitt me through your Lordship's Goodness to hope for a Recommendation to the Commander in Chief, as I am well advanced on the List as Master & Commander, & your Lordship is no Stranger what a great & desirable step it is to get *Post* which I hope will be some little Apology for the Liberty I take, & allow me to assure your Lordship I shall allways attain a most gratefull Sense of the many Obligations I lay under & be happy if any Opportunity should offer of convincing your Lordship of my Sincerity.

197.   From Captain Thomas Farnham

Alexander at Spithead
Novembr. ye 29th. 1781

My Lord

I have the Honr. to inform your Lordship the Lords of the Admiralty have been pleased to appoint me acting Captain of the *Alexander* of seventy four Guns in the Absence of Ld. Longford, who is gone to Ireland; which induces me through your Lordship's former favours to take the Liberty to request you would be pleased to sollicit Lord Sandwich to confirm me Post; as I think there never can be a more favourable Opportunity then the present; but submit that to your Lordships Consideration. I should suppose my being constantly employ'd upwards of twenty years, & three years a Master & Commander, should intitle me to some little Claime for Promotion from Lord Sandwich, but I expect very little from that, as nothing but Interest will do. Should I my Lord be so happy as to succeed, I shall ever most gratefully acknowledge the many Obligations I lay under, & with pleasure convince your Lordship of my Sincerity.

P.S. The *Alexander* is going out with Admiral [Richard] Kempenfelt with twelve sail of the Line and the Fleet is nearly ready for Sea and are as follows

	Guns		Guns
Edgar	74	*Queen*	98
Courageux	74	*Alexander*	74
Britannia	100	*Hercules*	74
Victory	100	*Medway*	64
Union	90	*Valiant*	74
Duke	98	*Renown*	50 with seven Frigates

198.   From Captain Thomas Farnham

Brune at Spithead Febry. ye. 8th. 1782

My Lord

I was favoured with yours of the fourth of last month[1] and allow me to assure you, I am fully satisfyed with your Lordship's wish to serve me, I would have answerd yours before but was in daily expectation of seeing Ld. Longford down to join the *Alexander*; but did not arrive till Sunday last, and sailed on Wednesday with four other ships to reinforce Sr. Richard Bickerton's Fleet for the East Indies, the wind continues fair and its to be hoped they will get out of the Channel to day, the West Indies Fleet is not ready for Sea, but will sail on Sunday if the Wind answers.

In conversation the other Day with Sr. Thos. Pye the Commanding Officer here understood yr. Lordship had got me employed & wish'd to get me forward in the Service, in consequence of which, he has been pleased to appoint me Acting Captain of the *Brune* Frigate, her Captn. being sick on shore & will not be able to join her again: She is old & wants repair, & is under orders to be payed off at Woolwich; & as we have many Instances of Captns. being confirmed in similar Vacancies, I am in hopes your Lordship may bring it about as it takes not Vacancy from Lord Sandwich, and only gives me rank, which is all I wish, as she will not be more than a month in Commission; I can only say My Lord I shall have the fullest sense of the many Obligations I am under, & ever endeavour to merit your future favours.

1. Not entered in the letter book.

199. From Lord Amherst

Whitehall March ye. 8th. 1782

Lord Amherst presents his Compts. to Lord Denbigh has the Honour & Pleasure of acquainting his Lordship, that the King has been pleased, in the most gracious manner, to appoint Lord Feilding to succeed Major [Benjamin] Lambert in the 19th. Regt. of light Dragoons, of which Lord Amherst gives Lord Denbigh, Lady Denbigh & Lord Feilding Joy.

200.   **To Lord Amherst**

South Street Friday Evening
March ye. 8th. 1782

Lord & Lady Denbigh's most grateful thanks to Lord Amherst for his very friendly & kind Notification [No. 199] of their Son's Promotion, which they will never forget: The gracious Manner in which his Majesty has been pleased to confer the Favour adds greatly to their Satisfaction. Lord D: has sent the note to Lord Feilding who is at the House of Commons.

201.   **From Captain William Feilding**

New York June ye. 13th. 1782

My Lord

By a Letter I have just rec'd from my Sister (which is the first I have rec'd from any Body since I left England) I am inform'd that your Lordship has not rec'd any Letters from me of late which surprises me much, as Mr. Oliver & self have allways wrote at the same Time. I wrote to your Lordship last Novbr. by the *Robust*, but she springing a Leak, was obliged to go to the West Indies, after putting Ld. Cornwallis & Genl. [Benedict] Arnold on board a Transport, which Transport was taken off the Lizard by a French Privateer, and the mail from New York sunk. We then sailed on a Cruize to the Southward, of near four Months, & no Opportunity offering since but by the *Pearl* who carried Sr. H: Clinton home. We are kept constantly at sea, & know of nothing going on a Shore, as the Ships when they arrive from a Cruize seldom go to [New] York, but get their Stores, Provisions & water at the Hook. Our Army at present I hear is to act in the Defensive, but that I believe will not last long, as the Rebels will not suffer Mr. Morgan[1] to pass with Dispatches from Sr. G: Carleton[2] to Congress, and seem to treat every Overture of Peace with Disdain, without their Independance is acknowledged; which I hope will never happen. They are collecting all their force (including the French) near the White Plains, as they say, with an Intention to attack New York this Summer, as Count de Grasse[3] with his fleet and Army were expected on the Coast of America, and that the Idea of attacking Jamaica, was a Blind for us to send Troops from our Army to it's Relief: But Sr. G: Rodney's late glorious Action[4] in the West Indies, will disappoint them this year; & I am in hopes will be a means for the French to recall their Troops from America. The Accounts from Jamaica say, the French have got such a Beating that no great Fleet ever got before, & that they have lost 15,000 men, killed, wounded & taken Prisoners. A report prevails here, that Admiral Drake's Division has fallen in with the four cripled ship that went to Curaçao, and had taken three & sunk one. Another Report by different Vessels from the West Indies says, that the *St. Esprit* was lost in the Mona Passage, and every soul perished. The French and Spaniards have 42 sail of the Line at Cape François, but the former are in very bad condition and the troops very sickly. I d) not imagine that many of Count de Grasse's Fleet will see France again. In our last Cruize of six weeks, we had the Honour of Prince William's[5] Company on board. He is a very fine youth, and bids fair to be a very shining Character in the profession; his Activity, & Attention to his Duty is much to be admired; he keeps a very strict watch, and is the first Aloft when any thing is going forward: Weather makes no difference to him. As we expect to sail in a few Days on a Cruize, I am much affraid we shall not have His Royal H:[ighness] Company: as he got a Fall a Fortnight ago and put his right Shoulder out, but is recovering very fast, and wishes to go with us. Mr. Washington & Congress are going to commit such an Act of Cruelty, and Breach of Faith that cannot be equalled in civilized Nations: Some time ago, the Loyal Refugees took a Rebel Captain prisoner, hung him, in the Room of a Captain of theirs that the Rebels had hung a little Time before; for which Mr. Washington & Congress are going to make the Innocent suffer for the guilty; and ordered the Captain's of Lord Cornwallis's Army that were prisoners to draw for their Lives, but they refused, in consequence of which Congress drew for them, and the unfortunate Lot has Fallen upon Captain [Charles] Asgill of the Guards, who was immediately ordered into close Confinement, and sent to Headquarters; and is to be hanged in a few Days (on the same Spot where Major [John] Andre suffered) if Captain Lippincott of the Refugees (who commanded the party that hung their Captain) is not given up.[6] In my two last Letters I requested your Lordships Interest with Lord Sandwich in behalf of my Nephew, but as his Lordship is out,[7] I am affraid I shall not be able to get him to the Marines. I hope your Lordship will forgive me, if I improperly ask your Lordship, if you have any Interest with Sr. Guy Carleton, to recommend my Nephew to him for an Ensigncy in his Army. I daily see Ensigncy's given to Officers Children, and others who are not on the Spot, and number of Vacancy's Frequently happen, and many get Commissions who have not the least Pretentions to them. A Brother Officer of mine has lately got his Son a Commission who is at home at School.

P.S. The Men of War in general have been pretty successfull, but I can't say much for the *Warwick* tho' she has very good Stations but was unfortunate. The last Cruize we lay 6 weeks in and off the Dela-ware, waiting for the *South Carolina* a Rebel Ship of 44 Guns (built in France, and 28-36 Pounders on her main Deck & 500 men) from the Havana with a Convoy; two Days after our Cruize was out, and return'd to [New] York, She arrived at Philadelphia. She had 200,000 Dollars on board, besides a very valuable Cargo. Mr. Oliver is very well, but was left behind ye. last Cruize, he having a very bad Leg, which had very nigh cost him his Life which proceeded from a Bite of a Musquito; he begs his Respects to your Lordship.

1. Dr. Maurice Morgan, Sir Guy Carleton's secretary.
2. General Sir Guy Carleton replaced Clinton as commander-in-chief of the British army in America after Yorktown.
3. Lieutenant-général François-Joseph-Paul, Comte de Grasse, commander-in-chief of the French Squadron in the West Indies.
4. The Battle of the Saints.
5. William, Duke of Clarence. The future King William IV.
6. In retaliation for the alleged murder on March 30, 1782, of a Loyalist soldier named Philip White, a party of the Associated Loyalists led by Captain Richard Lippincott procured the release of Captain Joshua Huddy of the New Jersey militia from a British prisoner of war compound, and on April 12, 1782, hung Huddy on the New Jersey coast with a placard on his chest reading, "Up Goes Huddy for Philip White." Washington, upon learning of the execution, demanded that the British surrender Lippincott to the American army. When the British refused, Washington had Captain Charles Asgill selected at random from among the British captains who had surrendered at Yorktown. Asgill was placed under close arrest and the British were informed that unless justice was done he would be hung in retaliation for the death of Huddy. After months of negotiation and the intervention of the French government, the "Huddy affair" blew over and Asgill was released.
7. The North government fell in March 1782 and Sandwich was no longer First Lord of the Admiralty.

202.   From Captain William Feilding

New York August ye. 2d. 1782

My Lord

I have just time to acquaint your Lordship by the Ship *Sr. Guy Carleton*, that the French Fleet consisting of 12 Ships of the Line and two Frigates are on the American Coast, & had very nigh taken the *Centurion* two Days ago. Captain Slater[1] in the *St. Margaretta* engaged & took the French Frigate *L'Amazon* in sight of part of their fleet, but was the next morning obliged to leave the prize to them. The *Amazon* has above one hundred Men killed & wounded, including the first & second Captain killed, the remainder of the Officers with 70 men Captn. Slater has brought in with him. The *St. Margaretta's* Loss was but 5 Men kill'd and as many wounded. The *Lyon, Warwick, Centurion* with several Frigates are moored close to the Bar at the Hook to prevent the French from coming in if possible, besides several small Transports ready to sink in the Channel upon the[ir] Appearance off [New] York. We are in hourly expectation of Rodney or Hood from Jamaica. God send they may soon arrive, or else we shall be in a doleful situation.

P.S. A Fortnight ago the *Warwick* in Company with the *Astraea* and *Carysfort* chased a French 64 *L'Eville* two Days & nights, & was very near bringing him to action but he beat the *Warwick* in sailing and the Frigate was inferior. She was from the Havana & had some small American under her convoy: She is gone for Brest.

1. Captain Elliot Salter, R.N.

203.   From Captain William Feilding

New York August ye. 10th. 1782

My Lord

I wrote to your Lordship the 2d. instant [No. 202] by the Ship *Sr. Guy Carleton* acquainting your Lordship that the French Fleet was on the American coast, and that the Hook was secured from their coming in, by Transports to be sunk on the Bar, and the Men of War to cover them. They have not as yet made their Appearance off the Hook, therefore it is imagined they are either gone to the Chesapeake or Boston, dreading the Approach of the Fleet from Jamaica. On the Arrival of the Packet Sr. Guy Carleton & Admiral [Robert] Digby acquainted General Washington & Congress that Independance would be granted to America. The Inhabitants of [New] York & Loyall Refugees are very much hurt at this sudden change of Affairs, saying that their Loyalty to their King and Mother Country, has sold them, & made them worse than slaves, that great Britain has convinced the world she was superior to her Enemies by sea, & had lately gained a compleat Victory of over the Fleet of France, that the American Army was reduced very low, and their Trade wholly destroy'd, & that the French & Dutch had lost all their possessions in the East: And that in the very Hour of prosperity, & triumph over all her Enemies, grants Independance to the undutiful Americans, & sues for Peace with all the other Powers at war with her. Nothing but long faces & dejected Countenances to be seen. Washington's whole force including the French (I am told) does not exceed 5,000, and was decreasing daily; while that of the British is 14,000, besides what is at Charleston & Halifax. I have sent your Lordship [No. 202] the particulars of the *St. Margaretta*'s Action with the French Frigate *L'Amazon*, and of the chase the *Warwick*, *Astraea* & *Carysfort* had after *L'Eville* French 64. I have just heard from New York, that the Inhabitants hearing Independance was to be granted to America waited on Sr. G: Carleton to know weither such report was true, who desired, they would meet him the next day at Head Quarters for an Answer, when Mr. Morgan (the General's Secretary) read to several Thousands the inclos'd Letter,[1] which infused Melancholy in the Face of every Spectator, and the whole dispersed very much displeased, and immediately sent Word to the General that they would do no more Duty in Town (The Militia of [New] York then doing Garrison Duty and the Army was in Camp) as they were not to be protected: on which some of the Troops were immediately order'd to Town to relieve the Guards & Posts. Many very respectable Characters & Friends to old England are ruined, and are sure to meet no Mercy from Congress. A paper has been stuck up at the Coffee-House saying if Sr. G: Carleton and Prince William will open the Campaigne, the whole of the Inhabitants &c. &c. will join the Army and sacrifice their Lives rather than live under the American Government. The

Assurance & *Adamant* are just arrived with the Troops from Savannah that place being evacuated and not an Inhabitant left behind.

1. Not entered in the letter book.

204. From Captain William Feilding

Warwick, New York Octobr. ye. 8th. 1782

My Lord

I have just rec'd Mr. Bulkeley's Letter informing me of the disagreable News of my Mother's Death, an Event I long expected. The distressed Situation of the Family in Yeoman's Row gives me great concern, and as far as I am able, shall, as I have allways done, give them every assistance in my Power. I have given Directions to a very particular friend of mine in London to pay Mrs. Farrell £ 40 Pr. An: from the Time of my Mother's Death, and £ 10 Pr. An: for my Nephew's schooling, which is as much as I conveniently can at present allow out of my Pay. Agreable to my Mother's most earnest request and my promise, she was buried with my Father at Waltham near Portsmouth; which funeral, with mourning and other expences I have ordered to be paid. I am under, the greatest Obligations to your Lordship for the many favours you have done me & mine, & am sorry for a late Change, it is not in your Power to serve my family at present. I have presented a Memorial to Sr. Guy Carleton in favour of my Nephew, which was backed by Captn. Elphinstone, and am in great hopes I shall succeed in a Commission for him. I have promised, as soon as he was appointed to a Regiment in this Country he should immediately join. The 14th. of last Month the *Warwick* in company with the *Lyon, Vestel* & *Bonetta* chased up the Delaware two French Frigates, *L'Aigle* of 42 Guns, & *La Gloire* of 32 Guns. The former under the Command of Commodore Count De la Touche,¹ got aground & struck to our Frigates, after cutting away all her Masts & Bowsprit; and skutling the Ship in five different Places; before our Ships could get up with *L'Aigle*, she landed the Duc de Lauzane,² Baron Viominel,³ the Marquis De Laval,⁴ and several French and American Officers, with £ 50,000, however we got the Ship off & have brought her safe to New York. She has Stores and Camp Equipage for the French Army, and is the largest Frigate ever built, being near three hundred Tons burthen more than the *Warwick*, with 28 twenty four Pounders on her main Deck. She will turn out a good Prize, £ 4,000 was left on Board. *La Gloire* escaped over the Shoals, and got up to Philadelphia, not without some Damage. Two days before we saw the French Frigates, the Squadron took a Ship of 22 guns *La Sophie* from France to Philadelphia, on board of which was Madame De la Touche, Lady to the Commodore. *L'Aigle* had 750 Men on board, when we chased her, and 630 when She struck. Admiral [Hugh] Pigot's Fleet is allmost ready for Sea, and will I believe leave this place for the West Indies, as soon as the French Fleet is ready and leaves Boston. I cannot at present think of going to England, as in all probability the next Campaigne will be a very interesting one; therefore, I mean, if the *Warwick* goes home with the Convoy to get a Change.

1. Lieutenat-général la Touche de Tréville, Comte de la Touche.
2. The Chevalier de Anne César Luzerne, French minister to the United States.
3. Major General Antoine Charles de Houx, Baron de Vioménil, the commander of the French troops in the assault on the British redoubts at Yorktown.
4. A major in the French army.

205. From Lord Keppel

Lord Keppel's Compts. to Lord Denbigh and begs to assure his Lordship that He will with much readiness advance the Grandson[1] of the late Admiral Feilding to a Commission in the Marines when the young Gentleman Iye conformable to the Admiralty Rules will permit.

Admiralty Octbr. ye 26th 1782

1. George John Farrell.

206.   From Captain William Feilding

Warwick, New York Novbr. ye 9th. 1782

My Lord

I am Honoured with your Lordship's Letter[1] of the 18th of July
being the first I have receiv'd since I left England; except the one I got
from Mr. Bulkeley acquainting me of the Death of my Mother,
which I fear will be severely felt by the Family in Yeoman's Row: I
am greatly oblig'd to your Lordship for your kind intentions to serve
them, and lament much that the late Change prevents your Lordship
assisting my Family so much as you could wish. The *Warwick* will
soon go Home with a Convoy, I shall therefore endeavour to get to
the *Centurion* a very desirable ship, where I hope to be more fortunate than in the *Warwick*. I hope your Lordship will agree with me
that I can be of more use to my distressed Family by staying in this
Country then by going Home, as by being in a cruizing Ship I may
be enabled to assist them. Admiral Pigot is sailed for the West Indies
with fourteen sail of the Line; and Lord Hood with the remainder
(13) will sail as soon as the French Fleet will move from Boston,
which is hourly expected. Prince William goes with Lord Hood in the
Barfleur, which I believe pleases his Royal Highness much, as he will
there learn more of his Duty as an Officer in the Management of a
Fleet (which is the great Line) then by staying in a cruizing Ship on
the coast of America. Every thing respecting this place is kept a
profound Secret; sometimes it is said, that the City will be evacuated
in the Spring, and that America will be left to herself; & by the arrival of the last Packett a report prevails that the General['s] hands are
untied, & that a vigorous Campaigne will take place early next year,
which is the earnest Wish of every well-Wisher to Old England. The
very Idea of giving Independance to America would ruin thousands of
Families, many of whom have sacrificed very affluent Fortunes to
maintain their Loyalty. I am very happy to hear that Lady D: is perfectly recover'd, & that Lord F & Mr. Charles are well, to whom I
beg my best respects.

1. Not entered in the letter book.

207.   From General Hon. Henry Conway[1]

General Conway presents his Compts. to Lord Denbigh, and has the Pleasure to acquaint him that the King has consented to Lord Feilding's Appointment to the Lieutenant Colonelcy of the twenty second Light Dragoons in the Room of Lord Sheffield.[2]

Little Warwick Street
15th of January 1783

1. M.P. for Higham Ferrers, 1741-1745; Penryn, 1747-1754; St. Mawes, 1754-1761; Thetford, 1761-1774; Bury St. Edmunds, 1775-1784; Commander-in-Chief of the Army, March 1782-December 1783.
2. John Barker Holroyed, 1st Baron Sheffield.

208.   To Captain William Fielding

South Street London January ye. 18th. 1783

Dear Will

I have rec'd your Letter [No. 206] and as a Soldier you are perfectly in the right in continuing in America; however as I firmly believe Peace will be soon concluded, I would advise you to return to England, & should be happy to hear of your safe Arrival. I have the pleasure to inform you that I got a Commission in the Marines for your Nephew young Farrell and that he is appointed to the Portsmouth Division, & moreover that I have obtained for him, through our Friend [John] Bowater Leave of Absence for six Months, by which Time I hope you'll be at Home to take care of him. I am very sorry to hear that you & young Oliver are not on board the same Ship, however when an opportunity offers, I Trust you will have an Eye over him, as I have a great regard for the young Man, and for his Family. On the 30th of ye. last Month it was his Majesty's Pleasure to appoint Lord Feilding Lieutenant Colonel Commandant to the 22d. Regt. of Light Dragoons, in the Room of Lord Sheffield, who has sold out of the Army.

209.   From Captain William Feilding

New York April ye. 14th. 1783

My Lord

I have the pleasure to acquaint your Lordship we are just arrived from our last Cruize, and have brought in with us an American Ship from the Havana, bound Philadelphia, which we took off the Capes of Delaware three Days before the Expiration of the Time limited for taking Prizes. And on the first of April we drove a large Ship on Shore at Cape Henlopen from the Havana with Sugar, which the Americans set on fire. I volunteered to go on board to put the fire out which I accomplished; in doing which I had near lost my Life, as the Americans before they left the Ship, fired several Vollies of small Arms· at the boat, as did the Militia from the Shore, but fortunately I had no Man hurt. As it was strong Ebb-Tide was not able to get her off, soon after I put the fire out she over-set. The Packett arrived the 5th. instant with the Articles of Peace & Independance to America. It is impossible to describe the Melancholly Effect the News had upon Thousands of Loyalists, & Refugees, who are oblig'd to abandon their Country, & seek an Assylum in Nova-Scotia. A Fleet of Transports sailed this Day for [St.] Augustine for the Evacuation of that Place, a distressing Circumstance to many hundred Famillies (who had fled there for protection) from Charleston, and who will now be at the Mercy of Congress, not having Vessells to carry them from thence, any where else. When this place is to be evacuated I know not; as I understand there is not a sufficient Number of Transports to carry off the Troops & Stores at once, by near sixty Thousand Tons, besides assisting the Refugees. I have rec'd by this Packett a letter [No. 208] from your Lordship informing me you have got my Nephew George a Commission in the Marines which gives me infinite Satisfaction; and for which, and many other Favours I am greatly obliged to your Lordship; and hope the young Man will do Honour to your Lordship's reccommendation. I hope to be at Home by Midsummer as in all Probability the large ships will be ordered Home first. I am very happy to hear that Ld. Feilding has got the twenty second Light Dragoons and sincerely congratulate him on his Promotion. By a Letter I have rec'd from my Sister I am much concerned to hear of the Death of Lady Denbigh. The *L'Aigle* Frigate (on board of which is young Oliver) is gone to Antigua, she having sprung all her Masts in a gale of Wind of[f] Bermuda. I do not hear of her taking any Prizes during her Winter's Cruize I suppose she will not return here again.

210.   From Captain William Feilding

New York June ye. 17th. 1783

My Lord

Every thing has remained here, in the same state as when I wrote to your Lordship last [No. 209]. If there is not a sufficient Number of Transports sent from England, it will be impossible to leave this place before Xtmas: As there is still several Thousand Loyalists & Refugees to be sent to Nova Scotia, the River & Island of St. Johns, and to Canada. Those who have lately been sent to the above places are perfectly well satisfied with the appearance of the Country, and of the prospect of once more enjoying happiness undisturbed by a vile set of Miscreants (as your Lordship will be able to see from the inclosed papers[1]) as they would suffer every persecution from the Country People should the[y] stay behind. Some have attempted to go & take possession of their Estates, but have met with a very rough reception and sent back again. Several who left Charleston at the Evacuation and went to Jamaica, were invited back again, with Assurances of being restored to their property, which they gladly accepted; but were greatly disappointed to find the reverse on their Arrival. By the Resolves of the different States, it will be impossible that several of the Articles of the Treaty can be fulfilled by Congress.

I hope soon to have the pleasure of seeing your Lordship, as we expect to sail ten Days after this.

1. Not entered in the letter book.

211.   From Captain William Feilding

Portsmouth, Sepbr. ye 19th. 1783

My Lord

The 16th of August we sailed from New York with a Convoy of three thousand Hessian Troops. On the 7th instant we fell in with the

Torbay a leaky Ship from Halifax who took us from the Convoy, to stay by her during her passage: And I have the pleasure to acquaint your Lordship that the two ships arrived safe at Spithead last Night. The Inhabitants of [New] York are in great distress at the Evacuation of the place taken place in November, as the most of them fear they shall not be able to settle their affairs by that Period. The American States are daily finding Bills of high Treason against the Inhabitants of [New] York, Long Island and Staten Island merely for living within the British Lines. Therefore but few of the many Thousands belonging to the above Islands can stay after the British quits New-York. I hear by the *Torbay* that the Americans have attack the Loyalist lately settled at Port Roseway Nova Scotia; but they being aprised of their intention were prepared to receive them and drove them off.

As soon as I am landed and my little Matters settle at Quarters shall apply for leave: As a Captn's Guard [dutys] mount daily in the Dock Yard. I have got a brother Officer to take my Duty in my Absence. The day before I left I received a Letter from Lord Feilding dated in November last, to whom I beg my best respects.

212. From Captain William Feilding

No. 119 Jermyn Street St. James
Octobr. ye 14th. 1783

My Lord

The Day after I wrote to your Lordship [No. 211] the *Centurion* sailed for the Downs with part of the Convoy of Hessian Troops: and after being there a week I took the Opportunity of taking my party to Portsmouth, in the *Scipio*. On my arrival, I heard a Letter had been there, from your Lordship; and sent to me at Chatham, supposing the Ship had gone to the Medway to be paid off; and I did not receive it till the End of last week.

I arrived in Town this Evening, and as soon as I have settled with the American Agents, for some Prize Money, that is due to me, & have got some Cloaths made, I shall with great pleasure accept of your Lordship's kind Invitation to Newnham. I am with my best Compts. to Mr. Feilding & Bowater, My Lord, your Lordship's much oblig'd & very humble Servt.

INDEX

Agnew, Lt. Col. James, 57
Allen, Capt. John, 169
Alleyne, Mr., 4
Amherst, Gen. Jeffery, 1st Baron, 19, 60, 62, 161, 180, 181, 185, 188, 214, 215
Ancaster, Robert Bertie, 4th Duke of, 190
Anderson, Lt. Robert, 60
Andre, Maj. John, 216
Arbuthnot, Vice-Adm. Marriot, 79, 80, 171, 189, 209
Arnold, Brig. Gen. Benedict, 63, 81, 92, 124, 125, 131, 215
Asgill, Capt. Charles, 216, 217
Associated Loyalists, 217
Aylesford, Lord, 135

Bajazet, 130
Banks, Capt. Francis, 90, 91, 92
Barceló, Antonio, 198
Barré, Lt. Col. Issac, 89, 90
Barrington, Lt. William, 141
Barrington, William Wildman Barrington, 2nd Viscount, 17, 19, 40, 63, 87, 90, 110, 111, 119, 125, 149, 150, 151, 155, 158, 176, 177
Barton, Mr. & Mrs., 186
Bassett, Maj. Richard, 57
Batt, Maj. Thomas, 105, 114
Beaufort, Henry Somerset, 5th Duke of, 42
Bere Alston, 20, 206, 207
Berkeley, Lt. George, 41, 42
Berkley, Lt. James, 66, 67, 161, 186

Bickerton, Capt. Sir Richard, 12, 109, 110, 111, 132, 159, 168, 214
Bird, Col. John, 124
Boston, Mass., 14, 27, 28, 29, 33, 34, 35, 36, 39, 45, 49, 50, 51, 54, 55, 56, 58, 61, 62, 63, 64, 68, 70, 72, 75, 77, 79, 80, 82, 85, 90, 91, 92, 108, 114, 115, 120, 134, 135, 140, 145, 155, 162, 171, 173, 176, 209, 219, 221, 222
Bouillé, Gov. Gen. François-Glaude, Marquis de, 210, 212
Bourmaster, Lt. John, 14, 54, 55
Bowater, Capt. Edward, 8, 9, 10, 11, 12, 13, 15, 47, 48, 49, 75, 94, 102, 106, 109, 110, 111, 146, 159, 164, 165, 168, 169, 171, 172, 174, 175, 176, 178, 179, 181, 191, 192, 193, 195, 196, 200, 201, 209, 212
Bowater, Maj. John, 8, 15, 16, 22, 64, 68, 70, 74, 82, 84, 86, 87, 92, 94, 95, 100, 102, 104, 106, 107, 111, 118, 121, 124, 125, 130, 132, 138, 139, 143, 145, 151, 156, 157, 158, 162, 163, 165, 166, 173, 175, 176, 179, 180, 181, 191, 223
Bowater, Mary, 8, 66
Bowater, Richard, 8, 37, 38, 86, 102
Bowlby, Mr., 42
Braithwaite, Capt. Richard, 163
Brereton, Capt. William, 169, 171

A new historical discovery which sheds light on the political and military aspects of the American Revolution.

The Lost War consists of the unprecedented find by the historian Marion Balderston, who describes in her preface how "For nearly two hundred years they had stayed there in the library of the Earl of Denbigh's home in Warwickshire, England—buried treasure, too heavy to lift easily and the writing inside difficult to read. But they are pure gold to students of the late eighteenth century and to anyone interested in why England lost her most important colony."

The "buried treasure" Mrs. Balderston describes is revealed in this book: more than two hundred hitherto undivulged letters—never intended for public scrutiny—from British Officers in America during the revolution, as well as some from political figures, to Basil Feilding, Earl of Denbigh, the Tory political power—and his replies to them.

Because these letters were never meant to be disclosed, they have a candidness and immediacy not found in dispatches by senior officers.

The eminent historical authority, Professor David Syrett in his remarkable account of their background writes: "Because he wanted reliable independent information, Denbigh set up what amounted to a private news gathering organization. . . . The result is a collection of correspondence, much of which is unique, for many of the letters contain vivid accounts of naval, military, and political events at the time of the American Revolution. . . . Intermixed with discussions about promotions are first hand accounts of some of the great events of the age. On occasion, the information contained in these letters made Denbigh one of the best informed men in England."

The renowned historian, Henry Steele Commager has here written a probing exploration both of their meaning as historical revelation and their significance for our time. Of these letters, Professor Commager writes that "they suggest some answers to the fascinating question why the greatest military power of its day should have found, in the American wilderness, only defeat. . . . It reminds us that the psychology of the Americans in Vietnam has long anteced- ents. . . . Victory for the British (as for the Americans in Vietnam) was always just around the corner, and always inevitable. . . .

"What was perhaps most baffling—it is reflected here in many letters—is that the Americans could lose Boston, New York, Philadelphia, Charleston, without losing the war. . . .

"As Philip Guedalla reminded us, half a century ago, Lord Sandwich and Lord George Germain have some claim to be honored as Fathers of the American Repub- lic for their contributions to American mili- tary victory were as valuable as those of any American military men except Wash- ington himself. This is a consideration that Professor Syrett brings out with great per- suasiveness."

Besides Marion Balderston's exciting de- scription of her discovery of the great treas- ure (uncovered through a casual remark by a friend in the Warwickshire County Record Office); Henry Steele Commager's superb introduction; and David Syrett's masterly analysis of the interconnections of the patronage system in England with its military and national politics, all the letters are given in seven chronological sections. In addition, in order to give the reader a guide by which the work is threaded together into a sequential story, each section is intro- duced by an account of the major events which surrounded the writing of these pri- vate letters in those momentous years.

These rare documents—with their wealth of detail, their local color, their vivid de- scriptions of battles and discussion of major figures and events—comprise a unique view of that perennially enthralling era, now made public for the first time.